Java 2

The Cram Sheet

This Cram Sheet contains the distilled, key information for the Sun Certified Programmer for the Java 2 Platform exam. Review this information last thing before entering the test room, paying special attention to those areas where you feel you need the most review. If you transfer any of the tasks from this sheet onto a blank piece of paper before beginning the exam, you can refer to it while taking the test.

JAVA SOURCE CODE

1. If a **package** statement is present, it must be the first non-comment statement in the file.

2. You don't have to import the **java.lang** package. However, either every other package you use must be named in an **import** statement, or you must use the fully qualified name of the class every time it is mentioned. An **import** statement can use an asterisk (*) to import all classes in the package or explicitly name the imported class, as in the following example:

```
import java.util.* ; // or
import java.util.Hashtable ;
```

3. Each source code file can have only one class declared **public**. If there is a **public** class in a file, the file name must match the class name exactly. Resolution of Java names *always* considers case.

MODIFIER KEYWORDS

4. The Java keywords that control the accessibility of a class and class members (variables, methods, and inner classes) are as follows:

   - **public** Any part of a program can access this class or class member.

   - **protected** Only methods in the same package or in subclasses can access **protected** class members. This keyword is *not* applied to classes.

   - **private** Only methods in the same class can access a private member. This keyword is *not* applied to classes.

   - *(none)* If no access modifier is present, the class or member is visible only from classes in the same package. This is sometimes called "package" or default visibility.

5. The **abstract** modifier. An **abstract** method just declares the return type and signature of a method, but not its body. Any class containing an **abstract** method must be declared **abstract**. Interfaces are always **abstract**, but the keyword is optional in the declaration. Variables can't be declared **abstract**.

6. The **final** modifier. A **final** method can't be overridden, and a **final** variable can't have its value changed after initialization. A local variable or method parameter must be declared **final** if it is to be used by an inner class declared inside a method.

7. The **static** modifier. Methods, variables, and nested classes can be declared **static**, in which case they belong to the class as a

whole, not any particular instance. Blocks of code outside a method can be declared **static** for the purpose of initializing **static** variables.

ENTITY NAMES

8. The only nonalphabetic characters allowed to start a name are $ and _ (underscore). The compiler will try to convert any string of characters starting with a numeral into a number.

PRIMITIVE VALUES

9. Integer variable types. Java integer primitives are always signed except for the **char** primitive type. Note that the maximum positive magnitude is always one less than the maximum negative magnitude. The default value for an integer primitive is zero. The ranges are as follows:

• **byte**	8-bit	-128	127
• **short**	16-bit	-32768	32767
• **char**	16-bit	\u0000	\uFFFF
• **int**	32-bit	$-(2^{31})$	$2^{31} - 1$
• **long**	64-bit	$-(2^{63})$	$2^{63} - 1$

10. Integer literals are assumed to be of type **int** unless the letter L or l is appended.

11. Floating-point variable types **float** and **double** use 32 and 64 bits, respectively, and conform to the IEEE 754 floating-point standard. The default value of a floating-point primitive is zero.

12. Floating point literals are assumed to be of type **double** unless the letter F or f is appended.

13. The boolean primitive type can only have **true** and **false** values. The default value of a boolean is **false**.

ARITHMETIC OPERATIONS

14. When evaluating an arithmetic expression with two operands, the compiler converts primitives by widening according to these rules:
    a. If either is of type **double**, the other is converted to **double**.
    b. Otherwise, if either is a **float**, the other is converted to **float**.
    c. Otherwise, if either is of type **long**, the other is converted to **long**.
    d. Otherwise, both operands are converted to **int**.

15. Division by zero in integer arithmetic produces a runtime **ArithmeticException.**

16. Division by zero in floating point-arithmetic: No exception occurs; instead, the result is one of the special values, **NaN**, **NEGATIVE_INFINITY** or **POSITIVE_INFINITY** that is defined in the **Float** and **Double** wrapper classes.

17. **NaN** stands for Not a Number; the only way to see if a floating-point result is **NaN** is to use the **Float.isNaN** or **Double.isNaN** **static** method.

18. Special floating-point values. In addition to **NaN**, the **Float** and **Double** classes define **MAX_VALUE**, **MIN_VALUE**, **POSITIVE_INFINITY**, and **NEGATIVE_INFINITY**.

LOGIC OPERATIONS

19. The logic AND operators **&** and **&&**. The **&&** operator will "short-circuit" an evaluation and will not evaluate the right-hand term if the left-hand result is **false** because the final result is bound to be **false**.

20. The logic OR operators **|** and **||**. The **||** operator will "short-circuit" an evaluation and will not evaluate the right-hand term if the left-hand result is **true** because the final result is bound to be **true**.

21. The **if** and **while** statements require a **boolean** input, so C tricks that evaluate zero as false do not work.

BITWISE OPERATIONS

22. The shift operators, **>>**, **>>>**, and **<<**. These operators work with integer primitives only; they shift the left operand by the number of bits specified by the right operand except that they never shift more than 31 places for **int** and 63 places for **long** values. The **>>** right shift extends the sign so a negative number stays negative, whereas the **>>>** operator shifts in zero bits, creating a positive number.

REFERENCE VARIABLES AND ARRAYS

23. Objects, interfaces, and arrays are "reference" data types. The default value of a reference variable that has not been initialized is the special value **null**.

Java 2

Bill Brogden

The Coriolis Group, LLC
14455 N. Hayden Road, Suite 220
Scottsdale, Arizona 85260

480/483-0192
FAX 480/483-0193
http://www.coriolis.com

Library of Congress Cataloging-in-Publication Data
Brogden, William B.
      Java 2 exam cram / by Bill Brogden.
            p.   cm.
      Includes index.
      ISBN 1-57610-291-2
      1. Electronic data processing personnel--Certification.   2. Java
(Computer program language)--Examinations--Study guides.   I. Title.
QA76.3.B76   1999
005.13'3--DC21
                                                          98-26340
                                                              CIP

Printed in the United States of America
10 9 8 7 6 5

President, CEO
Keith Weiskamp

Publisher
Steve Sayre

Acquisitions Editor
Shari Jo Hehr

Marketing Specialist
Cynthia Caldwell

Project Editor
Michelle Stroup

Technical Reviewer
Tom McQueary

Production
Coordinator
Kim Eoff

Cover Design
Jody Winkler

Layout Design
April Nielsen

 CORIOLIS

CORIOLIS

14455 North Hayden Road, Suite 220 • Scottsdale, Arizona 85260

Coriolis: The Training And Certification Destination ™

Thank you for purchasing one of our innovative certification study guides, just one of the many members of the Coriolis family of certification products.

Certification Insider Press™ has long believed that achieving your IT certification is more of a road trip than anything else. This is why most of our readers consider us their *Training And Certification Destination*. By providing a one-stop shop for the most innovative and unique training materials, our readers know we are the first place to look when it comes to achieving their certification. As one reader put it, "I plan on using your books for all of the exams I take."

To help you reach your goals, we've listened to others like you, and we've designed our entire product line around you and the way you like to study, learn, and master challenging subjects. Our approach is *The Smartest Way To Get Certified™*.

In addition to our highly popular *Exam Cram* and *Exam Prep* guides, we have a number of new products. We recently launched Exam Cram Live!, two-day seminars based on *Exam Cram* material. We've also developed a new series of books and study aides—*Practice Test Exam Crams* and *Exam Cram Flash Cards*—designed to make your studying fun as well as productive.

Our commitment to being the *Training And Certification Destination* does not stop there. We just introduced *Exam Cram Insider*, a biweekly newsletter containing the latest in certification news, study tips, and announcements from Certification Insider Press. (To subscribe, send an email to **eci@coriolis.com** and type "subscribe insider" in the body of the email.) We also recently announced the launch of the Certified Crammer Society and the Coriolis Help Center—two new additions to the Certification Insider Press family.

We'd like to hear from you. Help us continue to provide the very best certification study materials possible. Write us or email us at **cipq@coriolis.com** and let us know how our books have helped you study, or tell us about new features that you'd like us to add. If you send us a story about how we've helped you, and we use it in one of our books, we'll send you an official Coriolis shirt for your efforts.

Good luck with your certification exam and your career. Thank you for allowing us to help you achieve your goals.

Keith Weiskamp
Publisher, Certification Insider Press

About The Author

Bill Brogden is LANWrights, Inc.'s VP of Technology and Development. A full-time programmer and writer based in Leander, Texas, Bill has over 20 years' experience in the programming field. He's worked for clients as diverse as The Psychological Corporation, Litidex, and Cox Newspapers, and has written programs ranging from text indexing and retrieval software to multi-user BBSs. Bill has written significant software in Fortran, Forth, C, C++ and—of course—Java.

Bill enjoys nothing better than learning and exploring new technologies, so when Java came along, he jumped right in. In addition to writing Java-related books, Bill also acts as a SysOp on the CompuServe Java User's forum (GO JAVAUSER), where he has donated his expertise for the past two years.

Acknowledgments

I would like to thank Ed Tittel for his encouragement and support of the idea of an *Exam Cram* book for Java. Thanks also to Dawn Rader and Margaret Berson for straightening out my tangled syntax. Thanks also to Tom McQueary for his technical review. Most of all, I would like to thank my wife, Rebecca, for her continued support.

—*Bill Brogden*

Contents At A Glance

Table Of Contents

Introduction

Welcome to *Java 2 Exam Cram*. This book is intended to prepare you for taking and passing the Sun Certified Programmer for the Java 2 Platform exam, number 310-025 as administered by the Sylvan-Prometric testing organization. This Introduction explains Sun's certification program in general and talks about how the *Exam Cram* series can help you prepare for certification exams.

Exam Cram books help you understand and appreciate the subjects and materials you need to pass certification exams. *Exam Cram* books are aimed strictly at test preparation and review. They do not teach you everything you need to know about a topic. Instead, the series presents and dissects the questions and problems that you're likely to encounter on a test. In preparing this book, I've worked from preparation guides and tests and from a battery of third-party test preparation tools. The aim of the Exam Cram series is to bring together as much information as possible about certification exams.

Nevertheless, to completely prepare yourself for any test, I recommend that you begin by taking the Self-Assessment included in this book immediately following this Introduction. This tool will help you evaluate your knowledge base against the requirements for the Sun Certified Programmer for the Java 2 Platform exam under both ideal and real circumstances.

Based on what you learn from that exercise, you might decide to begin your studies with some classroom training, or to pick up and read one of the many study guides available from third-party vendors, including The Coriolis Group's *Exam Prep* series. I also strongly recommend that you install, configure, and fool around with the Java 2 (Java Development Kit 1.2) software and documentation, because nothing beats hands-on experience and familiarity when it comes to understanding the questions you're likely to encounter on a certification test. Book learning is essential, but hands-on experience is the best teacher of all!

Who Is This Book For?

This book is for you if:

➤ You are a programmer who is already familiar with Java to some extent and are seeking certification. Maybe you have written a couple of applets or applications and worked through one or two of the introductory books.

➤ You have been working with Java on and off for a couple of years. You have even done a fairly large application, but it was with Java 1.0 and you have not done much with Java 1.1 or Java 2.

➤ You are an experienced Java programmer but you have heard that even experienced programmers can fail the exam because it covers a lot of basics that you don't use every day.

➤ You see that more and more employment ads, especially for the more interesting Internet-related jobs, mention Java and you think that "Sun Certified Programmer" would help your resume.

This book is *not* for you if:

➤ You are just getting started in programming and have little experience in any language.

➤ You have done a lot of programming but none of it in an object-oriented language.

➤ You have a theoretical understanding of Java but want to work with a lot of code examples so you will feel comfortable.

➤ You are curious about this suddenly popular language called Java and what to find out what the fuss is about.

If you fall into the category that indicates this book is not for you, you should start your Java certification path somewhere else. Please consider my other book, *Java 2 Exam Prep* (The Coriolis Group, ISBN: 1-57610-261-0) because it is full of programming exercises and has even more sample exam questions.

Sun's Java Certifications

Sun has several forms of certification for Java as listed on the Web page at http://suned.sun.com/usa/cert_test.html. There is now a multi-corporation initiative for Java certification. Corporations involved are IBM, Novell, Oracle, and Sun. The Sun Certified Programmer exam is the first step in the proposed certification standard. The main Web page is at **http://java.sun.com/cert-initiative/**. Here is the list of Java certifications that are possible:

➤ Sun Certified Programmer for the Java Platform (JDK 1.0.2)

➤ Sun Certified Programmer for the Java Platform (JDK 1.1)

➤ Sun Certified Programmer for the Java Platform (Java 2)

➤ Sun Certified Developer for the Java Platform (JDK 1.0.2)

➤ Sun Certified Developer for the Java Platform (JDK 1.1)

➤ Sun Certified Architect for Java Technology (Java 2 Platform)

The certified developer tests involve a programming project that you can work on in your own time, followed by an exam with questions related to your design decisions. The architect certification appears to involve more theoretical design considerations.

Signing Up To Take The Exam

After you have studied this book, taken the example exam, and feel ready to tackle the real thing, you first have to deal with Sun's Education branch. Sun will take your money ($150 in the U.S.) and give you a voucher number. You will have to provide a unique ID number, such as your Social Security number. All of this can be done by telephone with a credit card. The number to call for U.S. residents is (800) 422-8020. For other locations, start at the following Web page to locate a Sun representative: http://suned.sun.com/usa/cert_reg.html.

Sun will give you a voucher number that you can use to sign up for the test and will then mail you paperwork with the voucher number (but you can sign up with just the voucher number so you don't need to wait for the mail).

Signing Up With Sylvan Prometric

After you have gotten a voucher number, you can contact Sylvan to locate a nearby testing center that administers the test and get an appointment. Here are the most recent telephone numbers for various areas:

➤ Asia & Australia 61-2-9414-3663

➤ Germany 49-2159-9233-50

➤ Japan 813-3269-9620

➤ Latin America 1-612-820-5200

➤ USA and Canada 1-800-795-3926

➤ UK 44-181-607-3850

To schedule an exam, call at least one day in advance, but do not count on getting an early appointment. In some areas of the U.S., tests are booked up for weeks in advance. To cancel or reschedule an exam, you must call at least 12 hours before the scheduled test time (or you may be charged). When calling Sylvan Prometric, please have the following information ready for the telesales staffer who handles your call:

➤ Your name, organization, and mailing address.

➤ A unique Test ID. (For most U.S. citizens, this will be your Social Security number. Citizens of other nations can use their taxpayer IDs or make other arrangements with the order taker.)

➤ The name and number of the exam you wish to take. (For this book, the exam number is 310-025, and the exam name is "Sun Certified Programmer for the Java 2 Platform.")

➤ The voucher number you obtained from Sun.

You may also locate a testing center on the Web. The main Web page for Sylvan-Prometric is http://www.sylvanprometric.com/. A very complete locator system is provided at http://www.sylvanprometric.com/testcenterlocator/zipcode.asp.

When using this system to locate a nearby test center use "Sun Micro Educational Services" for the "Testing Partner" input, then select the exam (310-025) and the state. This produces a list of cities, testing centers, and contact numbers. Pick one of these and it will even give you a map to the testing center.

Taking The Test

When you show up for your appointment, be sure that you bring two forms of identification that have your signature on them, including one with a photograph. You won't be allowed to take any printed material into the testing environment, but you can study The Cram Sheet from the front of this book while you are waiting. Try to arrive at least 15 minutes before the scheduled time slot.

All exams are completely closed-book. In fact, you will not be permitted to take anything with you into the testing area, but you will be furnished with a blank sheet of paper and a pen. I suggest that you immediately write down on that sheet of paper all the information you've memorized from the Cram Sheet.

You will have some time to compose yourself, to record memorized information, and even to take a sample orientation exam before you must begin the real thing. I suggest you take the orientation test before taking your first exam, but because they're all more or less identical in layout, behavior, and controls, you probably won't need to do this more than once.

About This Book

Each topical Exam Cram chapter follows a regular structure, along with graphical cues about important or useful information. Here's the structure of a typical chapter:

➤ **Opening Hotlists** Each chapter begins with a list of the terms, tools, and techniques that you must learn and understand before you can be fully conversant with that chapter's subject matter. I follow the hotlists with one or two introductory paragraphs to set the stage for the rest of the chapter.

➤ **Topical Coverage** After the opening hotlists, each chapter covers a series of at least four topics related to the chapter's subject title. Throughout this section, I highlight topics or concepts likely to appear on a test using a special Study Alert layout, like this:

This is what a Study Alert looks like. Normally, a Study Alert stresses concepts, terms, software, or activities that are likely to relate to one or more certification test questions. For that reason, any information found offset in a Study Alert format is worthy of unusual attentiveness on your part.

Pay close attention to material flagged as a Study Alert; although all the information in this book pertains to what you need to know to pass the exam, I flag certain items that are really important. You'll find what appears in the meat of each chapter to be worth knowing, too, when preparing for the test. Because this book's material is very condensed, I recommend that you use this book along with other resources to achieve the maximum benefit.

➤ **Practice Questions** Although I talk about test questions and topics throughout each chapter, this section presents a series of mock test questions and explanations of both correct and incorrect answers. I also try to point out especially tricky questions by using a special icon, like this:

Ordinarily, this icon flags the presence of a particularly devious inquiry, if not an outright trick question. Trick questions are calculated to be answered incorrectly if not read more than once, and carefully, at that.

Although they're not ubiquitous, such questions make regular appearances on the exams. That's why I say exam questions are as much about reading comprehension as they are about knowing your material inside out and backwards.

➤ **Details And Resources** Every chapter ends with a section titled "Need To Know More?", which provides direct pointers to Sun and third-party resources offering more details on the chapter's subject. In addition, this section tries to rank or at least rate the quality and thoroughness of the topic's coverage by each resource. If you find a resource you like in this collection, use it, but don't feel compelled to use all the resources. On the other hand, I only recommend resources I use on a regular basis, so none of our recommendations will be a waste of your time or money.

The bulk of the book follows this chapter structure slavishly, but there are a few other elements that I'd like to point out. Chapter 15 is a sample test that provides a good review of the material presented throughout the book to ensure you're ready for the exam. Chapter 16 is an answer key to the sample test that appears in Chapter 15. Additionally, you'll find a glossary that explains terms and an index that you can use to track down terms as they appear in the text, as I mentioned before.

Finally, the tear-out Cram Sheet attached next to the inside front cover of this Exam Cram book represents a condensed and compiled collection of facts, figures, and tips that I think you should memorize before taking the test. Because you can dump this information out of your head onto a piece of paper before answering any exam questions, you can master this information by brute force—you only need to remember it long enough to write it down when you walk into the test room. You might even want to look at it in the car or in the lobby of the testing center just before you walk in to take the test.

Typographic Conventions

Listings of Java programs and code fragments will be in a monospaced font. In some cases, I have used a line number at the start of each line of code to facilitate referring to a particular statement as in the following example:

```
1.   int n = 42 ;
2.   long j =  4096L ; // appending L or l makes it a long
3.   long k =  0xFFFFFFL ;
4.   byte b2 =  010 ;  // an octal literal
```

If you are typing code into an editor to experiment with one of my examples, do not type the line numbers.

When Java keywords, class names, and other words or phrases that could literally occur in a Java program are mentioned in the text, they are bolded. For example, "classes similar to **java.lang.Integer** are provided to wrap **byte, short,** and **long** integer primitives." Many classes and Java keywords are similar to words used in normal discussions, such as **Integer** in the preceding sentence. The bolding convention is used to alert you to the fact that the word or phrase is being used in the Java programming sense. You should also pay close attention to the occurrence of uppercase letters. The use in Java of **Boolean** and **boolean** is *not* interchangeable. Finally, I will occasionally use *italics* to emphasize a term, particularly on the first use.

How To Use This Book

The order of chapters is what I consider to be a logical progression for someone who wants to review all of the topics on the exam. If you feel that you are already up to speed with Java at the JDK 1.1 level, the main thing you will need to review is the Collections API as discussed in Chapter 10. In any case, you should try all of the questions in the chapters and the sample test in Chapter 15.

Providing Feedback

If you find errors, sections that could be worded more clearly, or questions that seem deceptive, please feel free to let me know by email at wbrogden@bga.com.

Earlier study guides for Java certification (not published by Coriolis) were marred by extensive typos and other errors. I have tried to double-check everything in this book, but if some errors did slip through, they will be documented as soon as I find out about them and reported at http://www.lanw.com/books/errata/default.htm.

Self-Assessment

Since Sun first released Java freely over the Internet, over a million curious programmers have downloaded the Java Development Kit or bought a book with the intent to teach themselves how to program in Java. Although many schools are now teaching beginning programming using Java, most Java programmers have been largely self-taught.

Sun's program for certifying Java programmers is designed to help both programmers and potential employers by providing benchmarks of programmer confidence. In addition to the programmer certification this book is devoted to, Sun also offers developer and architect certifications. Offering these certifications is part of Sun's plan to make Java the language of choice for many applications, especially those involving networks.

Java In The Real World

Due to the rapid expansion of applications and toolkits, Java is now being applied in a huge range of scenarios. A Java programmer might find himself or herself working in many different areas such as the following:

➤ Client Server projects using applets on Web browsers and Java-based Web server

➤ Applications with graphical user interfaces that have nothing to do with the Internet

➤ Applications that run on non-traditional systems with the Java card language subset or even the Java ring

No matter which area you are interested in, the language basics as tested in the Sun Certified Programmer for the Java 2 Platform exam will be important.

The Ideal Programmer Certification Candidate

One thing the ideal candidate does not have to have is years of experience. The certification test does not cover esoteric items that you only pick up by burning the midnight oil while slaving over a two-year project. Instead, the test requires sound knowledge of the fundamentals. The ideal candidate for the certification exam will be able to do the following:

➤ Know all of the Java keywords and how they are used.

➤ Be able to create legal Java identifiers and reject illegal ones.

➤ Know the distinction between primitives and reference variables.

➤ Know how to create and initialize primitive variables, strings, and arrays.

➤ Know the range of values and limitations of all Java primitive variables.

➤ Understand what is meant by the *scope* of variables.

➤ Know the conventions that govern the way the JVM starts and runs applications and applets.

➤ Know what every Java mathematical, logical, and bitwise operator with primitives does.

➤ Be able to apply the functions in the Math class.

➤ Know what every Java operator with reference variables does, especially the operators that work with strings.

➤ Be able to decide when to use the equals method and when to use the == operator.

➤ Correctly use casts with primitive variables and reference variables.

➤ Use the primitive wrapper classes in the java.lang package and predict the consequences of the immutability of wrapper class objects.

➤ Choose the right access modifiers to control the visibility of classes, variables, and methods.

➤ Know the implications of declaring a class or method to be abstract.

➤ Know the implications of declaring a class, method, or variable to be final.

➤ Know the implications of declaring a method or variable to be static.

➤ Understand how to design programs using the concept of interfaces.

➤ Be able to use the interfaces specified in the java.lang and java.util packages.

➤ Predict when a default constructor will be created for a class.

➤ Distinguish between overloading and overriding of methods and be able to write both types of code.

➤ Understand the uses of all forms of inner classes.

➤ Use all of Java's program flow control statements including break and continue.

➤ Create, throw, catch, and process exceptions and be able to predict which exceptions the compiler will require specific provision for.

➤ Understand the benefits of encapsulation and inheritance in object-oriented design and be able to design classes demonstrating the "is a" and "has a" relationships.

➤ Be able to predict when objects may be garbage collected and know the implications of Java's garbage collection mechanism.

➤ Know how to create finalize methods and predict when a finalize method will run.

➤ Be able to write code that creates and starts threads using both the Runnable interface and extensions of the Thread class.

➤ Use the synchronized keyword to prevent problems with multiple threads interacting with the same data.

➤ Write code using the wait, notify, and notifyAll methods to coordinate threads.

➤ Select the correct interface or class from the Collections API to accomplish a particular task.

➤ Write user interfaces with the AWT classes and layout managers that present a required appearance and behavior.

➤ Write code that implements listener interfaces to receive events and extract information from them.

➤ Understand how File class objects are used.

➤ Write code using streams to read and write text files.

Assessing Your Readiness

People come to Java from a variety of backgrounds; however, even years of experience are not a guarantee of good preparation for the test. In fact, even experienced Java programmers may have problems with the test if they have let their fundamental skills slip.

Programming Background

1. Do you have significant experience with C or C++? [Yes or No]

    No C experience: People frequently ask if they should learn C before starting Java, my emphatic answer is *no*, Java is easier to learn than C. The idea that Java users should know C may have gotten started before there were good books for beginners in Java. Many schools have switched to Java for beginner programming courses.

    Yes: The syntax of Java will be familiar, just watch out for some traps that I point out in the book. Don't expect any of your C tricks to work in Java.

2. Do you have significant experience with creating object-oriented programs? If yes, proceed to question 3.

    If you do not have significant experience with creating object-oriented programs, Java is the right place to start because it is so much simpler than C++. There are several good books available. *Thinking in Java* by Bruce Eckel is widely recommended as a good starting book if your object-oriented programming background is weak. You can download it for free from www.bruceeckel.com or purchase it on paper (Prentice-Hall, 1998, ISBN 0-13-659723-8).

    A very convenient resource is the design of the Java language itself. Study the way the graphical interface components in the java.awt package make use of inheritance. The source code for all of these classes comes with the JDK download.

Experience With Java

3. Have you written Java programs as applets, graphical applications, and non-graphical applications? If not, you must expand your experience in this area because each type of program has its own unique requirements. Working with Java 1.1-level applets is adequate experience.

4. Is your experience entirely with Java 1.1 or 1.02? If so, you must act to get some experience with Java at the JDK 1.2 level.

5. Do you have a good set of up-to-date Java resources? At a minimum, you should have downloaded the Java Development Kit and documentation from the Sun Web site (http://java.sun.com)—this is still referred to as JDK 1.2 in spite of the fact that Sun marketing literature refers to Java 2.

   You should download the current copy of Sun's Java tutorial from http://java.sun.com/docs/books/tutorial/index.html. They are continually adding to this, so refresh it if your copy is more than two months old. This tutorial comes with many sample programs in a range of complexities. For test preparation you should concentrate on the simple ones.

   Books that were written for the JDK 1.1 level of Java will still be useful for Java basics. The new collections related classes are most likely to be on the test, but are missing from existing books.

   Books that were written for the JDK 1.02 level of Java may do more harm than good due to the major changes in such important topics as event handling.

6. In your current Java projects, does the first pass of the compiler over your new class turn up frequent type casting errors and other mistakes related to Java basics? Use these errors to direct you to the topics you need to review.

7. Can you solve Java problems? For example, if you read the "help me" messages on the comp.lang.java newsgroup, does the correct solution for basic problems usually occur to you? (I'm not talking about problems involving Swing or databases or other advanced topics, just the basic problems.) Helping other programmers with Java problems is a great way to assess your own knowledge.

I Think I'm Ready, What Next?

Before you put up some money and schedule the test, try some of the mock Java exams that can be found at various places on the Web. When you can do well on these tests and can check off every item on the list presented at the start of this chapter, you're ready to sign up. Good luck!

Java And The Sun Certification Test

Terms you'll need to understand:

➤ Radio button

➤ Checkbox

➤ Text entry questions

Techniques you'll need to master:

➤ Assessing your exam-readiness

➤ Preparation based on the objectives

➤ Practice, practice, practice

➤ Pacing yourself

➤ Don't panic

➤ Informed guessing

This book is intended to prepare you for taking and passing the Sun Certified Programmer for the Java 2 Platform exam. In this chapter, I cover the way the test is administered, suggestions for test-taking strategy and tactics, how to prepare for the test, and a short history of the various versions of the Java language.

Subsequent chapters explore various aspects of Java that are likely to appear on the test or are essential to understanding the Java programming language. This book is not intended to cover all aspects of Java, that is a task that takes a whole bookshelf these days.

Assessing Exam-Readiness

I strongly recommend that you read through and take the Self-Assessment included with this book (it appears just before this chapter, in fact). This will help you compare your knowledge base to the requirements for passing the Sun Certified Programmer exam, and it will also help you identify parts of your background or experience that may be in need of improvement, enhancement, or further learning. If you get the right set of basics under your belt, obtaining Sun certification will be that much easier.

Once you've worked through the *Exam Cram*, have read the supplementary materials as needed, and have taken the practice test, you'll have a pretty clear idea of when you should be ready to take the real exam. The practice test included in this book is considered slightly harder than the real one. We strongly recommend that you keep practicing until your scores top the 70 percent mark; 75 percent would be a good goal to give yourself some margin for error in a real exam situation (where stress will play more of a role than when you practice). Once you hit that point, you should be ready to go. But if you get through the practice exam in this book without attaining that score, you should keep taking the practice test and studying the materials until you get there.

The Test Environment

Tests are administered by the Sylvan Prometric organization using typical Windows-based computers. You will be in a quiet environment with one or more testing stations in a separate room. Typically, this room will have a large picture window that enables the test coordinator to keep an eye on the test takers to make sure people are not talking to each other or using notes. Naturally, you are not allowed to take any notes into the room.

There will be scratch paper or an erasable plastic sheet with a felt tip marker. You can use this to write down key information; however, you are not allowed to take any notes out of the exam. If there is any topic you have a hard time remembering, you might want to scan the Cram Sheet from the front of this book just before taking the test and then make a few quick notes when you get into the testing room.

The computer will be a pretty typical system with mouse and keyboard. The initial screen gives you the option to run a quick tutorial test. If you have never taken one of these tests before, you should take the tutorial. The real test timer does not start until you have specifically chosen to start the real test. You are allowed 120 minutes to answer 59 questions. This is plenty of time if you have studied the material.

Question Types

Questions are presented on the screen in a scrollable window. There are three different styles of questions:

➤ **Multiple Choice With Radio Buttons** This type of question presents a number of possible choices labeled with lowercase letters and presented with a round radio style button. You can answer by either clicking the button with the mouse or typing the letter on the keyboard. Only one item can be chosen.

➤ **Multiple Choice With Checkboxes** In this type of question, the number of correct answers may vary from one to all of them. To indicate this, you will be presented with square checkboxes instead of radio buttons. All correct answers must be checked for you to get any credit for the question, no partial credit is awarded for partially correct selections.

➤ **Text Entry Questions** This type of question presents a one-line text area for you to type the answer. Pay close attention to what the question is asking for so you don't type more than what it wants. In most cases, a list of possible words is presented as part of the question so what you have to do is select the correct words and type them in the right order. Remember that Java is case-sensitive.

Here is a sample multiple-choice question that requires you to select a single correct answer. Following the question is a brief summary of each potential answer and why it is either right or wrong.

Question 1

> Here are some statements about the **java.lang.System** class. Which of the following statements is correct?
>
> ○ a. You must initialize **System** with a path and filename if you want to use the **System.err** output.
>
> ○ b. The **System.timer** method allows timing processes to the nearest microsecond.
>
> ○ c. The **System.arraycopy** method works only with arrays of primitives.
>
> ○ d. The **System.exit** method takes an **int** primitive parameter.

Answer d is correct. The **System.exit** method takes an **int** primitive value that can be used as an error code returned to the operating system. Answer a is incorrect because the **System.err** print stream is automatically created by the JVM. Answer b is incorrect because there is no **System.timer** method and the **System** method that does return the time is only precise to the millisecond. Answer c is incorrect because **System.arraycopy** works with both primitive and reference arrays.

Let's examine a question that requires choosing multiple answers. This type of question provides checkboxes rather than radio buttons for marking all appropriate selections.

Question 2

> Which of the following statements about the **java.util.Vector** and **java.util.Hashtable** classes are correct? [Check all correct answers]
>
> ❑ a. A **Vector** can hold object references or primitive values.
>
> ❑ b. A **Vector** maintains object references in the order they were added.
>
> ❑ c. A **Hashtable** requires **String** objects as keys.
>
> ❑ d. A **Hashtable** maintains object references in the order they were added.
>
> ❑ e. Both **Vector** and **Hashtable** use **synchronized** methods to avoid problems due to more than one **Thread** trying to access the same collection.

Answers b and e are correct. Answer b is correct and answer d is incorrect because a Vector maintains the order in which objects are added but a **Hashtable** does not. Answer e is correct—this is an accurate statement. Answer a is incorrect because a **Vector** can only hold references, not primitives. If you need to store primitive values in a **Vector** you must create wrapper objects. Answer c is incorrect because any object may be used as a **Hashtable** key (although **Strings** are frequently used).

Navigating The Test

There are clickable buttons near the bottom of the screen that are used to move to the next question or back to the previous one. Pressing the Enter key also moves you to the next question.

There is a checkbox at the top of the screen that lets you mark a question to consider later. Before the test is finished, you will be given a chance to review all of the questions or go directly to those you have marked. You should mark a difficult question and leave it for later rather than spending too much time on it. It is quite possible that a later question will provide a clue and remind you of the correct answer.

Finishing And Scoring

The test is scored in the 10 categories described in the test objectives document at the Sun certification Web site, as discussed in "The Test Objectives" section, later in this chapter. After you complete the test, your test results will be printed out with a bar graph showing how you did in each category. Only the aggregate score determines whether you pass or fail. The lowest passing score is 71 percent, which corresponds to getting 42 questions out of 59 correct.

Test-Taking Techniques

The most important advice we can give you is to read each question carefully. Be sure you answer the question as written and don't jump to conclusions. For example, you may be asked to check all of the correct names for Java variables or the question may ask for all those which would cause a compiler error.

Some questions involve long code samples or other material that you will have to scroll the test window to see. Don't start by reading all of the question and code in detail, scan all of the possible answers first. It may turn out that keeping the possible answers in mind will help you understand what the question is really about.

Typos

It is possible (but not likely) that a typo in a question may make all of the possible answers impossible. In that case, make your best guess as to what was intended, answer the question and move on.

Guessing

Because scoring is based on the number right out of the total number in the test, it is better to guess than to leave a question blank. You can frequently eliminate some of the possible answers to improve the odds of guessing correctly.

Preparation For The Test

I feel that it will be very helpful for you to have a working copy of the JDK 1.2 available. As of this writing, the only source is the Sun Web site at http://java.sun.com/products/index.html.

The total installation file is over 20 MB, but you can download it in pieces if necessary. It takes a huge amount of disk space to install: over 65 MB after you have the installation file downloaded, so clean out your hard disk. You can also download the JDK documentation which is very complete but also very bulky.

Naturally, you should practice with the questions at the end of each chapter and the practice test in Chapter 15. There are also a fair number of Web sites devoted to preparation for the Java 1.1 and Java 2 programmer certification exams. I've listed some here, but more will probably appear, so try a Web search engine.

Practice With Mock Exams

There are some additional practice tests available. First on the list is from the main Sun certification page at http://suned.sun.com/usa/cert_test.html. This page has a pointer to a very short list of example questions. In addition, Marcus Green's Java Programmer Certification Page has a mock exam at http://www.software.u-net.com/javaexam/javaexam.htm.

Finally, I will be maintaining and adding to the mock exam at http://www.lanw.com/java/javacert. I used this practice test to evaluate sample questions for this book and to locate topics that most new Java programmers have a hard time with.

The Test Objectives

Sun publishes a rather general statement of the test objectives at http:// suned.sun.com/usa/cert_test.html. The major sections of the objectives list are the categories used for grading the test:

➤ Declarations and Access Control

➤ Flow Control and Exception Handling

➤ Garbage Collection

➤ Language Fundamentals

➤ Operators and Assignments

➤ Overloading, etc.

➤ Threads

➤ The java.awt package-Layout

➤ The java.lang package

➤ The java.util package

Note that none of the specialized libraries and toolkits, such the Swing graphics components, JDBC (Java Database Connectivity), or JavaBeans is mentioned. This test covers nothing but the basics, and it covers them thoroughly. Even programmers who have been working with Java for years and have created significant applications may get tripped up by basic language details they have forgotten.

Several certification test takers have remarked that many questions seemed designed to trap C and C++ programmers who don't really get the fundamental differences between C++ and Java. We have made special notes on topics that may cause trouble if you are thinking like a C programmer.

Comparison With The Java 1.1 Exam

The objectives for the Java 2 test are quite similar to those for the Java 1.1 exam. The main differences are:

➤ **Graphics** There is less emphasis on the AWT graphics capabilities in the Java 2 exam. However, you can count on some questions that require familiarity with the AWT classes, and especially the layout managers. This book covers that material in Chapters 11 and 12.

➤ **Utilities** The Java 2 exam will likely include some questions on the classes in the Collections API which is new for the Java 2 release. We cover these classes in Chapter 10.

If you have been working mainly with Java 1.1 and are wondering which exam to take, the Collections API is the only new material you will have to study to take the Java 2 exam. I recommend going ahead and taking the Java 2 exam, to gain the most recent certification.

What Happens When You Pass?

After your test is graded, there will be a button on the screen to print the results. Be sure you click that button a couple of times. The test administrator will stamp one copy (only one) with an "Authorized Testing Center" seal. Keep that one safe and use the other one to brag on. Sun will be notified automatically, which should start the ball rolling on you getting an official certificate from Sun. Until you get that, an online database at http://merchant.hibbertco.com/sun_certification/ is supposed to be able to verify your score.

When I passed the 1.1 programmer's exam, I got a nice certificate, a neat looking lapel pin, and some Java logo sheets for use on business cards and stationary. Sun says it may take up to six weeks to get any of this, so it is not surprising that I have not gotten back anything for passing the Java 2 exam. As of this writing, Sun seems to be re-evaluating their policy on logo sheets, so you should check with the Sun Education Web site for the latest information.

Will It Help You Get A Job?

There has been a lot of discussion on Java-related newsgroups on the value of certification when applying for a job. Some employers say that they like to see applicants that have passed the exam and some say they ignore certifications. Everybody agrees that years of experience with a variety of languages and successful projects weigh more than any certification.

I feel that the greatest value of the exam is that it gives you confidence that you have mastered the basics, but "Sun Certified Programmer" is a pretty nice thing to have on your resume.

How We Prepared This Book

The idea of an *Exam Cram* book for the Java Programmers exam got started in late 1997. Coriolis had originally planned a book on the Java 1.1 exam, but then Sun announced that there would be a new test when the Java Development Kit version 1.2 came out, so we thought we would wait for that. As you may know, the 1.2 release was delayed several times and the final version was not released until December, 1998, and is now called the Java 2 Platform.

This long lead-time gave us a unique opportunity. For over a year, we have offered a mock Java certification exam administered by a Java applet on the LANWrights Web site at http://www.lanw.com/java/javacert.

Using this Web site, we have been able to test proposed questions to be used in this book. Thanks to user feedback, we have been able to eliminate typos and ambiguous questions and to determine those topics that are most likely to cause trouble for the typical programmer. Thousands of tests have been administered and evaluated. We feel that this unique resource has enabled us to create example questions to emphasize those points which are most likely to cause you trouble.

Study Resources

To prepare for the exam, you should certainly have downloaded and installed the JDK 1.2 package from the Sun Web site. When in doubt about a detail in Java, by all means, try some example programs. The compact format of an *Exam Cram* book keeps us from publishing extensive example programs. If you want lots of examples, look for our *Java 2 Exam Prep* (The Coriolis Group, ISBN 1-57610-261-0), which includes a large number of projects illustrating various important points.

The Java 2 (JDK 1.2) package includes a large number of demonstration programs, many of them very elegant and spectacular. However, most of these programs are designed to demonstrate advanced Java features that are not a major part of the test, so your time may be better spent writing your own programs and making your own mistakes. There is nothing like tracking down the cause of a compiler error message to reinforce your understanding of basic Java concepts.

Java Books

A truly astonishing number of books have been published on various aspects of Java programming. Those that dealt with the 1.0 version of the language are not of much use anymore. Fortunately, practically all aspects of language basics have remained the same on the move from Java 1.1 to Java 2. Citations to these books appear at the end of each chapter. When contemplating buying a book, you should check one of the online bookstores to see if an updated version is available. There is a great Java section at http://www.computerliteracy.com/.

Java Developers Connection

Sun's Web site for developers has tutorials, articles on advanced topics, and the current bug list. This site also has early release versions of various advanced toolkits. You need to register but it doesn't cost anything. This site is located at http://java.sun.com/jcd/index.html.

Just The FAQs

There is a tremendous Java support community on the Web with many pages devoted to Java programming. Some of the most useful are those devoted to frequently asked questions (FAQs). The following list points to the best sites I've found:

➤ http://www-net.com/java/faq/ Has pointers to a number of Java FAQ collections.

➤ http://www.afu.com/javafaq.html One of the oldest and largest FAQs is maintained by Peter van der Linden.

➤ http://mindprod.com/ Another extensive collection of FAQs and a Java Glossary, maintained by Roedy Green.

➤ http://www.woj.com/tech/javacert/discussion/ Provides an ongoing discussion of the certification tests.

Notes On Java History

It has been quite a wild ride for those of us who have been following the fortunes of Java. There have been two major changes and any number of minor changes on the route from the first "beta" release in the spring of 1995 to the present Java 2. Although none of the following will be on the test, I am including the information in Table 1.1 on Java history to help orient you in the vast amount of Java related material you will find in the bookstores and on the Internet. When considering a book to buy, look at the publication date.

That brings us up to the present—now it's time for you to get to work!

Table 1.1	The history of Java.	
Year	**Month**	**Detail**
1995	May	Sun's first announcement of Java (1.0 alpha).
	August	Netscape licenses Java for the Navigator browser.
1996	January	Sun releases JDK 1.0 production version with major changes from beta. Every week brings new announcements of licensing deals, new APIs, and scads of publicity. Programmer and Developer certification tests become available.
	December	Sun announces JDK 1.1 with major changes and improvements.
1997	March	Release of draft specifications for Java 2D, the graphics toolkit that eventually ends up in Java 2. JDK 1.1.1 released.
	December	First public release of JDK 1.2 beta 2.
1998	March	JDK 1.2 beta 3 released.
	June	Preliminary list of objectives for the 1.2 programmers exam is much more complex than the 1.1 objectives.
	July	Beta release 4 includes major changes in the Collections API.
	September –November	Two "Release Candidate" versions appeared in this interval with major changes. Fortunately these changes were not related to the exam objectives.
	December	JDK 1.2 Final release. Sun is now calling the entire package Java 2 but the Sun technical documentation continues to refer to JDK 1.2.
1999	January	Final version of the test objectives released.
	February	Sun Certified Programmer for the Java 2 Platform exam released.

Language Fundamentals

Terms you'll need to understand:

- √ Package
- √ Import
- √ Main method
- √ Instance variable
- √ Reference variable

- √ Public
- √ Protected
- √ Private
- √ Javadoc
- √ Deprecated

Techniques you'll need to master:

- √ Distinguishing the correct order and usage of items in Java source code files
- √ Giving the correct form of a main method and using parameters passed on the command line to a Java application
- √ Identifying Java keywords from a list of keywords and non-keywords
- √ Recognizing legal and illegal Java identifiers

- √ Stating the range of values in the primitive types: **byte**, **short**, **int**, **long**, and **char**
- √ Knowing the state of member variables that have not been explicitly initialized
- √ Determining the value of an element of an array of any base type
- √ Using the standard Javadoc format documentation to identify and use methods and variables in classes and in superclasses

In this chapter, I review the basics of Java source code files: keywords and identifiers. Because Java borrows much of its syntax from C++, we will try to point out areas in which C++ programmers may go astray. I also cover the basics of Java variables and the behavior of Java "primitive" data types. Finally, I discuss the Javadoc format of the Java API (application programming interface) documentation and how to use it.

Although many different commercial Java development environments exist, the Java Development Kit (JDK), as released by Sun Microsystems, is the only one the Certified Java Programmer exam covers.

Structure Of Java Programs

Programming in Java consists of writing source code that defines one or more classes. Because Java is completely object-oriented, all Java code is inside a class definition. When a Java program runs, it uses these class definitions to create objects that contain all of the program variables and instructions.

 In Java, there is no such thing as a global variable or any function that is not part of a class, and therefore an object. Java groups the various utility calls you might expect to find in a system library into classes, frequently as "static" methods. The implications of the **static** keyword are discussed in Chapters 3 and 4.

Java programs are defined in source code files, which always have a file type of **java** and which follow strict rules for their naming and contents. You can create source code files with any editor that generates ASCII text. Each Java class is completely defined in a single file. More than one class can be defined in the file as long as there is only one public class.

Source Code Comments

There are three styles of comment notation used in Java. Any text between "//" and the end of the line is a comment. Text starting with "/*" and terminated with "*/" is used to make multiple line comments. The special form starting with "/**" and terminated with "*/" is used to create comments that can be processed by the *javadoc* program to produce HTML formatted documentation. Creating javadoc comments is beyond the scope of this book, consult the resources cited at the end of the chapter for more details.

Class Names, Packages, And Imports

Java uses the concept of *package*s to control naming of classes. For instance, many standard library math functions are in the **Math** class, which is in the

java.lang package along with the classes for other commonly used objects, such as strings. Therefore, **java.lang.Math** is the complete name of this class.

All Java programs are automatically assumed to use the **java.lang** package, but the compiler must be specifically instructed to use classes in other packages. This instruction is in the form of one or more **import** statements. The **import** statements tell the compiler where to look for classes. They don't require classes to be loaded, and they don't add to the final bulk of the compiled class files. You can import an entire group of classes in a package using the familiar wild card "*" to imply any name, as shown in line 1, which imports all classes in the **java.applet** package, or a specific class as shown in line 2:

```
1.    import java.applet.* ;
2.    import java.applet.AudioClip ;
```

Note that the **import** statements end with a semicolon, like all Java statements.

As an alternative to specifying a package in an **import** statement, you can use the fully qualified name of a class in an expression. For example, instead of the **import** statement in line 2 (in the previous code), you could refer to the **java.applet.AudioClip** class.

The result of compiling a Java source code file is the creation of a single class file for each class defined in the source code. The Java compiler turns your class definitions into bytecodes, which are in turn interpreted by a Java interpreter. The name of this file will be the name of the class, and the file type will be class. Case is significant when you're naming Java files and classes, and long file names must be supported by the operating system.

When you're creating your own classes, you can place them in a package by means of the package declaration. There can be only one package declaration in a Java file, and if it appears, it must be the first non-comment statement. If no package declaration appears, the class will belong to the default package. Because any **import** statements must precede any class definitions, the required order for these primary elements is as follows:

1. 0 or 1 package declaration

2. 0, 1, or many **import** statements

3. 1 or many class definitions, but at most one public class definition

Being able to apply these rules is one of the objectives of the Java Programmer Certification Exam.

More About Package Names

All of the standard Java library is in packages whose names start with **java,** and Sun has suggested rules for naming your own packages that are generally observed in the industry. For instance, custom classes provided in the Symantec development environment are in packages with names that start with **symantec.** The package name implies a directory structure in which the class files will be found. Packages also have significance in terms of the "visibility" of classes, as you will see in the following section.

Java Reserved Words And Keywords

Table 2.1 includes language keywords—the boolean literals and words that are reserved by the language definition but are not currently used. Note that keywords are always all lowercase. You will need to be extremely familiar with the words in this list.

Table 2.1 gives the total list of reserved words. In addition to the boolean literal values **true** and **false,** and the special value **null,** you will need to be able to distinguish the words that are reserved but not actually used, as shown in Table 2.2.

Table 2.1	All Java reserved words.			
abstract	do	implements	protected	transient
boolean	double	import	public	true
break	else	inner	rest	try
byte	extends	instanceof	return	var
byvalue	false	int	short	void
case	final	interface	static	volatile
cast	finally	long	strictfp	while
catch	float	native	super	
char	for	new	switch	
class	future	operator	synchronized	
const	generic	outer	this	
continue	goto	package	throw	
default	if	private	throws	

Table 2.2	Words reserved but not used currently.		
byvalue	future	inner	rest
cast	generic	operator	var
const	goto	outer	

Packages And Visibility

Our exploration of Java keywords starts with those (used) that affect the visibility of classes, variables, and methods. *Visibility* of a class controls the ability of other classes to create objects or gain access to the variables and methods in the class. This subject is covered in greater detail in Chapter 4.

➤ **Public visibility** A class, variable, or method declared **public** can be used by any class in the program.

➤ **Protected visibility** A variable or method declared **protected** can be used only by classes in the same package or in a derived class in the same or a different package.

➤ **Default, or package visibility** If none of the visibility keywords are used, the item is said to have *package visibility*, meaning that only classes in the same package can use it.

➤ **Private visibility** The **private** keyword is not used with classes, only with variables and methods. A private variable or method can only be used within a class.

Familiar But Wrong Words

You may run into words that sound as if they should be Java keywords because of your familiarity with C or C++, or because they are used in casual discussion of programming in Java. For example, the word "friend" is sometimes used in discussion of class relationships, but it is not a keyword. Other familiar words that are not used in Java include delete, inline, using, and virtual. Also, Java does not use any of the C preprocessor directives, such as **#include**, **#ifdef**, or **#typedef**. Furthermore, because pointer arithmetic is impossible in Java, **sizeof** is not used.

Identifiers

Words used in programs to name variables, classes, methods, or labels are *identifiers* and are subject to strict rules. None of the Java reserved words may be used as identifiers. An identifier can begin with a letter, a dollar sign, or an underscore character. Letters can be drawn from the Unicode character set, but the ASCII character set will probably be used on the test. The compiler generates an error if you try to use a digit or any punctuation other than the dollar sign and underscore to start an identifier. Identifiers are case-sensitive.

 Common errors that you may be asked to spot in test questions include inconsistent use of case in identifiers of classes or variables, and incorrect starting characters in identifiers.

The Java Interpreter And The JVM

In the Java Development Kit (JDK) environment, a Java program consists of class files that are interpreted by the Java Virtual Machine (JVM), which creates the objects defined in the class files and interacts with the host operating system to handle user input, file reading, and other hardware interactions. The JVM can detect many types of errors in class files, security violations, and runtime errors.

Web browsers that support Java contain a JVM that is independent of any JDK components you have installed in your system. A JVM in a Web browser has many security restrictions imposed on it and deals with the operating system indirectly through the browser.

Java programs can also be compiled to binary code, which does not need an interpreter, but the Java Programmer Certification Exam covers the JDK environment only.

Data Types In Java

Java has four kinds of named data types and two categories of variables. The data types are primitives, classes, interfaces, and arrays. Variables can either contain primitive values or refer to objects. *Reference variables* refer to objects—you can think of the variable as containing a handle to the object. Naturally, the internal workings of the JVM deal with real pointers to memory, but these details are all concealed from you as a programmer.

Instance Variables And Static Variables

When a class is used to create an object, we say that the object is an *instance* of the class. Variables associated with the object are *instance* variables. It is also possible to have variables that belong to a class as a whole. These are referred to as *class* or *static* variables. Essentially, when the JVM reads a class file, it creates a class type object to represent the class and the static variables that belong to that object.

Reference Variables

Reference variables are declared in Java with a statement that gives the type of object to which the variable is expected to refer. For example, consider the following statements that declare two variables:

```
1.   Object anyRef ;
2.   String myString ;
```

The types of references these variables can hold depend on the object hierarchy. Because every class in Java descends from **Object, anyRef** could refer to any object. However, because **String** cannot be subclassed, **myString** can refer to a **String** object only. The rules about the relation of the declared type of a variable and the types of object references it can hold are discussed in detail in Chapter 6.

The contents of a newly declared reference variable depend on where it is declared. For instance, in variables and class variables, the content is the special value **null**. Variables that are declared inside code blocks are uninitialized. The Java compiler is able to detect the possibility of an uninitialized variable being used and issues an error.

References to a given object may be stored in any number of reference variables. The declared type of a variable may not match the type of the object it is referring to, but the object never forgets the class of which it is an instance.

Primitives

Java provides for certain common data types as primitives instead of objects to achieve acceptable performance. Java has four basic types of primitives: integers, character types, floating-point types, and boolean types. The character type represents 16-bit Unicode characters and can be considered as an unsigned integer for many purposes. The integer types are all treated as signed, and range in size from 8 to 64 bits. The floating-point types are in the standard IEEE 754 format in 32- and 64-bit size. These formats are the same regardless of the hardware.

Integer Primitives

Table 2.3 characterizes the integer primitives. You should become very familiar with these characteristics. Note that the only integer primitive that is not treated as a signed number is **char,** which represents a Unicode character. Member variables of the **integer** primitive type are initialized to zero by default.

Table 2.3	Numeric primitives and their ranges.		
Type	**Contains**	**Size**	**Range Of Values**
byte	signed integer	8 bits	−128 to 127
short	signed integer	16 bits	−32768 to 32767
char	unsigned Unicode character	16 bits	\u0000 to \uFFFF
int	signed integer	32 bits	-2^{31} to $2^{31} - 1$
long	signed integer	64 bits	-2^{63} to $2^{63} - 1$

Floating-Point Primitives

Table 2.4 summarizes the characteristics of the floating-point primitives. Questions about the floating-point primitives tend to be related to the initialization and manipulation of floating-point variables. Member variables of the floating-point types are initialized to zero by default.

Boolean Primitive Variables

The two possible values for a boolean are, of course, **true** and **false**. Member variables of the boolean type are initialized to **false** by default. Unlike integers in C, integers in Java can never be interpreted as boolean values, so expressions used for flow control must evaluate to boolean.

Arrays

You can think of a Java array as a special type of object that knows the data type it contains and the number of these items it can hold. Arrays can hold primitives, references to regular objects, and references to other arrays. Be sure to remember that addressing elements in an array start with zero. One of the major safety features of Java is that every attempt to address an array element is checked to ensure that the bounds are not exceeded.

Declaring An Array

Array variables may be declared separately from any initialization of the array elements. Here are some examples of array declarations:

```
1.  int[] counts ;
2.  String names[] ;
3.  boolean flags[][] ;
```

Statement 1 declares that the variable **counts** is an array of **int** primitives. Statement 2 declares that the variable **names** is an array of references to **String**

Table 2.4	**Floating-point primitives.**		
Type	**Contains**	**Size**	**Approximate Maximum And Minimum**
float	single precision IEEE standard	32 bits	$\pm\, 3.4 \times 10^{38}$ to $\pm\, 1.4 \times 10^{-45}$
double	double precision IEEE standard	64 bits	$\pm 1.8 \times 10^{308}$ to $\pm 4.9 \times 10^{-324}$

objects. Note that the square brackets can follow either the array name or the array type. Statement 3 declares that the variable **flags** is a two-dimensional array of boolean primitives. Note that in these statements, we have not set the size of the arrays, and no memory has been allocated for the array items.

Creating An Array

The size of an array is fixed when it is created with the **new** operator or with special combined declaration and initialization statements. Here are examples of creating some arrays (note that lines 2 and 3 combine declaration and array creation):

```
1.   counts = new int[20] ; // assuming counts was declared int[]
2.   String names[] = new String[100] ;   // combines declaration and
                                           // creation
3.   boolean[][] flags = new boolean[8][8] ;
```

When arrays of primitives are created, they are filled with the default values: **zero** for numerics and **false** for booleans. Reference variable arrays, on the other hand, are filled with the special value **null**. After you have created an array, you can use the length variable to find out the number of elements the array has.

Initializing An Array

Arrays of primitives are automatically initialized to the default values, but reference variable arrays contain references to objects only after you create each individual object. In other words, there is no way to "bulk" initialize. In the following code, statement 1 declares and creates an array of **Point** objects, but there are no objects in the array until statement 2 runs. Statement 3 illustrates use of the length variable belonging to the array:

```
1.   Point spots[] = new Point[20];
2.   for(int i = 0 ; i < 20 ; i++){spots[i] = new Point(i,0);}
3.   int count = spots.length ;
```

Program Conventions

You will probably see some questions that involve the conventions for starting a Java application. The command line to start a Java application consists of the name of the Java interpreter, the name of the starting class (just the name—the class file type is assumed), and zero or more parameters. The JVM expects to find a method named **main** with the signature as follows:

```
public static void main(String[] args )
```

This method will be the first one executed by the JVM. The command-line parameters are turned into an array of **String** objects that is passed to the **main** method. The array is typically named **args**, but it could be named anything. For example, the command to run an application named **MyApp** with a word and two numbers as input parameters would look like this:

```
>java MyApp Texas 1.03 200
```

The main method would get an array of **String** objects with three elements, which you would address as **args[0]**, **args[1]**, and **args[2]**. The array is still generated if there are no parameters, but it will have a length of zero. Note the differences from C: You find the number of parameters by looking at the length of the array, and the first element is not the name of the class but the first command-line parameter.

> *Note: You can have methods named **main** that have other signatures. The compiler will compile these without comment, but the JVM will not run an application that does not have the required signature.*

Applet Conventions

Java programs running in a Web browser environment are called applets and have a different set of conventions for program initialization and argument passing. Instead of providing a **main** method in an arbitrary class, the programmer must derive a class from **java.applet.Applet**. The JVM in the browser creates an instance of this class and expects to find the following method:

➤ **public void init()** This method is called once, just after the applet object has been created and before anything has been shown on the screen.

➤ **public void start()** This method is called when the applet is first shown and whenever it becomes visible after being hidden.

➤ **public void stop()** This method is called whenever the applet is hidden.

➤ **public void destroy()** This method is called when the JVM is about to permanently dispose of the applet.

Instead of the **args[]** array of **Strings**, an applet has access to named parameters that are supplied in the HTML tags that define the Web page containing the applet.

Utilization Of Javadoc Format API Documentation

Java has an automatic documentation feature that, as far as we know, is not duplicated in any other language. If source code comments are formatted with a few simple rules, the Javadoc utility provided with the JDK can create HTML files, which are automatically linked to the rest of the API documentation. This feature has been enhanced for the 1.2 JDK release to employ HTML frames and tables for greater ease of use. The great advantage of this approach is that if the rules are followed, keeping the documentation up-to-date is almost automatic.

Although you will not be required to know how to create the Javadoc documentation, you will have to know how to use it to find information about variables and methods in classes and how to navigate in the object and package hierarchy. The best way to learn this is to download the documentation (www.javasoft.com/products/index.html), install it, and then just play with it.

As an example of using the Javadoc documentation, suppose that you wanted to find out the variables and methods available for an **ActionEvent** object. (The **ActionEvent** class is part of the **java.awt.event** package.) Using a Web browser, you would open the documentation index, which lists the packages in alphabetical order.

On opening the link to the **java.awt.event** package, you would find an alphabetical listing of the classes in the package. Navigate to the correct package and then to the screen shown in Figure 2.1. It shows where the **ActionEvent** class fits in the object hierarchy.

Further down this page you would find alphabetical listings of the variables and methods in the class. These are given in summary tables linked to more detailed explanations. However, this is not a complete picture of the variables and methods available to an **ActionEvent** object because, as shown in the figure, it inherits from **AWTEvent**, which inherits from **EventObject**, which inherits from **Object**. Note that although the primary organization of the documentation is by package, the parent classes of **ActionEvent** are in three other packages. By clicking on the links, you can navigate to the details of each of these classes.

Figure 2.1   Browsing in the Javadoc-formatted Java API documentation at the main entry for the **ActionEvent** class.

In addition to the regular class details, there is also documentation for Interfaces, Exceptions, and Errors that belong to a given package. The Javadoc
documentation as distributed by Sun does have limitations in that only public
and protected variables and methods are listed. If you want to see all of the
variables and methods, you have to consult the source code.

Deprecated Classes And Other Items

In the transition from Java 1.0 to 1.1 and JDK 1.2, new naming conventions
and other revisions to the standard library resulted in some classes, variables,
and methods becoming outdated. Although they are still in the library to support older programs, their use is *deprecated*, meaning that they should not be
used. The Javadoc API documentation provides a convenient listing of deprecated items, and also marks them in the class documentation. You can have
every use of a deprecated method tagged by using the "-deprecation" option
with the javac compiler.

Practice Questions

Question 1

Let's suppose you are writing a utility class and your company's policy is to keep utility classes in a package named "conglomo.util". Select the correct code fragment to start a class file for a class that uses classes in the **java.awt** and **java.util** standard library packages.

○ a.

```
1.    package java.conglomo.util
2.    import java.awt.*
3.    import java.util.*
```

○ b.

```
1.    package conglomo.util ;
2.    import java.awt.* ;
3.    import java.util.* ;
```

○ c.

```
1.    import java.awt.* ;
2.    import java.util.* ;
3.    import conglomo.util.* ;
```

Answer b is correct. Note that the package statement *must* be the first compiler-usable statement. It can follow comment lines and blank lines but must precede all **import** statements. Answer a is incorrect because the fragment has several errors. Line 1 tries to put your package in with the Java standard library, which is not allowed, and none of the lines is terminated properly with a semi-colon. Answer c is incorrect because the fragment fails to declare the package. These are the statements other classes would use to import from the **conglomo.util** package.

Question 2

In a Java application, what are the appropriate modifiers and return type for the **main** method declaration? Write down the keywords in the correct order, choosing from the following keyword list:

```
private     protected     public     abstract
static      boolean       void       synchronized
final       Object        native     transient
```

The correct form for the **main** method in an application is as follows:

```
public static void main(String[] args)
```

or

```
static public void main(String[] args)
```

The **main** method must be a **static** member of the class so it is available when the class is loaded. The return type is **void** by convention. If you want to return an error code to the system, use **System.exit()**. **Main** must be public by convention.

Question 3

> What will be the result of trying to compile and run an application in which the following is the only declaration of a **main** method? (Assume the rest of the class is correct.)
>
> ```
> 1.  public static void main(){
> 2.    System.out.println("hello world");
> 3.  }
> ```
>
> ○ a. The class will compile without error but the program will not run.
>
> ○ b. The class will compile and run, writing "hello world" to the standard output.
>
> ○ c. The compiler will report an error.

Answer a is correct. The code compiles, but the runtime system will report an error because it is expecting the exact method signature:

```
public static void main(String args[])
```

The compiler looks for only the correct syntax. It does not know how this class will be used, so it cannot enforce the method signature.

Question 4

Assume that the following program has been compiled and the **Demo.class** file is in the current directory.

```
1.    public class Demo {
2.        public static void main(String args[]
            ){
3.            int n = 1 ;
4.            System.out.println("The word is " +
                args[ n ] );
5.        }
6.    }
```

Select the correct command line to execute the program and produce the output line:

"The word is gamma".

○ a. Demo alpha beta gamma delta

○ b. java Demo alpha beta gamma delta

○ c. java Demo beta gamma delta

○ d. java Demo.class beta gamma delta

○ e. java Demo.class alpha beta gamma delta

Answer c is correct; "gamma" will be the second string in the **args** array which has the index 1. Answer a is wrong because it does not start the Java interpreter. Answer b is wrong because gamma is the third string in the **args** array. Answers d and e are wrong because you don't use the class file type when starting the Java interpreter.

Question 5

Which of the following are *not* reserved words in Java? [Check all correct answers]

❏ a. **transient**

❏ b. **include**

❏ c. **goto**

❏ d. **union**

The words **include** and **union** are not reserved words in Java. Therefore, answers b and d are correct. C programmers should pay particular attention to learning which familiar C terms are not Java keywords. The Java keyword **transient** is used to label variables that should not be saved during serialization of an object. Therefore, answer a is incorrect. Java reserves **goto** but does not currently use it. Therefore, answer c is incorrect.

Question 6

> What is the range of values that can be stored in a byte primitive variable?
>
> ○ a. 0 to 255
>
> ○ b. −127 to 128
>
> ○ c. −128 to 127

The correct answer is c. Byte variables use 8 bits and are signed. Answers a and b are incorrect.

Question 7

> What is the range of values that can be stored in a long primitive?
>
> ○ a. 0 to $2^{32} - 1$
>
> ○ b. $- 2^{32}$ to $2^{32} - 1$
>
> ○ c. $- 2^{63}$ to $2^{63} - 1$

The correct answer is c. Long variables use 64 bits and are signed. Answers a and b are incorrect.

Question 8

> Which of the following would be an illegal identifier for a Java variable? [Check all correct answers]
>
> ❏ a. my_stuff
>
> ❏ b. _yourStuff
>
> ❏ c. $money
>
> ❏ d. %path
>
> ❏ e. 2enchantedEvening

The illegal identifiers are **%path** and **2enchantedEvening**. Therefore, answers d and e are correct. The leading numeral in e leads Java to expect a number and causes a compiler error. The only leading punctuation characters allowed are $ and underscore, so d causes an error. **my_stuff**, **_yourStuff**, and **$money** are legal identifiers. Therefore, answers a, b, and c are incorrect.

Question 9

> Which of the following is an organizing principle of Java's Javadoc format documentation for information on the methods in a given class?
>
> ○ a. Relative frequency of use of the various methods.
>
> ○ b. Lists of methods in a class in alphabetic order.
>
> ○ c. Separate listing of private, protected, and public methods in a class.

The correct answer is b. All methods are listed in alphabetic order. The obscure methods, which practically nobody uses, are listed with the common ones. Therefore, answer a is incorrect. The documentation does not list private variables and methods because there is no way for you to use them in a program. Therefore, answer c is incorrect.

Need To Know More?

Flanagan, David: *Java in a Nutshell, 2ⁿᵈ Edition*. O'Reilly & Associates, Inc., Sebastopol, CA, 1997. ISBN: 1-56592-262-X. This is the most compact desktop reference book documenting the Java language. Chapter 2, "How Java Differs from C" is recommended for programmers coming to Java from C and C++.

ftp://ftp.javasoft.com/docs/tutorial.zip

An excellent tutorial in HTML form can be downloaded from this site. (Although this document is updated frequently, it may not be entirely current with JDK 1.2 information.)

http://java.sun.com/docs/books/jls/html/index.html

The definitive Java language specification document is maintained in HTML form on the Sun Microsystems Web site.

http://java.sun.com/products/jdk/1.2/index.html

The Java API documentation in Javadoc-generated form can be downloaded from Sun Microsystems. Although this site changes a lot, the last time I looked, it was a good starting point.

Java Operators With Primitives And Objects

3

Terms you'll need to understand:

√ Assignment

√ **equals**

√ **instanceof**

Techniques you'll need to master:

√ Constructing numeric literals in decimal, octal, and hexadecimal formats

√ Constructing string literals in the quoted format

√ Constructing char literals in Java's Unicode format

√ Understanding the effect of assignment and mathematical operators on primitives and objects

√ Understanding the operation of logical and bitwise operators in expressions

√ Understanding the implications of the various forms of the AND and OR logical operators

√ Understanding the correct usage of the == comparison operator with primitives and objects

√ Predicting the operation of the **equals** method with combinations of various objects

√ Declaring, constructing, and initializing arrays of any type

Java uses operators and literals in a style that will be very familiar to all C programmers. In this chapter, I will review the way Java uses literals to initialize primitive variables, create objects, and pass values to methods. I will review all of the Java operators used in expressions with both primitives and objects. You should not assume that the behavior of operators will be the same as in C. Pay particular attention to the difference between the == operator and the **equals** method; this seems to confuse many programmers.

Using Literals

Literals are used to create values that are assigned to variables, used in expressions, or passed to methods. You will need to know the correct ways of creating integer, floating-point, character, boolean, and string literals.

Numeric Literals

Literal numbers can appear in Java programs in base ten, hexadecimal, and octal forms, as shown in the following example code statements, which combine declaring a variable and initializing it to a value. Notice that an unmodified integer value is assumed to be the 32-bit **int** primitive, but a value containing a decimal point is assumed to be the 64-bit **double,** unless you append an F or f to indicate the 32-bit **float** primitive.

```
1.   int n = 42 ;
2.   long j =  4096L ; // appending L or l makes it a long
3.   long k =  0xFFFFFFL ;
4.   byte b2 =  010 ;  // an octal literal
5.    double f2 = 1.023 ;  // double is assumed
6.    float f2 = 1.023F ;   // F or f makes it a float
```

As in line 1, an unmodified literal integer is assumed to be in base ten format. In line 3, a number starting with a leading zero followed by an upper- or lowercase X is interpreted as a hexadecimal number. In line 4, a number with a leading zero and no X is interpreted as an octal number. Appending an upper- or lowercase L indicates a **long** integer.

Tricky Assignment Facts

The compiler does a variety of automatic conversion of numeric types in expressions, but in assignment statements it gets quite picky as a defense against common programmer errors. In the following code, lines 1 and 3 would cause a compiler error.

```
1.  int n2 = 4096L ;  // would require a specific (int) cast
2.  short s1 = 32000 ;  // ok
3.  short s2 = 33000 ;  // out of range for short primitive
```

In spite of the fact that 4096 would fit in an **int** primitive, the compiler would object to line 1 because the literal is in the **long** format. It would require a specific cast to allow the statement. The compiler also pays attention to the known range of primitives, passing line 2 but objecting to line 3. You could force the compiler to accept line 3 with a specific (**short**) cast, but the result would be a negative number due to the high bit being set.

Numeric Wrapper Classes

Each of the primitive data types has a corresponding wrapper class in the Java standard library. Java uses these classes for several purposes. The static variables of a wrapper class hold various constants, and the static methods are used for convenient conversion routines such as the **toString** method, which returns a **String** representing a primitive value. You can also create objects that contain a primitive value, using either literals or primitive variables as in the following examples.

```
1. Integer cmd = new Integer( 42 );
2. Boolean flag = new Boolean( false );
3. Character ch = new Character( '\u000a' );
4. Long lx = new Long( x ) ; // where x is a long variable
```

The values contained in a wrapper object cannot be changed, so they are not used for computation. Wrapper objects are useful when you want to store primitive values using Java's utility classes—such as **Vector, Stack,** and **Hashtable**—that work only with objects. The names of the wrapper classes are **Byte, Short, Character, Integer, Long, Float, Double,** and **Boolean.** As you can see, the names reflect the primitive values they contain but start with a capital letter.

 The most important thing to remember about the wrapper class objects is that the contained value cannot be changed. These objects are said to be *immutable.*

Character Literals

Even though typical Java code looks as if it is made up of nothing but ASCII characters, you should never forget that Java characters are, in fact, 16-bit Unicode characters. The following code shows legal ways to declare and initialize **char** type primitive variables.

```
1.   char c1 =  '\u0057' ; // the letter W
2.   char c2 = 'W' ;
3.   char c3 = (char) 87 ; // the letter W
4.   char cr = '\r' ; // carriage return
```

Line 1 illustrates Unicode representation of a character indicated by the leading \u sequence. The numeric value is always a four-digit hexadecimal number in this format. Line 2 uses single quotes surrounding the literal character, and an integer is cast to the **char** primitive type in line 3. Line 4 shows a literal representing a non-printing character with an escape sequence.

You can also mix in Unicode characters and special characters with ASCII strings using the \u escape sequence (as shown in the following section on string literals). Table 3.1 summarizes Java escape sequences that can be used in strings or to initialize character primitives.

String Literals

Because Java does not deal with strings as arrays of bytes, but as objects, the compiler has to do a lot of work behind the scenes. The following example code shows declaration and initialization of **String** variables with literals:

```
1.   String name = "" ;  // an empty string, but still an object
2.   String type = ".TXT" ;
3.   String longtxt =  "A great long bunch of text \n"
4.        + "to illustrate how you break long lines." ;
```

Table 3.1 Java escape sequences.	
Escape Sequence	**Character Represented**
\b	Backspace
\t	Horizontal tab
\n	Newline (linefeed)
\f	Form feed
\r	Carriage return
\"	Double quote
\'	Single quote
\\	Backslash
\xxx	A character in octal representation; xxx must range between 000 and 377.
\uxxxx	A Unicode character, where xxxx is a hexadecimal format number. Note that this is the only escape sequence that represents a 16-bit character.

At the end of line 3 in the previous code you will notice the sequence \n; this is an example of an escape code sequence used to insert special characters—in this case, a line feed. Line 4 illustrates the special meaning of the + operator when used with strings; this is discussed in the later section "String Objects And The + Operator." Here is an example of a **String** literal with the Unicode representation of a capital Greek letter delta inserted between two double quote characters.

```
String tx = "Delta values are labeled \"\u0394\" on the chart.";
```

 Remember that string literals create **String** objects, not byte arrays. Most of the things you are used to doing with strings in C will not work in Java.

Boolean Literals

Fortunately, boolean literals are simple. Only the Java reserved words **true** and **false** can be used. Note that these words are always all lowercase. If you wrote

```
boolean flag = True ;
```

the compiler goes looking for a boolean variable named True.

 C programmers should remember that integer variables can never be interpreted as boolean values. All of your tricks that depend on zero being interpreted as false must be left behind.

Numeric Operators

I have created and initialized some variables. Now I'll look at Java's facilities for numeric operations. They will look very familiar to C programmers, but there are some differences. Operators performing arithmetic or numeric comparison are shown in Table 3.2. The precedence gives the order in which the compiler does operations, with 1 being the first.

Increment And Decrement

Java follows the C convention with the increment and decrement operators, which directly modify the value in a primitive variable by adding or subtracting 1. When this operator appears in a larger expression, the order in which the modification occurs depends on the position of the operator, as shown in the following code fragment:

```
1.  int x = 5 ;
2.  int y = x++  ; // y gets the value 5, before incrementing x
3.  int y2 = ++x  ;  // y2 gets the value 7, after incrementing
```

Unary + And - Operators

As distinct from the arithmetic add and subtract operators, the unary + and - operators affect a single operand. Unary - changes the sign of a numeric expression to the right of the operator. Unary + has no effect on an expression; it is included for completeness and because some programmers like to use it to emphasize that a number is positive.

Arithmetic Operators

In general, the arithmetic operators +, -, /, and * work as you would expect, but you will need to know the conventions that the compiler uses to convert various primitives before performing operations. As with C, the operator appears between its two operands.

Table 3.2   Numeric operators in Java.

Precedence	Operator	Description
1	++	Increment by 1 (or 1.0)
1	--	Decrement by 1 (or 1.0)
1	+	Unary plus
1	-	Unary minus
2	*	Multiplication
2	/	Division
2	%	Modulo
3	+	Addition
3	-	Subtraction
5	<	Less than
5	>	Greater than
5	<=	Less than/equal
5	>=	Greater than/equal
6	==	Equals (identical values)
6	!=	Is not equal to
13	op=	op assignment (+=, -=, *=, and so on)

Widening Conversions

Widening conversions of a number are those that don't lose information on the overall magnitude. For instance, the integer primitives **byte, char,** and **short** can all be converted to an **int** primitive, and an **int** primitive can be converted to a **long** integer without loss of information. An **int** can be converted to a **float** primitive, but there may be some loss of precision in the least significant bits. This conversion is carried out according to the IEEE standard.

When evaluating an arithmetic expression with two operands, the compiler converts primitives by widening according to these rules:

1. If either is of type **double,** the other is converted to **double.**

2. Otherwise, if either is a **float,** the other is converted to **float.**

3. Otherwise, if either is of type **long,** the other is converted to **long.**

4. Otherwise, both operands are converted to **int.**

Conversion With Casting

You can always direct the order and direction of number conversions with specific **casts.** As an example, consider the following code fragment:

```
1.   float x = 123 ;
2.   byte b = 23 ;
3.   float y = x + b ;
4.   b = (byte) y ;
```

In line 3, the compiler converts b to a **float** before performing the addition. However, you have to include the specific **cast** operation to get the compiler to accept line 4 because converting a **float** to an 8-bit **byte** involves potential loss of magnitude and precision.

The Modulo Operator

You can think of the % operator as yielding the remainder from an implied division of the left operand (dividend) by the right operand (divisor). The result will be negative only if the dividend is negative. Note that if the operands are integers, the **ArithmeticException** can be thrown if the divisor is zero, just as in integer division.

Using % with floating-point primitives produces results similar to the integer operation, but note that the special floating-point values, such as **NaN** and **POSITIVE_INFINITY,** can result.

Numeric Comparisons

The numeric comparisons <, >, <=, >=, !=, and == work pretty much as expected with Java primitives. If the operands are two different types, the compiler promotes one according to the rules for arithmetic operators. Remember that the result of a numeric comparison is a boolean primitive.

The <, >, <=, and >= operators are meaningless for objects, but the == and != operators can be used. When used with object references, == results in **true** only if the references are identical. I will return to this subject later in this chapter because it is very important.

 Be sure you master the differences between the == comparison with primitives and with objects. In my experience, this difference has been one of the most frequent sources of errors.

Arithmetic Errors

In general, Java lets you make a variety of arithmetic errors without warning you. If your code conducts operations that overflow the bounds of 32-bit or 64-bit integer arithmetic, that's your problem. Division by zero in integer arithmetic is the only error that produces a runtime exception, namely, an ArithmeticException.

On the other hand, floating-point operations meet the requirements of the IEEE standard for representing values that are out of the normal range. These special values are defined for **float** primitives as constants in the **Float** class, as shown in Table 3.3. The string representation is what you would get from the **Float.toString** method. The **Double** class defines similar constants for double primitive values.

Table 3.3 Special floating-point values.		
Constant	**Interpretation**	**Corresponding String**
Float.MAX_VALUE	The largest number representable	3.40282e+038
Float.MIN_VALUE	The smallest number representable	1.4013e-045
Float.NEGATIVE_INFINITY	Negative divided by zero	-Infinity
Float.POSITIVE_INFINITY	Positive divided by zero	Infinity
Float.NaN	Not a Number	NaV

Not A Number

The special **NaN** value is particularly tricky to handle. **NaN** can result from mathematical functions that are undefined, such as taking the square root of a negative number. You cannot directly compare the **NaN** value with anything. You must detect it with the special **Float.isNaN** or **Double.isNaN** methods, as in the following example. This example shows the right way and one of the many wrong ways to detect the **NaN** value.

```
1. float x = (float) Math.sqrt( y ) ; // where y may be negative
2. if( x == Float.NaN ) x = 0.0 ;  // WRONG, always false
3. if( Float.isNaN( x ) ) x = 0.0 ; // the right way to detect NaN
```

String Objects And The + Operator

For convenience in working with strings, Java also uses the + and += operators to indicate concatenation. When the compiler finds an expression in which a string appears in association with a + operator, it turns all items in the expression into strings, concatenates the strings, and creates a new **String** object. The compiler has a complete set of conventions used to turn primitives and objects into **Strings**, but the only operators that can be used are the + and += operators.

The methods used to turn primitives into strings are found in the wrapper classes that Java has for each primitive. (Wrapper classes are discussed in detail in Chapter 10.) For instance, in the following code fragment, the compiler knows to use the **toString** method in the **Float** class to create a **String** representation of the **pi** primitive, and it knows how to add the Unicode character for the Greek letter pi to the **String**.

```
1. float pi = 3.14159f ;
2. String tmp = "Pi = " + pi + " or " + '\u03c0' ;
```

Objects And toString()

The root of the Java object hierarchy, the **Object** class, has a **toString**() method that returns a descriptive string. Therefore, every object has a **toString** method by inheritance. This default **toString** method produces a rather cryptic result, so many of the standard library classes implement a **toString** method that is more appropriate for the particular class. The net result is that the compiler will always be able to use the + operator in any combination of **Strings** and objects.

Strings Are Immutable

The contents of a **String** object cannot be changed. In the following code, it looks as if I am changing a **String** object. What is actually happening is that there is a **String** object created in line 1 with a reference in the variable named **filename**. In line 2, the contents of that **String** are concatenated with the literal ".txt" and a reference to the new **String** object is stored in the variable **filename**.

```
1. String filename = "mystuff" ;
2. filename += ".txt" ;
```

Questions involving the immutability of **String** objects frequently cause trouble for beginning Java programmers. Chapter 10 contains more examples and practice questions on this subject.

The null Value And Strings

The Java mechanism that adds various items together to create **Strings** is able to recognize that a reference variable contains the special value **null,** instead of an object reference. In that case, the string "null" is added.

Bitwise And Logic Operators

Table 3.4 summarizes the operators that can be used on individual bits in integer primitives and in logical expressions. The term *logical expressions* refers to expressions in which all of the operands can be reduced to boolean primitives. Logical operators produce a boolean primitive result.

Table 3.4	Bitwise and logic operators.		
Precedence	**Operator**	**Operator Type**	**Description**
1	~	Integral	Unary bitwise complement
1	!	Logical	Unary logical complement
4	<<	Integral	Left shift
4	>>	Integral	Right shift (keep sign)
4	>>>	Integral	Right shift (zero fill)
5	instanceof	Object, type	Tests class membership
6	==	Object	Equals (same object)
6	!=	Object	Unequal (different object)
7	&	Integral	Bitwise AND
7	&	Logical	Logical AND
8	^	Integral	Bitwise XOR
8	^	Logical	Logical XOR

(continued)

Table 3.4   Bitwise and logic operators *(continued).*

Precedence	Operator	Operator Type	Description
9	|	Integral	Bitwise OR
9	|	Logical	Logical OR
10	&&	Logical	Logical AND (conditional)
11	||	Logical	Logical OR (conditional)
12	?:	Logical	Conditional (ternary)
13	=	Variable, any	Assignment
13	<<=	Binary	Left shift with assignment
13	>>=	Binary	Right shift with assignment
13	>>>=	Binary	Right shift, zero fill, assignment
13	&=	Binary	Bitwise AND with assignment
13	&=	Logical	Logical AND with assignment
13	|=	Binary	Bitwise OR with assignment
13	|=	Logical	Logical OR with assignment
13	^=	Binary	Bitwise XOR with assignment
13	^=	Logical	Logical XOR with assignment

Bitwise Operations With Integers

The bitwise operators change the individual bits of an integer primitive according to the familiar rules for AND, OR, and XOR (Exclusive OR) operations (as summarized in Table 3.5). The operands of the &, |, and ^ operators will be promoted to **int** or **long** types if necessary, and the result will be an **int** or **long** primitive, not a boolean. Because each bit in an integer primitive can be modified and examined independently with these operators, they are frequently used to pack a lot of information into a small space.

In thinking about the action of bitwise operators, you may want to draw out the bit pattern for various values. To keep them straight, it helps to draw groups of four bits so the groups correspond to hexadecimal digits. Questions on the test will not require you to remember all of the powers of two, but being able to recognize the first few helps. Here is an example of the use of the & or AND operator:

```
short flags = 20 ; // 0000 0000 0001 0100  or  0x0014
short mask = 4 ;   // 0000 0000 0000 0100
short rslt = (short)( flags & mask ) ;
```

Table 3.5	Bitwise logic rules.		
Operand	**Operator**	**Operand**	**Result**
1	AND	1	1
1	AND	0	0
0	AND	1	0
0	AND	0	0
1	OR	1	1
1	OR	0	1
0	OR	1	1
0	OR	0	0
1	XOR	1	0
1	XOR	0	1
0	XOR	1	1
0	XOR	0	0

Note that because operands are promoted to **int** or **long**, the **cast** to **short** is necessary to assign the value to a **short** primitive variable **rslt**. Applying the rule for the AND operator, you can see that the bit pattern in **rslt** will be "0000 0000 0000 0100" or a value of 4. C programmers who are used to checking the result of a bitwise operation in an **if** statement, such as line 1 in the following code, should remember that Java can only use boolean values in logic statements as shown in line 2.

```
1.  if( rslt ) doSomething()  ; // ok in C, wrong in Java
2.  if( rslt != 0 ) doSomething() ; // this is ok in both
```

Table 3.6 shows the result of applying the various bitwise operators to example operands. Note that in the last line, the ~ or complement operator sets the highest order bit, which causes the integer to be interpreted as a negative number. I am using **short** primitives here to simplify the table, but the same principles apply to all of the integer primitives.

If you have not done much bit manipulation in your programming experience, you might want to write some small Java programs to become familiar with the concepts. Note that the **Integer** and **Long** wrapper classes have **toBinaryString** and **toHexString** methods that will help with the output.

Table 3.6	Illustrating bitwise operations on some short primitives (16-bit integers).		
Binary	**Operation**	**Decimal**	**Hex**
0000 0000 0101 0100	op1	84	0x0054
0000 0001 0100 0111	op2	327	0x0147
0000 0000 0100 0100	op1 & op2	68	0x0044
0000 0001 0101 0111	op1 | op2	343	0x0157
0000 0001 0001 0011	op1 ^ op2	275	0x0113
1111 1110 1011 1000	~op2	-328	0xFEB8

The Unary Complement Operators

The ~ operator takes an integer type primitive. If smaller than **int**, the primitive value will be converted to an **int**. The result simply switches the sense of every bit. The ! operator is used with **boolean** primitives and changes **false** to **true** or **true** to **false**.

The Shift Operators, >>, >>>, And <<

These operators work with integer primitives only; they shift the left operand by the number of bits specified by the right operand. The important thing to note with these operators is that the value of the new bit is shifted into the number. For << (left shift), the new bit that appears in the low order position is always zero. Sun had to define two types of right shift because the high order bit in integer primitives indicates the sign. The >> right shift propagates the existing sign bit, which means a negative number will still be negative after being shifted. The >>> right shift inserts a zero as the most significant bit. Table 3.7 should help you to visualize what is going on.

Table 3.7	The results of some bit-shifting operations on example 32-bit integers.
0000 0000 0000 0000 0000 0000 0110 0011 starting x bits = 99	
0000 0000 0000 0000 0000 0011 0001 1000 after x << 3 (792)	
0000 0000 0000 0000 0000 0000 0001 1000 after x >> 2 (24)	
1111 1111 1111 1111 1111 1111 1001 1101 starting y bits = -99	
1111 1111 1111 1111 1111 1111 1111 1001 after y >> 4 = -7	
0000 0000 0000 1111 1111 1111 1111 1111 after y >>> 12 = 1048575	

When doing bit manipulations on primitives shorter than 32 bits, remember that the compiler promotes all operands to 32 bits before performing the operation.

One final note on the shift operators: If the right operand is larger than 31 for operation on 32-bit integers, the compiler uses only the five lowest order bits, that is, values of 0 to 31. With a 64-bit integer as the right operand, only the six lowest order bits are used, that is, values of 0 to 63.

Shift And Bitwise Operations With Assignment

Note that the assignment operator = can be combined with the shift and bitwise operators just as with the arithmetic operators. The result is as you would expect.

Operators With Logical Expressions

The &, |, ^ (AND, OR, XOR) operators used with integers also work with **boolean** values as expected. The compiler generates an error if both operands are not **boolean**. The tricky part (which you're almost guaranteed to run into) has to do with the && and || "conditional AND" and "conditional OR" operators.

When the & and | operators are used in an expression, both operands are evaluated. For instance, in the following code fragment, both the (x >= 0) test and the call to the **testY** method will be executed.

```
if(( x >= 0 ) & testY( y ) )
```

However, the conditional operators check the value of the left operand first and do not evaluate the right operand if it is not needed to determine the logical result. For instance, in the following code fragment, if x is -1, the result must be **false** and the **testY** method is never called.

```
if(( x >= 0 ) && testY( y ) )
```

Similarly, if the || operator finds the left operand to be **true**, the result must be **true**, so the right operand is not evaluated.

These conditional logical operators, also known as the short circuit logical operators, are used frequently in Java programming. For example, if it is possible that a **String** object reference has not been initialized, you might use the following code where the test versus **null** ensures that the **equalsIgnoreCase** method will never be called with a **null** reference.

```
//  ans is declared to be a String reference
if( ans != null && ans.equalsIgnoreCase( "yes") ) {}
```

Logical Operators With Assignment

Only the &, |, and ^ logical operators can be combined with =, producing &=, |=, and ^= operators. Naturally, the left operand must be a **boolean** primitive variable.

The *instanceof* Operator

The **instanceof** operator tests the type of the left operand versus the type named by the right operand, returning **true** if they are identical. The left operand must be the name of a reference variable, such as a class, an interface, or an array reference. The right operator cannot be an object. It must name a reference type.

This operator is extremely handy in programming in cases in which an object reference may belong to several different classes. For example, suppose the following method could be called with several types of event objects descended from **AWTEvent**. The **instanceof** operator ensures that the correct method is called.

```
public void myEventProcess( AWTEvent evt ){
 if( evt instanceof ActionEvent )  processAction( evt );
 if( evt instanceof AdjustmentEvent ) processAdjustment(evt);
}
```

Remember that the **instanceof** operator can be used with interfaces and arrays as well as classes.

The Conditional Assignment Operator

The conditional assignment operator is the only Java operator that takes three operands. It is essentially a shortcut for a structure that takes at least two statements, as shown in the following code fragment. Assume that x, y, and z are **int** primitive variables that have been initialized.

```
1.  // long way
2.  if( x > y ) z = x ;
3.  else z = y ;
4.  //
5.  // short way
6.  z = x > y ? x : y ;
```

The operand to the left of the ? must evaluate as **boolean** and the other two operands must be of the same type, or convertible to the same type, which will be the type of the result. The result will be the operand to the left of the colon if the **boolean** is true; otherwise, it is the right operand.

More About Assignment

I have seen the use of the = operator in simple assignment such as x = y + 3. You should also note that the value assigned can be used by a further assignment operator, such as in the following statement, which assigns the calculated value to four variables.

```
a = b = c = x = y + 3 ;
```

Testing Object Equality

It is a source of great confusion to novice programmers that Java has two ways of thinking about the equality of objects. When used with object references, the == (double = sign) operator returns **true** only if both references are to the same object. This is illustrated in the following code fragment in which I create and compare some **Integer** object references:

```
1.   Integer x1 = new Integer( 5 ) ;
2.   Integer x2 = x1 ;
3.   Integer x3 = new Integer( 5 ) ;
4.   if( x1 == x2 ) System.out.println("x1 eq x2" );
5.   if( x2 == x3 ) System.out.println("x2 eq x3" );
```

Executing this code will print only "x1 eq x2" because both variables refer to the same object. To test for equality of content, you have to use a method that can compare the content of the objects.

The equals Method

In the Java standard library classes, the method that compares content is always named **equals** and takes an **Object** reference as input. For example, the **equals** method of the **Integer** class (paraphrased from the original for clarity) works like this:

```
1. public boolean equals(Object obj){
2.    if( obj == null ) return false ;
3.    if( !( obj instanceof Integer ) ) return false ;
4.    return this.value == ((Integer)obj).intValue() ;
5. }
```

Note that the **equals** method does not even look at the value of the other object until it has been determined that the other object reference is not null and that it refers to an **Integer** object. The **equals** method in the **Object** class (the root of the entire Java hierarchy of classes) returns true only if

```
this == obj
```

so in the absence of an overriding **equals** method, the == operator and **equals** methods are equivalent.

 Remember that the **equals** method compares content only if the two objects are of identical type. For example, an **equals** test by an **Integer** object on a **Long** object always return **false** regardless of the numeric values. Also note that the signature of the **equals** method expects an **Object** reference as input. The compiler reports an error if you try to call **equals** with a primitive value.

The == With Strings Trap

One reason that it is easy to fall into the error of using == when you want **equals** is the behavior of **String** literals. The compiler optimizes storage of **String** literals by reusing them. In a large program, this can save a considerable amount of memory. In the following fragment, the **String** literal "YES" appears in both line 1 and line 2, but the compiler only creates one **String** object, referred to by both s1 and s2. Thus, line 3 prints out "equal" and it appears to have been tested for equality of content with the == operator. However, the test in line 6 is always false because two distinct objects are involved.

```
1.  String s1 = "YES" ;
2.  String s2 = "YES" ;
3.  if( s1 == s2 ) System.out.println("equal");
4.  String s3 = new String( "YES" );
5.  String s4 = new String( "YES" );
6.  if( s3 == s4 ) System.out.println("s3 eq s4");
```

Array Initialization

An array in Java is a type of object that can contain a number of variables. These variables can be referenced only by the array index—a non-negative integer. All of these contained variables, or elements, must be the same type, which is the type of the array. Every array has an associated **length** variable, established when the array is created, which you can access directly. If you try to address an element with an index that is outside the range of the array, an exception is generated. Java arrays are one-dimensional, but an array can contain other arrays, which gives the effect of multiple dimensions.

You can have arrays of any of the Java primitives or reference variables. The important point to remember is that when created, primitive arrays will have default values assigned, but object references will all be **null**.

Declaration

Like other variables, arrays must be declared before you use them. Declaration can be separate from the actual creation of the array. Here are some examples of declaring variables that are arrays of primitives (lines 1-3) and objects (lines 4,5). If this code fragment was executed, line 6 would print "counts = null" because the array object has not yet been constructed.

```
1. int counts[] ;
2. int[] counts ; // 1 and 2 are equivalent
3. boolean flags  [    ] ;  // extra spaces are not significant
4. String names[] ;
5. MyClass[][] things ; // a two-dimensional array of objects
6. System.out.println( "counts = " + counts );
```

Construction

You cannot do anything with an array variable until the array has been constructed with the **new** operator. The statement that constructs an array must give the size, as shown in the following code fragment, assumed to follow lines 1-6 in the previous code. The code in line 9 (in the following code) assumes that an integer primitive **nStrings** has been initialized.

```
7. counts = new int[20] ;
8. flags = new boolean[ 5 ] ;
9. names = new String[ nStrings ] ;
```

After this code executes, the array references will have array objects of known types, but exactly what is in the array depends on the type. Integer and floating-point primitive arrays will have elements initialized to zero values. Arrays of the **boolean** types will have elements of **false** values. Arrays of object types will have **null** references.

You can combine declaration of an array variable with construction, as shown in the following code examples:

```
1. float rates[] = new float[33] ;
2. String files[] = new String[ 1000 ] ;
```

You must remember the distinction between the status of arrays of primitives and the status of arrays of object references after the array is constructed. Arrays of primitives have elements that are initialized to default values. Arrays of objects will have the value **null** in each element. You are practically guaranteed to have a related question on the exam.

Combined Declaration Construction And Initialization

Java allows a statement format for combined declaration, construction, and initialization of arrays with literal values, as shown in the following code examples. Note that the **String** array defined in lines 2, 3, and 4 is two-dimensional.

```
1. int[] fontSize = { 9, 11, 13, 15, 17 } ;
2. String[][] fontDesc  = {
3.    {"TimesRoman", "bold"}, {"Courier","italic"},
4.    {"ZapfDingBats", "normal"} } ;
```

Initialization

To provide initial object references or primitive values other than the default, you have to address each element in the array. In the following code, I declare and create an array of **Rectangle** objects, and then create the **Rectangle** objects for each element.

```
1. Rectangle hotSpots[] = new Rectangle[10];
2. for( int i = 0 ; i < hotSpots.length ; i++ ){
3.     hotSpots[i] = new Rectangle(10 * i, 0, 10, 10);
4. }
```

The following Study Alert is an example question related to object arrays. This example caused many errors in my testing. I feel this difficulty illustrates two important points about taking the exam:

➤ Read the question carefully.

➤ Remember that the wrapper class names, although spelled like the primitives, always start with a capital letter.

 What will happen when you try to compile and run the following application?

```
1. public class Example {
2.    public Boolean flags[] = new Boolean[4] ;
3.    public static void main(String[] args){
```

```
4.      Example E = new Example();
5.      System.out.println( "Flag 1 is " + E.flags[1] );
6.   }
7. }
```

a. The text "Flag 1 is true" will be written to standard output.

b. The text "Flag 1 is false" will be written to standard output.

c. The text "Flag 1 is null" will be written to standard output.

d. The compiler will object to line 2.

Most people forgot that **Boolean** is a wrapper class for **boolean** values and thus the array creation statement in line 2 merely created the array. All of the references in that array are initialized to **null**. Therefore, answer c is correct.

Practice Questions

Question 1

What will be the result of calling the following method with an input of 2?

```
1.  public int adder( int N ){
2.    return  0x100 + N++ ;
3.  }
```

○ a. The method will return 258.

○ b. The method will return 102.

○ c. The method will return 259.

○ d. The method will return 103.

Answer a is correct. The hexadecimal constant 0x100 is 256 decimal. The post increment of N will have no effect on the returned value. The method would return 102 if the literal constant were decimal, but it is not. Therefore, answer b is incorrect. Answers c and d are incorrect arithmetic.

Question 2

What happens when you attempt to compile and run the following code?

```
1.  public class Logic {
2.    static int minusOne = -1 ;
3.    static public void main(String args[] ){
4.      int N = minusOne >> 31 ;
5.      System.out.println("N = " + N );
6.    }
7.  }
```

○ a. The program will compile and run, producing the output "N = -1".

○ b. The program will compile and run, producing the output "N = 1".

○ c. A runtime ArithmeticException will be thrown.

○ d. The program will compile and run, producing the output "N = 0".

Answer a is correct. The >> operator extends the sign as the shift operation is performed. The program would compile and run, producing the output "N = -1" if the >>> operator, which shifts in a zero bit, had been specified, but it was not. Therefore, answer b is incorrect. With respect to answer c, an Arithmetic-Exception is typically thrown due to integer division by zero, not by a shift operation. Therefore, answer c is incorrect. Answer d does not occur because the >> operator extends the sign as the shift is performed.

Question 3

Which would be the result of running the following method with an input of 67?

```
1.  public int MaskOff( int n ){
2.      return n | 3 ;
3.  }
```

○ a. The method would return 3.

○ b. The method would return 64.

○ c. The method would return 67.

○ d. The method would return 0.

Answer c is correct. The bit pattern of 67 is 1000011, so the bitwise OR with 3 would not change the number. The method would return 3 if the bitwise AND operator '&' was used, but this is the OR operator. Therefore, answer a is incorrect. The method would return 64 if the XOR operator '^' was used, but it was not. Therefore, answer b is incorrect. Answer d cannot result from the OR of 67 with 3.

Question 4

How many **String** objects are created in the following code?

```
1.  String A, B, C ;
2.  A = "1234" ;
3.  B = A ;
4.  C = A + B ;
```

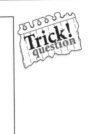

○ a. 1

○ b. 2

○ c. 3

○ d. 4

The correct answer is b. Both **A** and **B** refer to the same **String** object, whereas **C** refers to a **String** created by concatenating two copies of **A**. Therefore only two **String** objects have been created and all other answers are incorrect.

Question 5

Which of the following versions of initializing a **char** variable would cause a compiler error? [Check all correct answers]

❑ a. char c = - 1 ;

❑ b. char c = '\u00FF' ;

❑ c. char c = (char) 4096 ;

❑ d. char c = 4096L ;

❑ e. char c = 'c' ;

❑ f. char c = "c" ;

Answers a, d, and f are correct. In answer a, the literal creates a negative **int** that the compiler recognizes as being outside the normal range of **char** (the only unsigned integer primitive). In answer d, an explicit cast would be required to convert the literal **long** into a **char**. In answer f, the string literal could only be used to initialize a **String** object. The other options are legal assignments to a **char** primitive. Therefore, answers b, c, and e are incorrect.

Question 6

What happens when you try to compile and run the following code?

```
1.  public class EqualsTest{
2.    public static void main(String args[]){
3.      Long LA = new Long( 7 ) ;
4.      Long LB = new Long( 7 ) ;
5.      if( LA == LB )
          System.out.println("Equal");
6.        else System.out.println("Not Equal");
7.    }
8.  }
```

○ a. The program compiles but throws a runtime exception in line 5.

○ b. The program compiles and prints "Equal".

○ c. The program compiles and prints "Not Equal".

Answer c is correct. When used with objects, the "==" operator tests for identity. Because **LA** and **LB** are different objects, the test fails. All other answers are incorrect.

Question 7

What happens when you try to compile and run the following code?

```
1.  public class EqualsTest{
2.    public static void main(String args[]){
3.      char A = '\u0005' ;
4.      if( A == 0x0005L )
          System.out.println("Equal");
5.        else System.out.println("Not Equal");
6.    }
7.  }
```

○ a. The compiler reports "Invalid character in input" in line 3.

○ b. The program compiles and prints "Not Equal".

○ c. The program compiles and prints "Equal".

Answer c is correct. The compiler promotes variable A to a long before the comparison. The compiler does not report "Invalid character in input" in line 3 because this is the correct form for initializing a **char** primitive. Therefore, answer a is incorrect. Because answer c is correct, answer b cannot possibly be the correct answer.

Question 8

In the following code fragment from an applet, we know that the **getParameter** call may return a **null** if there is no parameter named size. Which logical operator should replace X in line 5 to ensure that a **NullPointerException** is not generated if **tmp** is **null**?

```
1.  int sz ;
2.  public void init(){
3.    sz = 10 ;
4.    String tmp = getParameter("size");
5.    if( tmp != null X tmp.equals("BIG"))
        sz = 20 ;
6.  }
```

○ a. Replace 'X' with '&'

○ b. Replace 'X' with '&&'

○ c. Replace 'X' with 'I'

○ d. Replace 'X' with 'II'

The correct answer is b, the "short-circuited" AND operator. All of the other operators would attempt to run the **equals** method on the **tmp** variable, even if it was **null**, thus causing a **NullPointerException**. Therefore, answers a, c, and d are incorrect.

Question 9

What would happen if you tried to compile and run the following code?

```
1.  public class EqualsTest{
2.    public static void main(String args[]){
3.      Long L = new Long( 7 );
4.      if( L.equals( 7L ))
          System.out.println("Equal");
5.      else System.out.println("Not Equal");
6.    }
7.  }
```

○ a. The program would compile and print "Equal".

○ b. The program would compile and print "Not Equal".

○ c. The compiler would object to line 4.

○ d. A runtime cast error would occur at line 4.

Answer c is correct. The compiler knows that the **equals** method takes an **Object** rather than a primitive as input. Because the program does not compile, answers a, b, and d are incorrect.

Question 10

What would happen if you tried to compile and run the following code?

```
1.  public class EqualsTest{
2.    public static void main(String args[]){
3.      Object A = new Long( 7 );
4.      Long  L = new Long( 7 ) ;
5.      if( A.equals( L ))
          System.out.println("Equal");
6.      else System.out.println("Not Equal");
7.    }
8.  }
```

○ a. The program would compile and print "Equal".

○ b. The program would compile and print "Not Equal".

○ c. The compiler would object to line 5.

○ d. A runtime cast error would occur at line 5.

Answer a is correct because the **Long** object created in line 3 does not lose its identity when cast to **Object** A, so the **equals** method knows the class is correct and compares the values. Because answer a is correct, answer b is obviously incorrect. Answers c and d do not occur because this is the correct form for comparing objects with the **equals** method. Therefore, they are incorrect.

Need To Know More?

Flanagan, David: *Java in a Nutshell, 2nd Edition*. O'Reilly & Associates, Inc., Sebastopol, CA, 1997. ISBN: 1-56592-262-X. Chapter 2, "How Java Differs from C," and Chapter 13, "Java Syntax," are pertinent to this chapter.

http://java.sun.com/docs/books/jls/html/index.html

The definitive Java language specification document is maintained in HTML form on the Sun Microsystems Web site.

http://java.sun.com/docs/white/index.html

A comparison of Java to C and C++ and other useful documents on the basic language can be found here.

http://java.sun.com/products/jdk/1.2/index.html

The Java API documentation in Javadoc-generated form can be downloaded from Sun Microsystems. Although this site changes a lot, the last time I looked, it was a good starting point.

Creating Java Classes

Terms you'll need to understand:

√ Access modifiers

√ Extends

√ Implements

√ Scope of variables

√ Automatic variables

√ Default constructor

Techniques you'll need to master:

√ Constructing a class definition using the modifiers public, abstract, and final

√ Constructing definitions of classes that implement interfaces

√ Declaring methods using the modifiers public, private, protected, static, final, native, and synchronized, as well as understanding the consequences

√ Declaring variables using the modifiers public, private, protected, static, final, and transient

√ Using variables declared inside code blocks

√ Understanding the circumstances governing the use of default constructors

Classes are the core concept of the Java language. Because all programming in Java consists of defining classes, it is essential to understand how to create a class. Points that are likely to arise in exam questions include the visibility of variables and methods in a class and other program elements as controlled by access modifier keywords. You should also clearly understand the differences between instance variables, static variables, and variables declared inside code blocks.

Defining A Class

Java classes are always defined inside a single source code file. As discussed in Chapter 2, **package** and **import** statements at the start of the file tell the compiler which resources can be used to compile the class. A class is defined with a declaration followed by a block of code inside a bracket pair. At the start of the declaration, keywords describe where the class fits in the Java class hierarchy and control the accessibility of the class. The components of a class declaration are as follows:

➤ **Class modifiers** An optional set of keywords.

➤ **Class keyword** The word "class" must appear here.

➤ **Class name** A Java name that must be unique within the package.

➤ **Superclass name** Optionally, the word "extends" followed by the name of the parent class. If this does not appear, the class extends **java.lang.Object**.

➤ **Interfaces implemented** Optionally, the word "implements" followed by a list of interface names.

➤ **Class body** The code that declares the fields and methods of the class.

Table 4.1 summarizes the meaning of various Java keywords used in class declarations. You will have to be very familiar with this material.

It is good practice for the test to work out the implications of various combinations of keywords in class declarations. Here are some examples to play with:

```
public abstract class ToneGenerator implements Runnable
class DataTable extends Observable
final class ErrorCodes
```

Abstract Classes

A class must be declared **abstract** if it has one or more methods declared **abstract**. Language designers use **abstract** classes to establish a pattern that can

Table 4.1	Summary of Java keywords used in class declarations.
Keyword	**Implication**
public	This class will be visible to all classes in the program. If this word is not used, this class will be visible only within the package.
abstract	This class contains at least one **abstract** method; it cannot be used to create an object.
final	This class cannot be subclassed. This word cannot be used with **abstract**.
extends	The class name following this keyword is the parent of this class. If this word is not used, the **Object** class will be the parent.
implements	This class provides for all the methods required by the interfaces that follow this keyword. Any number of interfaces can be implemented.

be filled out with concrete methods for a specific situation. For example, the **java.awt.Graphics** class is **abstract** because graphics methods depend on the specific hardware and operating system of a particular system. The Java Virtual Machine (JVM) supplies a specific class that is a subclass of **Graphics**, with methods suited to the specific system.

Final Classes

A class declared **final** cannot be used as a parent for another class. You may be wondering why anyone would declare a class as **final**. Frequently, this is done for security reasons. For example, the **java.lang.StringBuffer** class is declared final because experience has shown that misapplication of string-manipulating methods in C has been at the root of hard-to-find security holes in network applications. Because **StringBuffer** is final, no hacker can slip in an object that is derived from **StringBuffer** and does not have built-in security checks.

Class Modifier Restrictions

Classes cannot be *protected*, *private*, *native*, *static*, or *synchronized*. The words "abstract" and "final" cannot appear together because an **abstract** class, by definition, has declared methods that do not have implementations. Note that some compilers do not catch erroneous use of some keywords on class definitions.

The Class Body

In the class body are the declarations of the *members* of the class. These include fields (variables), methods, static initializers, and constructors. You can also have class definitions *inside* a class body. These *nested* classes are considered to be a member of the enclosing class and have a special relationship with it. Nested classes are discussed in Chapter 5.

Class Members

Access to class members of all types is controlled by access modifier keywords as follows:

➤ **public** A **public** member is accessible from any class in the program.

➤ **protected** A **protected** member can be accessed only by classes in the same package and classes derived from the current class—no matter which package they are in.

➤ **private** A **private** member can only be accessed from within the class.

➤ **default** If none of the other access modifier keywords appears, the default of access only by classes in the same package applies. You may see the word *friendly* used in connection with the default access, but friendly is *not* a Java keyword.

Other keywords that can be applied to class members are **static, final, abstract, native, transient, volatile,** and **synchronized**. The implications of these keywords are discussed in the following sections.

Fields

Fields are named variables, such as primitives and reference variables. Fields declared with the keyword **static** belong to the class and occur only once, as opposed to instance variables, which belong to class instances. Static variables are sometimes referred to as *class* variables. The **final** keyword means that the field cannot be changed once initialized.

The following code fragment illustrates the use of **static** and **final**. Lines 2 and 3 define Java equivalents to what would be called constants in other languages.

```
1.   class Widget extends Object {
2.     public static final int TYPEA = 1 ;
3.     public static final int TYPEB = 2 ;
4.     private static int count = 0 ;
5.     static void addOne(){ count++ ; }
6.     static final String name = "Widget" ;
7.     // more code here
8.   }
```

Note that if the word "final" is attached to a reference variable, the associated object must be created in the declaration statement, as in line 6. In this case,

final means that the initial object reference cannot be replaced by another object reference—not that the object cannot be modified.

Classes With Only Static Members

It is quite feasible to have classes that have only static members, do not have constructors, and cannot be used to create an object. An example of this is the **Math** class in the Java standard library, which is used to provide the typical mathematical functions. You address the static variables and methods with notation similar to that used with instance variables but with the name of the class instead of an instance reference, as shown in the following code:

```
1. area = Math.PI * rad * rad ; // addressing a static constant
2. root = Math.sqrt( area ) ; // addressing a static method
```

Variable Initialization

Both instance variables and class (static) variables have default initialization values that are used if the variable declaration statement does not include initial values. Class variables are initialized when the class is loaded by the JVM, and instance variables are initialized when an object is created. In contrast, there is no default initialization for variables that are declared inside the scope of methods or smaller code blocks.

 It is essential to know the default initializations of static and instance variables.

➤ Integer primitives are initialized to 0.

➤ Floating-point primitives are initialized to 0.0.

➤ Boolean primitives are initialized to false.

➤ Reference variables are initialized to null.

More On Variable Modifiers

The modifiers **abstract, native,** and **synchronized** are not used with variables. The keyword **transient** is used to indicate variables that do not need to be saved when an object is saved using the object serialization methods. The keyword *volatile* is used to signal to the compiler that the designated variable may be changed by multiple Threads and that it cannot take any shortcuts when retrieving the value in this variable.

Methods

Methods are defined with a method declaration. The elements in a method declaration are access modifier, additional modifiers, return type, method name, parameter list, and exceptions. The combination of name and parameter list constitutes the method *signature*. Table 4.2 summarizes the keywords that can be used in a method declaration. Note that if one of the access modifiers—**public**, **private**, or **protected**—does not appear, the default is visibility within the package.

Method Code

If the method is not declared abstract, the declaration is followed by a block of code enclosed in a bracket pair. An abstract declaration is followed by a semicolon. If the method is declared as returning a value, all paths through the code must terminate in a **return** statement that returns the correct type of value. If the method is declared with a void return type, **return** statements are optional; however, if they appear, they must not return a value.

Table 4.2 Summary of Java keywords used with methods.	
Keyword	**Implication**
public	The method is visible to all classes in the program.
private	The method is visible only inside the class.
protected	The method is visible to classes inside the package and to subclasses.
final	The method cannot be overridden in subclasses.
abstract	The method is declared without an implementation.
static	The method is independent of any object of the class, but can address only static variables.
native	The implementation must be provided in machine language for a specific system.
synchronized	A **Thread** entering this method obtains a lock on the object, which prevents other Threads from entering any synchronized code for the object.
throws	This word introduces a list of checked exceptions that the method may throw. Exceptions are discussed in Chapter 7.
void	If the method does not return a value, the word "void" must appear as the return type.

Method Overloading

Java allows multiple methods in a class with the same name as long as they have different parameter input lists. This is called *overloading* a method. You can see many examples of overloading in the Java standard libraries. For instance, the **java.awt.Graphics** class has six different **drawImage** methods.

Method Overriding

When a method in a derived class has the same name and signature as a method in the parent class, we say that the parent class method is overridden. A good example of this in the Java standard library is the **toString** method defined in the **Object** class. Many classes override **toString** with more informative versions.

Local Variables

Local variables, also known as "automatic" variables, are declared inside methods or smaller blocks of code. The storage for these variables does not exist in an object but in the environment of the Thread executing the method. The rules for initialization of and access to these variables are quite different from those for instance variables. My experiments with model tests have indicated that many people are weak on initialization and scope of local variables. The term *scope* refers to the section of code in which a variable can be referred to. A variable declared in a block of code, such as a method, has a scope within that block of code.

Initialization

Local variables are not initialized automatically; the programmer must provide a value for all variables before they are used. The compiler will report an error if there is any path through your code that does not initialize a variable before it is used, as illustrated in the following code fragment where **nameTable** is a **Hashtable** object:

```
1. public String lookup( String abrev ){
2.    String fullname ;
3.    if( nameTable.containsKey( abrev ) ) {
4.       fullname = (String) nameTable.get( abrev ) ;
5.    }
6.    return fullname ;
7. }
```

The purpose of the **lookup** method is to return the full name if the abbreviation is a key in the **nameTable**. However, the compiler detects that there is a path through the code in which **fullname** will not be initialized and reports an error. One solution to the problem is to initialize **fullname** in line 2; another is to provide an **else** branch that sets **fullname** after line 5.

Scope Of Local Variables

Remember that the scope (visibility) of local variables is restricted to the code block in which they are declared. For instance, in the following code fragment, the compiler will object to the use of **val** in lines 5 and 7 because the scope of the variable is inside the **try** block:

```
1. public int parseParam( String s ){
2.    try {
3.       int val = Integer.parseInt( s );
4.    }catch(NumberFormatException e ){
5.       val = -1 ;
6.    }
7.    return val ;
8. }
```

Another common mistake related to scope is the attempt to use a loop variable outside the code block of the loop. For example, in the following code fragment, the loop counter **i** will be meaningless outside the loop, and the attempt to use it in line 5 will cause a compiler error:

```
1. public int findNdx( String name ){
2.    for( int i = 0 ; i < nameList.length ; i++ ){
3.       if( name.equals( nameList[i] ) break ;
4.    }
5.    return i ;
6. }
```

Final Local Variables

The only modifier that can be applied to a local variable is **final**. The implication is the same as with other variables—once the variable has been set, it cannot be changed. Final local variables are of interest mainly in *inner classes*, which are discussed in Chapter 5.

Static Initializers

In addition to declaring and initializing a **static** variable in the same statement, you can create a special block of code that runs when the class is loaded by the JVM. This is typically used to initialize more complex structures. For instance, if you wanted to create a **Hashtable** for rapid lookup of state names from two-letter abbreviations, you can create and initialize the **Hashtable** with code like the following (and adding 47 more states):

```
static String[] states = { "Texas", "Florida", "Oklahoma" } ;
static String[] abrev = { "TX", "FL", "OK" } ;
public static Hashtable statesByAb ;
static {
  statesByAb = new Hashtable();
  for( int i = 0 ; i < abrev.length ; i++ ){
     statesByAb.put( abrev[i], states[i] );
  }
} // end of static initializer block
```

The **statesByAb Hashtable** would be available as soon as the class was loaded. Because it is declared **public**, it can be used by any method in any class.

Constructors

Constructors are chunks of code used to initialize a new object. All Java classes must have at least one constructor, either declared in the class or as an implicit default constructor. Although constructors look like methods, they are considered separately. Constructors always have the name of the class and no return type. You can control access to constructors with the access modifiers **public**, **protected**, and **private**, just as you can with other methods. Unlike methods, constructors cannot have the modifiers **abstract**, **static**, **final**, **native**, or **synchronized**. Constructor declarations can have a list of thrown exceptions.

Constructing a new object involves allocating the right amount of memory and initializing variables. Because your custom class may inherit from a long hierarchy of classes, constructing even a simple-looking object may involve a lot of work by the JVM. Fortunately, the compiler takes care of most of the details.

A class can have any number of constructors as long as they have different signatures. The restriction is that each constructor must have a different parameter list. Constructors are not inherited, so each derived class must specifically implement any constructors it needs; however, a derived class can make use of the constructors of its parent class using the **super** keyword. For example, the **java.awt.Rectangle** class has the following constructor:

```
public Rectangle( int x, int y, int width, int height )
```

If I wanted to write a class, **MyRect**, extending **Rectangle**, one possible constructor is as follows:

```
public MyRect( int w, int h ){
   super( 0,0,w,h );
   // other initialization code here
}
```

Note that if an invocation of the **super** constructor is used, it must be the first line of the constructor code. Any other use of the **super** constructor causes a compiler error.

The Implied Super Constructor

The Java compiler does a lot of extra work in compiling constructor code. If the first line of the code body does not have an invocation of the **super** constructor, the compiler inserts "super()", an invocation of the *default* constructor that takes no parameters belonging to the parent class.

Default Constructors

If no other constructors are declared in a class, the compiler will create a default constructor that takes no parameters and simply calls the parent class constructor, which takes no parameters. This can lead to problems, as exemplified in the following simple example:

```
1. class Base extends Object {
2.    int type ;
3.    Base( int n ) { type = n ; }
4. }
5. class XBase extends Base {
6.    String X = "" ;
7. }
```

Because the **Base** class has a constructor that takes a parameter (line 3), the compiler does not create a default **Base** constructor. Because the **XBase** class is defined without a constructor, the compiler attempts to provide a default constructor. However, there is no constructor taking no parameters in the **Base** class, so the compiler issues this error:

```
No constructor matching Base() found in Base
```

This rather odd-sounding error message has confused many beginning Java programmers. You will probably encounter one or more test questions related to default constructors.

Overloaded Constructors

A class can have any number of constructors as long as they have different parameter lists. One constructor can invoke another, but the statement has to be the first one in the code body. In the example shown in Listing 4.1, the constructor that takes a **String** and two **int** primitives invokes the constructor that takes two **int** primitives.

Listing 4.1   Code for a Java class that has two constructors.

```
import java.awt.* ;
  class Base extends Object {
    Point theP ;
    String str = "" ;
    Base( int x, int y ){
        theP = new Point( x, y );
    }
    Base( String txt, int x, int y ){
      this( x, y );
      str = txt ;
    }
  }
```

Points to keep in mind about constructors:

➤ If you don't define any constructor in the class code, the compiler will provide a default constructor that takes no parameters.

➤ You can invoke constructors in the parent class, but this must be done in the first line of code in the constructor body.

➤ A class can have multiple constructors, but they must have different parameter lists.

➤ A constructor can invoke another constructor in the class, but this must be done in the first line of code in the constructor body.

Interfaces

Interfaces are reference types like classes, but can have only abstract method declarations and constants as members. Interfaces are defined in the same way as classes, with a source code file having a ".java" file type that is compiled to a class file. Interfaces are also members of packages, just like classes. Java uses interfaces extensively to provide a convenient alternative to multiple inheritance. A Java class can implement any number of interfaces.

A class that implements an interface must provide implementations for all of the methods that the interface defines. An object of this class then has a sort of alternate identity and can be referred to as being of the interface type. For example, the **Runnable** interface, a member of the **java.lang** package, defines only a single method with the following signature:

```
public void run();
```

Another simple interface is the **ActionListener** interface in the **java.awt.event** package. The single method required by this interface has the signature shown in the following:

```
public void actionPerformed( ActionEvent e );
```

The CountDown Demonstration Class

Listing 4.2 shows a Java class that demonstrates several of the features I have been talking about. The function of the **CountDown** class is to animate a countdown message after a button has been clicked. To do this, it implements the **Runnable** interface so it can have a separate **Thread** to run a timer mechanism and the **ActionListener** interface so it can be notified when a button is clicked.

Listing 4.2 Complete source for the CountDown class.

```java
import java.awt.TextField ;
import java.awt.event.*;
public class CountDown extends java.lang.Object implements
     java.awt.event.ActionListener, java.lang.Runnable
{
  static int counters = 0 ;
  static synchronized int incCount(){ return ++counters; }
  TextField text ;
  int myN ;
  CountDown( TextField tf ){
    text = tf ; myN = incCount() ;
  }

  public void run()
  { for(int i = 10 ; i >= 0 ; i--){
      try{
        text.setText( Integer.toString( i ));
        Thread.sleep( 1000 );
      }catch(InterruptedException e ){}
    }
  }
  // required by ActionListener interface
  public void actionPerformed(ActionEvent e)
  { Thread t = new Thread( this );
    System.out.println("Start counter " + myN );
    t.start();
  }
}
```

The *CountDown* Constructor

Note that the constructor for **CountDown** takes a reference to a **TextField** object. **TextField** objects are used in Java applications and applets with graphical user interfaces to show a single line of changeable text. The constructor saves this reference in the instance variable named **text**.

Every time a new **CountDown** object is created, the counter is incremented in the **static incCount** method, and a unique number is returned to the constructor. Because the **incCount** method is synchronized, only one **Thread** at a time can use it to obtain a serial number; thus, every **CountDown** object has a unique **myN**.

If you are sure that only one **Thread** will be creating **CountDown** objects, you can leave off the **synchronized** keyword. If you browse through the source code for Java standard library components, such as **java.awt.TextField**, you will see that many classes use this technique to create a unique serial number.

The *ActionListener* Interface

The **CountDown** class has an **actionPerformed** method to satisfy the requirements of the **ActionListener** interface. In the **java.awt.Button** class, there is a method that has the following signature:

```
public synchronized void addActionListener( ActionListener a );
```

Note that the input parameter is a reference to an interface, not to a specific class. Any object that wants to get **ActionEvents** from a **Button** has only to implement the **ActionListener** interface and register with the **Button**.

The *Runnable* Interface

In order to satisfy the **Runnable** interface, **CountDown** has a **run** method. When a **Thread** is attached to an object having a **run** method and started, it automatically executes the **run** method. I will cover **Threads** and the **Runnable** interface in Chapter 9.

References To Interfaces

You can have variables declared as being of an interface type, as illustrated in the following code from an applet using **CountDown** objects:

```
CountDown cd1 = new CountDown( textField1 );
Runnable rcd1 = cd1 ;
ActionListener acd1 = cd1 ;
button1.addActionListener( acd1 );
```

Here you see three reference variables of three different types, all referring to the same object. You can also use the **instanceof** operator to see if a given object implements an interface.

Defining An Interface

Defining an interface is just like defining an **abstract** class with all **abstract** methods. Interfaces can have access modifiers of **public** or *blank*, just like classes. An interface can be defined as extending another interface, in a hierarchy similar to the class hierarchy, but there is no base interface analogous to the **Object** class.

Practice Questions

Question 1

> Which of the following class declarations are *incorrect* use of modifier keywords? [Check all correct answers]
>
> ❑ a. public synchronized class FastClass extends Thread
>
> ❑ b. private protected class FastClass
>
> ❑ c. public abstract class FastClass
>
> ❑ d. class FastClass extends Thread

Both a and b are incorrect usage, and thus correct answers; the **synchronized**, **protected**, and **private** keywords cannot be applied to classes. Answer c is correct usage but an incorrect answer; the **abstract** keyword indicates that there is at least one abstract method in the class. Answer d shows a legal class declaration and is thus an incorrect answer.

Question 2

> Given the following class:
>
> ```
> 1. class Widget extends Thingee{
> 2.     static final int maxWidgetSize = 40 ;
> 3.     static String Title ;
> 4.     public Widget( int mx, String T  ){
> 5.         maxWidgetSize = mx ;
> 6.         Title = T ;
> 7.     }
> 8.     // other code
> 9. }
> ```
>
> What will happen when you try to compile this code and run a program that creates a **Widget** as follows?
>
> ```
> 10.  Widget myWidget = new Widget( 50, "Bigger");
> ```
>
> ○ a. The program compiles and runs fine.
>
> ○ b. The program compiles but gets a runtime error in line 5.
>
> ○ c. The compiler objects to line 5.
>
> ○ d. The compiler objects to line 6.

Answer c is correct. The compiler knows that a variable declared as **static final** cannot be modified, so it generates an error. Answers a and b are incorrect because the compiler error occurs. Answer d is incorrect because line 6 is perfectly reasonable; objects are allowed to access and modify static (class) variables as long as they are not also declared **final**.

Question 3

Given the following listing of the **Widget** class:

```
1. class Widget extends Thingee{
2.     static private int widgetCount = 0 ;
3.     public String wName ;
4.     int wNumber ;
5.
6.     static synchronized int
           addWidget(){ widgetCount++ ;
7.         wName = "I am Widget # " +
             widgetCount ;
8.         return widgetCount ;
9.     }
10.    public Widget(){
11.        wNumber = addWidget();
12.    }
13. }
```

What happens when you try to compile the class and use multiple **Widget** objects in a program?

○ a. The class compiles and each **Widget** will get a unique **wNumber** and **wName** reflecting the order in which the **Widgets** were created.

○ b. The compiler objects to line 7.

○ c. The class compiles, but a runtime error related to the access of the variable **wName** occurs in the **addWidget** method.

Answer b is correct; the static method **addWidget** cannot access the member variable **wName**. Static methods can refer to static variables only, such as **widgetCount**. Answers a and c are incorrect because a compiler error is generated by line 7. Note that answer c is incorrect also because it is the compiler that catches incorrect use of access modifiers, such as static.

Question 4

Given the following listing of the **Widget** class:

```
1. class Widget extends Thingee{
2.    static private int widgetCount = 0 ;
3.    public String wName ;
4.    int wNumber ;
5.
6.    private static synchronized int
          addWidget(){
7.       return ++widgetCount ;
8.    }
9.    public Widget(){
10.      wNumber = addWidget();
11.   }
12. }
```

What happens when you try to compile the class and use multiple **Widget** objects in a program that uses multiple Threads to create **Widget** objects?

- ○ a. The class compiles and each **Widget** will get a unique **wNumber** reflecting the order in which the **Widgets** were created.

- ○ b. The compiler objects to the **addWidget** call of a static method in line 10.

- ○ c. A runtime error occurs in the **addWidget** method.

- ○ d. The class compiles and each **Widget** will get a **wNumber**, but we cannot guarantee that the number will be unique.

The correct answer is a. The use of **synchronized** in line 6 ensures that number assignment will not be interrupted, no matter how many **Threads** are trying to create **Widget** objects. Answer b is incorrect because line 10 is in the correct form, although **Widget.addWidget()** could also be used. Answer c is incorrect because the **addWidget** method has no code that can generate a runtime error. Answer d is incorrect because the use of **synchronized** in line 6 ensures that number assignment will not be interrupted, no matter how many Threads are trying to create **Widget** objects.

Question 5

Trying to compile the following source code produces a compiler warning to the effect that the variable **tmp** may not have been initialized.

```
1. class Demo{
2.    String msg = "Type is " ;
3.    public void showType( int n ) {
4.      String tmp ;
5.      if( n > 0 ) tmp = "positive";
6.      System.out.println( msg + tmp );
7.    }
8. }
```

Which of the following changes would eliminate this warning? [Check all correct answers]

❑ a. Make line 4 read

```
4.      String tmp = null ;
```

❑ b. Make line 4 read

```
4.      String tmp = "" ;
```

❑ c. Insert a line following line 5

```
6.      else tmp = "not positive" ;
```

❑ d. Remove line 4 and insert a new line after 2 so **tmp** becomes a member variable instead of a local variable in showType.

```
3.      String tmp ;
```

All of these changes will eliminate the warning and are therefore correct. Both a and b provide for initializing the reference when it is declared. Answer c ensures that **tmp** gets initialized no matter what the value of n. Answer d makes **tmp** a member variable that will be initialized to null by default.

Question 6

The following method definition is designed to parse and return an integer from an input string that is expected to look like "nnn,ParamName." In the event of a **NumberFormatException**, the method is to return -1.

```
1. public int getNum( String S ){
2.    try {
3.       String tmp =
             S.substring( 0,S.indexOf(',' ));
4.       return Integer.parseInt( tmp );
5.    }catch(NumberFormatException e){
6.       System.out.println("Problem in " + tmp
      );
7.    }
8.    return -1 ;
9. }
```

What happens when you try to compile this code and execute the method with an input string that does not contain a comma separating the number from the text data?

○ a. A compiler error in line 6 prevents compilation.

○ b. The method prints the error message to standard output and returns -1.

○ c. A **NullPointerException** is thrown in line 3.

○ d. A **StringIndexOutOfBoundsException** is thrown in line 3.

Answer a is correct because the scope of the **tmp String** is confined to the **try** block; thus, it cannot be used in line 6. The situation in answer b does not occur because of the compiler error related to the scope of the **tmp** variable. Answer c would not occur even if the scope of the **tmp** variable were fixed. Answer d would occur only if the scope of the **tmp** variable were fixed by declaring and initializing **tmp** in the first line of the method.

Question 7

Given the following class definition:

```
1. public class DerivedDemo extends Demo{
2.    int M, N, L ;
3.    public DerivedDemo( int x, int y ){
4.      M = x ; N = y ;
5.    }
6.    public DerivedDemo( int x ){
7.      super( x );
8.    }
9. }
```

Which of the following constructor signatures *must* exist in the **Demo** class for **DerivedDemo** to compile correctly? [Check all correct answers]

❏ a. public Demo(int a, int b)

❏ b. public Demo(int c)

❏ c. public Demo( )

The correct answers are b and c. The code in answer b is required because it is called in line 7. The code in answer c is required because a default (no arguments) constructor is needed to compile the constructor starting in line 3. The code in answer a is not required because no constructor with that signature is explicitly called.

Need To Know More?

 Flanagan, David: *Java in a Nutshell, 2nd Edition*. O'Reilly & Associates, Inc., Sebastopol, CA, 1997. ISBN: 1-56592-262-X. This is the most compact desktop reference book documenting the Java language. Chapter 3, "Classes and Objects in Java" is pertinent to this chapter.

 ftp://ftp.javasoft.com/docs/tutorial.zip

An excellent tutorial in HTML form can be downloaded from this site. (Although this document is updated frequently, it may not be entirely current with JDK 1.2 information).

 http://java.sun.com/docs/books/jls/html/index.html

The definitive Java language specification document is maintained in HTML form on the Sun Microsystems Web site.

 http://java.sun.com/products/jdk/1.2/index.html

The Java API documentation in Javadoc-generated form can be downloaded from Sun Microsystems. Although this site changes a lot, the last time I looked, it was a good starting point.

Nested Classes

Terms you'll need to understand:

√ Nested class

√ Inner class

√ Member class

√ Local class

√ Anonymous inner class

Techniques you'll need to master:

√ Distinguishing the various types of nested classes and what they are used for

√ Writing inner classes to handle events

The designers of Java decided at an early stage that Java classes would have single inheritance—in other words, each class has only one parent class. Sometimes in object-oriented programming, you wish a class could partake of the methods of more than one parent. In Java 1.0, this was supplied to some extent by the concept of interfaces, but in Java 1.1, the designers found it necessary to add the concept of nested classes.

Nested And Inner Classes

The main driving force for this change in the language was a major change in the way user interface events are handled. In Java 1.0, user interface events could be delivered only to classes in the user interface hierarchy. As Java applications got larger, this method was found to be slow and inflexible.

Starting with Java 1.1, events can be delivered to any object, but this implies great duplication of code in every class that needs to handle an event. Nested classes are the solution to avoiding this duplication of code and simplifying the process of adding an event handler to a class. Although nested classes can be used for a variety of purposes, you are most likely to see them as inner classes in connection with event handling.

What Is A Nested Class?

Generally speaking, a nested class is a member of another class. However, it is common to speak of the static members as nested and the nested classes that are members of instances of the enclosing class as inner classes. Indeed, you are most likely to read about inner classes only, but the more general term is nested classes.

The basic idea is simply that a top-level Java class, in addition to having member variables and member methods, can have a member class. This member class can inherit from any top-level class and implement any interface, independent of the object hierarchy of the enclosing class. Just as member methods in a class have unlimited access to all private and other variables and methods in the class, nested classes also have unlimited access.

Why Make A Nested Class?

You would want to create a nested class for two main reasons:

➤ You might need to make use of the special functionality of class A from within class B without complicating the inheritance hierarchy of either class. This is the reason for the use of inner classes to support the Java 1.1 event model.

➤ From the point of view of programming philosophy, if class A exists solely to help work with class B, you might as well make class A a member of class B. This helps to keep all of the code related to class B in a single source code file.

Why *Not* To Make A Nested Class

Nested classes are not a cure-all, and some Java programmers find them down-right ugly. Large nested classes make reading Java code harder than it already is, so keep your nested classes small for easier maintenance. Inner classes do make automatic code generation for event handling with the Java 1.1 model much easier, and your encounters with inner classes will probably be in the context of event handling.

How To Make A Nested Class

From a programmer's standpoint, you create a nested class by simply declaring a class inside the declaration of a top-level class or inside a block of code. From the Java compiler's standpoint, a lot of work has to be done. The Java compiler has to create a class file for both the enclosing class and the nested class. The name of the nested class is created by the compiler, starting with the name of the enclosing class. From the Java Virtual Machine (JVM) standpoint, only a slight change in the format of class files was needed to add nested classes; otherwise, the JVM treats a nested class just like any other.

Here is a summary of the different configurations of nested classes:

➤ **Nested static class** A named class declared **static**. It can directly access only static variables and methods. Considered a top-level class.

➤ **Nested interface** A named interface, typically used for defining methods used to access the enclosing class.

➤ **Inner class - member** A named class defined as a member of the enclosing class. Must be associated with an instance of the enclosing class. There can be multiple member inner classes in an enclosing class. Member inner classes can be declared as **public, private, protected, final,** or **abstract,** but cannot have the same name as the enclosing class.

➤ **Inner class - local** A named class defined in a code block in a method of the enclosing class. The inner class can access local variables in the method and parameters passed to the method only if the variables are declared **final**. Similar to a local variable, the inner class cannot be accessed outside the code block; in other words, the scope of the class is confined to the code block.

> ➤ **Inner class - anonymous** A class defined inside a single expression, having no name or constructor method. These classes can access local variables in the method and parameters passed to the method only if they are declared **final**.

Static Nested Classes

A static nested class is simply one that is declared inside another class and is declared with the **static** modifier. Like static methods, a static nested class can refer to static variables and methods only directly. It can refer to instance variables and methods only when given a reference to an object of the enclosing class type. The following code is a rough outline of the way a static class is declared:

```
class NormalClass {
    static class NestedClass {
        // methods and variables of NestedClass
    }
    // methods and variables of NormalClass
}
```

A Static Nested Class Example

Most of the examples of static nested classes I have seen have been a little forced, but I've found a more realistic example, one related to experiments in computer-based artificial life (ALife). In typical ALife experiments, the programmer creates a class representing an organism, then provides for creation of lots of individuals and lets them roam an artificial environment.

One approach to giving each individual a slice of CPU time is to give each one a **Thread**, but this has disadvantages, such as excessive overhead. In the following example, the static nested class is used to portion out execution time to each "live" object, using only one thread and taking advantage of the access the static nested class has to the enclosing top-level class static variables.

The **Bubble** class, as shown in Listing 5.1, creates a simple object that has a color, a radius, an x and y position, and an x and y rate of change variables. A **Bubble** object knows how to move and how to paint itself on the screen, but it is the **BubTimer** class that provides the **Thread** to execute the **move** method and time the calls to **repaint**.

The **BubTimer** class (emphasized in the listing) also provides for creating new **Bubble** objects and adding them to the **Vector** of active objects. Note that the **BubTimer.addBub** method can directly access the static variables and private methods of the **Bubble** class. In fact, to emphasize the special relationship of the nested class to the enclosing class, all of the instance variables and methods of the **Bubble** class are **private,** so only **BubTimer** can access them.

Listing 5.1   The **Bubble** class with the static nested BubTimer class.

```
import java.lang.*;
import java.awt.* ;
import java.util.* ;
public class Bubble extends java.lang.Object
{
  static Vector allBub = new Vector();
  static Dimension size ;
  public static class BubTimer extends Thread {
    Panel P ;
    BubTimer(Panel p ){ P = p ;
    }
    public void addBub(int x, int y ){
      allBub.addElement(
        new Bubble( Color.red, 20, x, y ) );
    }
    public void run(){
      while( true ){
        if( allBub != null && allBub.size() > 0 ){
          Enumeration e = allBub.elements();
          while(e.hasMoreElements()){
            ((Bubble)e.nextElement()).move();
          }
          P.repaint();
        }
        try {
          Thread.sleep(100);
        }catch(InterruptedException e){}
      }
    }
    public void paintAll(Graphics g ){
      if( allBub == null || allBub.size() == 0 ) return;
      Enumeration e = allBub.elements();
      while(e.hasMoreElements()){
        ((Bubble)e.nextElement()).paint( g );
      }
    }
  }

  // Bubble instance variables
  private Color clr ;
  private int radius, x, y, dx, dy ;
```

```
    private Bubble( Color c, int r, int xx, int yy ){
      clr = c ; radius = r ; x = xx ; y = yy ;
      dx = dy = r/2 ;
    }
    private void move(){
      x += dx ; y += dy ;
      if( x > size.width ) dx = -dx ;
      else if( x < 0 ) dx = -dx ;
      if( y > size.height) dy = -dy ;
      else if( y < 0 ) dy = -dy ;
    }
    private void paint(Graphics g){
      g.setColor( clr );
      g.fillOval( x, y, radius, radius );
    }
}
```

A Member Inner Class Example

Listing 5.2 shows a typical example of the use of an inner class to implement an interface, in this case the **ActionListener** interface, that requires only a single method: **actionPerformed**. (The role of **ActionListeners** in Java event handling is covered in Chapter 13.) This code was originally generated with Symantec's Visual Café development environment, so the inner class is named **SymAction**. **SymAction** extends **Object** (by default) and implements **ActionListener**.

In the **init** method, I create an instance of the **SymAction** class and connect it to the **button1** and **button2** objects with the **addActionListener** method. The sole function of **SymAction** is to receive events generated when a button is clicked, and to perform an appropriate method. In this example, **button1** clears a text field and **button2** sends data from the text field:

Listing 5.2   A Java applet making use of a named inner class to handle events.

```
import java.awt.*;
import java.awt.event.* ;
import java.applet.*;
public class Applet1 extends Applet{
...// variables
   public void init(){
      button1 = new Button("Clear");
      button2 = new Button("Send");
      textField1 = new TextField();
      // various initialization statements to create
```

```
      // the rest of the interface
      SymAction lSymAction = new SymAction();
      button1.addActionListener(lSymAction);
      button2.addActionListener(lSymAction);
   }
   class SymAction implements java.awt.event.ActionListener
   {
     public void actionPerformed( ActionEvent event)
     {
       Object object = event.getSource();
       if (object == button1) textField1.setText("");
       if( object == button2) doSend( textField1.getText() );
     }
   } // end of inner class definition
       // code left out to save space
} // end of enclosing class definition
```

If you were to compile the code in Listing 5.2, you would find that the compiler has created both an Applet1.class and an Applet1$SymAction.class. The formal name of the inner class would be **Applet1.SymAction**, but the extra period would confuse some operating systems, so the compiler uses a dollar sign instead.

Because the **SymAction** object is created in the context of an instance of **Applet1**, it has access to all variables and methods—both static and instance members. Even if **textField1** were declared **private**, the inner class object would have access.

A Local Inner Class Example

A local inner class is defined inside the scope of a code block—typically, the code block of a method, but it could be any code block. In the following method code, the purpose is to return a **Hashtable** object containing a subset of names and keys derived from two **String** arrays—**keys** and **names**—in the enclosing class:

```
Hashtable makeHash( String start ){
   class myHash extends Hashtable {
      public myHash(){
         super(10);
      }
      public void buildHash( String str ){
         for( int i = 0 ; i < keys.length ; i++ ){
            if( names[i].startsWith( str ) ){
               put( keys[i], names[i] );
            }
```

```
        }
      }
    } // end inner class definition
    myHash h = new myHash();
    h.buildHash( start );
    return h ;
}
```

Access To Local Variables

The introduction of local inner classes (classes declared inside the scope of a code block or statement) produced a problem for Java's designers. An object created in an inner class may live long after the code block has been exited and any local variables have been discarded. The inner class declaration could see these variables, but how could an inner class method refer to them? The solution was to provide a new meaning for the word "final." When the compiler finds a local variable declared **final**, it creates a special hidden copy of the variable that the inner class can refer to safely. This also applies to parameters that are input to the method in which the inner class is declared.

 Local inner classes and anonymous classes can refer to local variables only if they are declared **final**.

An Anonymous Inner Class Example

In Listing 5.2, the **SymAction** object was connected to two buttons. If you needed to connect only to a single button, you could use the even simpler anonymous style inner class, as shown in Listing 5.3, for **Applet2**. The class is defined and a single instance of it is created entirely within a single Java statement. It is anonymous because the class does not have a name and there is no named variable that holds a reference to it. The only reference to the object is in the list of **ActionListeners** that **button1** holds.

Listing 5.3   A Java applet making use of an anonymous inner class.

```
import java.awt.* ;
import java.awt.event.* ;
import java.applet.* ;
public class Applet2 extends Applet{
.../// variables
  public void init()
  {
    button1 = new Button("Clear");
```

```
        textField1 = new TextField();
        // various initialization statements to create
        // the rest of the interface
        button1.addActionListener(
          new ActionListener()
          { // start inner class definition
            public void actionPerformed( ActionEvent evt )
            { textField1.setText("");
            }
          }
        ); // end of addActionListener statement
    } // end of init method
    // code left out to save space
} // end of enclosing class definition
```

With anonymous inner classes, the compiler names the compiled class file sequentially. Therefore, in the previous example, it would create Applet2$1.class. In this example, the anonymous inner class had only one method because that is all that is required for the **ActionListener** interface. There is no limit on the number of methods and variables it could declare, but such code gets harder and harder to read as the number of variables and methods expands.

The observant student would have noticed the curious thing about the inner class declaration. It used the name of an interface, **ActionListener**, where a named class would have a class name and "implements ActionListener." In this case, the anonymous class extends **Object** by default and the compiler supplies the necessary code.

An anonymous inner class can also be declared as extending a class, but the syntax does not use the word "extends". In the following example fragment, which provides for handling **FocusEvents** in the **panel1** object, the parent class is **FocusAdapter**:

```
panel1.addFocusListener(
  new FocusAdapter()
  { public void focusGained( FocusEvent evt ) // override parent
      { // do something here
      }
  } // end anonymous inner class defintion
) ; // end addFocusAdapter statement
```

Access From Outside

Now that you have seen examples of the various types of nested classes, let's look at how a nested class can be accessed from outside the enclosing class.

Static Nested Class

Listing 5.4 shows an example of how to create an instance of the static nested class **BubTimer**, from Listing 5.1, in an Applet **start** method. Notice how the statement that creates the BT object addresses **BubTimer** as a member of the **Bubble** class. This code also illustrates the use of a named inner class, which extends the **MouseAdapter** class to capture mouse click events.

Listing 5.4   An applet using the **BubTimer** class.

```
import java.awt.*;
import java.applet.*;

public class BubApplet extends Applet
{
  Bubble.BubTimer BT ;
  public void init()
  {
    setLayout(null);
    setSize(426,266);
    Bubble.size = getSize();
    SymMouse aSymMouse = new SymMouse();
    this.addMouseListener(aSymMouse);
  }
  public void start(){
    BT = new Bubble.BubTimer((Panel)this );
    BT.addBub( 0,0 );
    BT.start();
  }
  public void paint(Graphics g){
      BT.paintAll( g );
  }
  class SymMouse extends java.awt.event.MouseAdapter
  {  public void mouseClicked(java.awt.event.MouseEvent evt)
    {  BT.addBub(evt.getX(), evt.getY());
    }
  } // end inner class
}
```

Using A Member Inner Class Object

The important thing to remember about inner classes is that an inner class object must always be associated with an instance of the enclosing class. Let's consider the following outline of a class:

```
public class NormClass {
  public class NestedClass {
```

```
      // methods and variables of NestedClass
   }
   // methods and variables of NormClass
}
```

It is possible for another class to create references to objects of these classes as follows:

```
NormClass nc = new NormClass() ;
NormClass.NestedClass nnc = nc.new NestedClass();
```

You can also create an instance of the inner class without specifically keeping a reference to an instance of the enclosing class. Of course, there has to be an enclosing class instance, but you don't have to keep a reference to it, as shown in the following code:

```
NormClass.NestedClass nnc = new NormClass().new NestedClass();
```

The new instance of **NormClass** will not be garbage-collected because the **NestedClass** object, **nnc**, keeps a reference to it. If the instance of **NestedClass** had to refer to the associated instance of **NormClass**, the following syntax would be used:

```
NormClass myPartner = NormClass.this ;
```

As another example, if both **NormClass** and **NestedClass** had a **String** variable "name", the **NestedClass** object could refer to them as follows:

```
System.out.println("My name is " + name ) ; // nested class name
System.out.println("My partner is " + NormClass.this.name ) ;
```

 You should know the correct ways to define various types of nested classes. Also, be aware of which variables and methods of the enclosing class each type of nested class has access to.

Practice Questions

Question 1

> You need to write code in an applet that will call the **submitData** method when **button1** is clicked. To do this, connect **button1** with an object that implements the **ActionListener** interface. Which of the following anonymous class declarations is the correct way to do this?
>
> ○ a.
>
> ```
> button1.addActionListener(
>        new ActionListener()
>        { public void
>            actionPerformed( ActionEvent evt )
>          {  submitData() ;
>          }
>        }
>     );
> ```
>
> ○ b.
>
> ```
> button1.addActionListener(
>        new Object implements ActionListener()
>        { public void
>            actionPerformed( ActionEvent evt )
>          {  submitData() ;
>          }
>        }
>     );
> ```
>
> ○ c.
>
> ```
> button1.addActionListener(
>        new ActionListener()
>        { submitData() ;
>        }
>     );
> ```

Answer a is the correct answer. Answer b is incorrect because the "Object implements" terminology is wrong. An anonymous inner class implementing an interface does extend **Object,** but the compiler provides the default. Answer c is incorrect because it does not have a method declaration.

Question 2

> Why would a responsible Java programmer want to use a nested class? [Check all correct answers]
>
> ❑ a. To impress the boss with his/her knowledge of Java by using nested classes all over the place.
>
> ❑ b. To keep the code for a very specialized class in close association with the class it works with.
>
> ❑ c. To support a new user interface that generates custom events.

Answers b and c are both good reasons to use a nested class. Although answer a has a certain attraction, the question specified a *responsible* programmer. Inappropriate use of nested classes can result in code that is hard to read and maintain.

Question 3

> When programming a local inner class inside a method code block, which of the following statements is true?
>
> ○ a. The inner class will have access only to static variables in the enclosing class.
>
> ○ b. The inner class can use any variables declared in the method.
>
> ○ c. The inner class can use only local variables that are declared final.
>
> ○ d. The inner class can use only local variables that are declared static.

Answer c is the only correct answer. Only local variables declared **final** can be used by the inner class. Therefore, answers b and d are incorrect. The inner class can have access to any static or instance variables. Therefore, answer a is incorrect.

Question 4

> The following is an outline of code for a top-level class. Assume that both classes have correct constructors taking no parameters.
>
> ```
> class NormalClass {
>    static class NestedClass {
>        // methods and variables of NestedClass
>      }
>    // methods and variables of NormalClass
> }
> ```
>
> Which of the following code fragments shows the correct way to declare and initialize a reference to a **NestedClass** object?
>
> ○ a.
>
> ```
> NormalClass.NestedClass myNC = new
>   NormalClass.NestedClass();
> ```
>
> ○ b.
>
> ```
> NestedClass myNC = new NormalClass().new
>   NestedClass();
> ```
>
> ○ c.
>
> ```
> NestedClass myNC = new NormalClass.NestedClass();
> ```

Answer a shows both a correct reference variable declaration and a correct constructor. Answers b and c have an incorrect declaration of the reference variable because the name of a nested class starts with the enclosing class name.

Question 5

You have been given the following programming problem with respect to a Java application. An existing class called **AB** now needs some additional functionality, which it is proposed to add with a nested or inner class, **ABC**. You have been able to establish the following requirements:

1. There will probably be more than one **AB** instance active in the application, so the solution has to work no matter how many **AB** instances there are.

2. **ABC** will need to have access to instance methods and variables as well as static variables.

3. More than one method in **AB** will have to have access to a method of **ABC**.

Which configuration of a nested class is the best bet for this problem?

○ a. A static class

○ b. A member inner class

○ c. An inner class defined in an AB method

○ d. An anonymous inner class

Answer b is the best approach because a member inner class can easily take care of all three requirements. Answer a is not indicated because of the requirement to access instance variables. Answers c and d are not indicated because of the requirement that more than one method in **AB** will need to use **ABC**.

Question 6

The following is an outline of code for a top-level class. Assume that both classes have correct constructors taking no parameters.

```
class BaseClass {
    public class NestedClass {
        // methods and variables of NestedClass
        }
    // methods and variables of BaseClass
}
```

Which of the following code fragments shows the correct way to declare and initialize a reference to a **NestedClass** object?

○ a.
```
BaseClass.NestedClass myNC = new
    BaseClass.NestedClass();
```

○ b.
```
NestedClass myNC = new BaseClass().new
    NestedClass();
```

○ c.
```
NestedClass myNC = new BaseClass.NestedClass();
```

○ d.
```
BaseClass.NestedClass nbc = new
    BaseClass().new NestedClass();
```

Answer d shows both a correct reference variable declaration and a correct constructor. This statement creates a **BaseClass** object, which the **NestedClass** must have. Answers b and c have an incorrect declaration of the reference variable because the name of a nested class starts with the enclosing class name. Answer a does not create a **BaseClass** object for the **NestedClass** to be associated with.

Question 7

In the following code for a class in which **methodA** has an inner
class, which variables would the statement in line 8 be able to use
in place of **XX**? [Check all correct answers]

```
 1. public class Base {
 2.    private static final int ID = 3 ;
 3.    private String name;
 4.    public void methodA( final int nn ){
 5.     int serialN = 11 ;
 6.     class inner {
 7.       void showResult(){
 8.         System.out.println("Rslt= " + XX );
 9.       }
10.     } // end class inner
11.     new inner().showResult();
12.   } // end methodA
13. }
```

❑ a. The **int ID** in line 2

❑ b. The **String** in line 3

❑ c. The **int nn** in line 4

❑ d. The **int serialN** in line 5

Answers a, b, and c are correct. Answers a and b are correct because inner
classes can access any static or member variable in the enclosing class. Answer
c is correct because, although it is a local variable, it is declared **final**. Answer d
is incorrect because the variable is not declared **final**.

Question 8

Which of the following statements is true?

○ a. An inner class can have the same name as its enclosing
class.

○ b. An instance of a non-static inner class always has an
associated instance of the enclosing class.

○ c. An anonymous inner class is always assumed to extend
Object.

Only answer b is correct. Answer a is incorrect because inner classes are prohibited from having the same name as the enclosing class. Answer c is incorrect because an anonymous inner class can extend any class; however, the declaration syntax does not use the word "extends".

Need To Know More?

 Flanagan, David: *Java in a Nutshell, 2nd Edition*. O'Reilly & Associates, Inc., Sebastopol, CA, 1997. ISBN: 1-56592-262-X. This is the most compact desktop reference book documenting the Java language. Chapter 5, "Nested Classes and Other New Language Features," is pertinent to this chapter.

 ftp://ftp.javasoft.com/docs/tutorial.zip

An excellent tutorial in HTML form can be downloaded from this site. (Although this document is updated frequently, it may not be entirely current with Java JDK 1.2 information.)

 http://java.sun.com/docs/books/jls/html/index.html

The definitive Java language specification document is maintained in HTML form on the Sun Microsystems Web site.

 http://java.sun.com/products/jdk/1.2/index.html

The Java API documentation in Javadoc-generated form can be downloaded from Sun Microsystems. Although this site changes a lot, the last time I looked, this was a good starting point.

Converting And Casting Primitives And Objects

6

Terms you'll need to understand:

√ **instanceof**

√ **interface**

√ Narrowing conversion

√ Object hierarchy

√ Widening conversion

Techniques you'll need to master:

√ Understanding how primitive data types are converted and cast

√ Understanding how object references are converted and cast

√ Understanding when an object reference cast is necessary

√ Understanding which cast operations are legal

You have already encountered some of Java's rules for converting between various primitive types in the discussions of initializing variables (Chapter 2) and mathematical expressions (Chapter 3). In this chapter, I will cover these conversions and the use of cast operations with primitives more formally. Java reference variables can refer to classes, interfaces, or arrays. This chapter covers the rules that govern how they can be converted and cast.

Converting And Casting Primitives

Every Java expression, whether arithmetic, a literal, or a method call, has a type. When the result of an expression has to be assigned to a variable or used in another expression, a different type may be required. The Java compiler is allowed to perform some type conversions automatically but will reject others unless the programmer provides a specific cast. In this section, I'll discuss the rules the compiler uses.

Widening Conversions

Generally speaking, the Java compiler is allowed to perform primitive conversions that do not lose information about the magnitude of the value. It is also allowed to perform some conversions of integers to floating-point values that lose some precision due to the impossibility of representing all integers in floating-point formats.

Signed Integer Conversion

Signed integer conversions proceed by simply extending the sign bit, so a byte with value minus 1 can become a **short, int,** or **long** with value of -1. Of course, if the integer is positive, the zero sign bit is extended, so the value stays positive.

Integers of **int** (32-bit) size or smaller can be converted to floating-point representation, but because a **float** also uses only 32 bits and must include exponent information, there can be a loss of precision. Integer types smaller than 32 bits are first converted to a 32-bit **int** and then to a **float**. In a similar fashion, when converting integer values to **double**, the integer is first converted to a **long** and then to a **double**.

Unsigned *char* Conversion

The **char** primitive type is the only integer that Java treats as unsigned. When converting a **char** type to **int** or **long**, the value is always positive. Because the **short** primitive is a signed integer, you cannot simply convert a **char** to a **short** with code such as line 2 in the following:

```
1. char ch = '\u8243' ;
2. short s = ch ;   // compiler objects
3. short x = (short) ch ; // ok
```

A specific cast is required, as shown in line 3. In this case, the high bit of the **char** is set; therefore, the short value is negative.

Float To Double Conversion

As you might expect, the compiler is free to convert **float** primitives to **double** whenever it wants to. This conversion does not cause the loss of any precision. If the **float** has one of the special values, NaN, **POSITIVE_INFINITY**, or **NEGATIVE_INFINITY**, the **double** ends up with the corresponding **double** special values.

When Are Conversions Done?

In addition to conversions done when assigning a value to a primitive variable and when evaluating arithmetic expressions, the Java compiler makes conversions as necessary to match the signature of methods. Consider the following code fragment, which makes use of the Java standard library **Math** class **static sin** method:

```
int x = 1 ;
double sinx = Math.sin( x );
```

The Java compiler looks up the signature of the method and finds that there is only one **sin** method in the **java.lang.Math** class:

```
public static native double sin( double d );
```

Because this requires a **double** as input, the compiler produces code that is the equivalent of the following (naturally, without any actual temporary variables):

```
int i = 1 ;
long tempL = i ;
double tempD = tempL ;
double sin = Math.sin( tempD );
```

Here's another example of the method signature controlling conversion of primitives. The Math **max** and **min** methods come in several different versions, one for each of **int, long, float,** and **double**. Therefore, in the following code that calls **Math.max** with one **int** and one **long** in line 3, the compiler converts the **int** primitive to a **long** value. The alternative in line 4 forces the compiler to cast the value of **n** to an **int** and calls the version of **max** that uses two **int** primitives:

```
1. int m = 93 ;
2. long n = 91 ;
3. long x = Math.max( m, n ) ;
4. int y = Math.max( m, (int)n );
```

Method Signatures And Return Values

Here are the signatures of some of the **Math** class methods:

```
public static int max( int a, int b );
public static long max( long a, long b );
public static float max( float a, float a );
public static double max( double a, double b );
```

The compiler chooses a method to use based on the input parameters, not on the **return** value. If you need to put the maximum of two **int** primitives in a **double** variable, the compiler uses the version of **max** that returns an **int** and converts the **return** value just before assigning it to the **double** variable.

Impossible Conversions

The following conversions with primitives are not allowed, although some of them might appear plausible to the C programmer:

➤ Any primitive type to any reference type

➤ The null value to any primitive type

➤ Any primitive to boolean

➤ A boolean to any primitive

Casting Primitives

When a Java expression calls for conversion of a primitive type to another type with a smaller range (*narrowing conversion*), the compiler will insist on a specific cast. At runtime, casts that lose information do not cause a runtime exception. It is up to the programmer to think through all the implications of the cast.

Cast Between Integer Types

Narrowing conversion of integer types simply lops off the excess bits. The sign of the converted primitive depends on the value in the sign bit position, and this result is independent of the original sign of the original value.

Cast From Floating-Point To Integer Types

The first step in converting a **float** or **double** to an integer type is conversion to either a **long**, if the destination is **long**, or **int** for all other integer types. The final step is dropping any excess bits. You can get some surprising results from these conversions because the special floating-point values, such as **NaN** (Not a Number) and **POSITIVE_INFINITY,** all turn into integer values without any complaint from the compiler or an exception. For example, the following code prints "Value = 0":

```
double d = Math.sqrt( -1.0 ); // i.e. Double.NaN
int x = (int) d ;
System.out.println("Value = " + x ) ;
```

Cast From *Double* To *Float*

Because a **double** can represent a much wider range of magnitudes than a **float,** the cast may produce some unexpected results. Java follows the IEEE 754 standard for these conversions, as follows:

➤ A **double** value too small to be represented as a **float** becomes a positive or negative zero.

➤ A **double** value too large to be represented as a **float** becomes positive or negative infinity.

➤ A **double** with the special **NaN** (Not a Number) value becomes the float NaN value.

Converting And Casting Reference Types

Java has three kinds of *reference* type variables: class type, interface type, and array type. A variable of type **Object** can hold a reference to any of these three types because **Object** is the root of the Java object hierarchy. This point is important because a Java method that is passed an **Object** reference may have a reference to just about anything.

In contrast to converting and casting primitives, converting and casting a reference to a variable does not change the object being referred to. Once created, an object can be referred to in a variety of ways, but the object type is not changed. However, the way in which Java expressions can use the reference is determined by the reference type.

The instanceof Operator

Objects always "know" what type they are. The programmer can use the **instanceof** operator to check the type of any object reference. For example, the following method can detect a class type (**String**), interface type (**Runnable**), and an array type (**long[]**) reference:

```
public int checkRefType(Object ref ){
  if( ref instanceof String ) return 1 ;
  if( ref instanceof Runnable ) return 3 ;
  if( ref instanceof long[] ) return 4 ;
  return 0 ;
}
```

instanceof With Two Objects

Suppose you have two objects, **objA** and **objB**, and you want to see if they are of the same class. You cannot use

```
if(  objA instanceof objB )
```

because the **instanceof** operator expects a type as a right operand. The solution is to use the Object method **getClass()** as shown in the following code. This statement determines whether the same **Class** object was used to create **objA** and **objB**.

```
if( objA.getClass() == objB.getClass() )
```

The Special null Value

Note that any reference variable can be set to the special **null** value, but **null** is not an instance of anything. All **instanceof** tests with a **null** reference produce **false**.

Conversion And Object Hierarchy

The conversions of object references that are allowed depend on the object hierarchy. Consider the following diagram showing the family tree of the **java.awt.FileDialog** class:

```
java.lang.Object
   |-- java.awt.Component
        |-- java.awt.Container
             |-- java.awt.Panel
             |-- java.awt.ScrollPane
             |-- java.awt.Window
                  |-- java.awt.Dialog
                       |-- java.awt.FileDialog
```

A reference to a **FileDialog** object can be assigned to a variable of any type higher in the hierarchy without a specific cast, as shown in the following code fragment:

```
Dialog myDialog = new FileDialog( this, "Open" );
Component tc = myDialog ;
```

This is called a *widening conversion* of a reference. Because the compiler can assure itself that this is a legal conversion, there is no runtime checking of this conversion. Widening conversions can also be performed when calling a method. For instance, the **add** method of the **Container** class has this signature:

```
public Component add( Component cmp );
```

This means that a call to this method can use a reference to a **Panel**, a **Window**, or a wide variety of other objects that inherit from **Component** without a specific cast or runtime check.

instanceof And The Object Hierarchy

The **instanceof** operator returns **true** for any type in the operand's parentage. For instance, consider the hierarchy shown in the previous section; if **testObj** were created as a **Panel**, the following expressions would return **true**:

```
testObj instanceof java.awt.Panel
testObj instanceof java.awt.Container
testObj instanceof java.awt.Component
testObj instanceof java.lang.Object
```

The freedom that the programmer has to convert any reference to an **Object** reference is the reason for the design of the Java utility classes for manipulating collections of objects. For example, the **Vector** and **Stack** classes can accept and return any reference as an **Object** reference. If you were writing a calculator program working in reverse Polish notation, you might keep a stack of operands with the following code, where **opStack** is a **java.util.Stack** object:

```
1. public void pushD( double d ){
2.    opStack.push( new Double( d ) );
3. }
4. public double popD(){
5.    Double dt = (Double) opStack.pop();
6.    return dt.doubleValue();
7. }
```

In line 2 we create a **Double** object with the **double** value d because **Stack** works with objects, not primitives. Note how line 5 has a specific cast of the reference returned by the **pop** method to type **Double** because **pop** returns an **Object** reference. If line 5 had been written

```
Double dt = opStack.pop() ;
```

a compiler error would have resulted. A specific cast is required for this narrowing conversion of a reference. As far as the compiler is concerned, the reference returned by **pop** is to an **Object** until proven otherwise. The compiler inserts a check of the type of the reference returned by **pop**. If this type is not compatible with a cast to **Double**, a **ClassCastException** will be thrown.

 The specific cast is necessary only when converting from a superclass to a subclass reference type. Conversions from a subclass to superclass are allowed anywhere.

Conversion With Interface References

Essentially, interface reference types can be converted only to interface types or **Object** references. For example, if your class **MyPanel** derived from **Panel** implements **Runnable**, you could use the following statements:

```
MyPanel  p = new MyPanel() ;
Panel tmp = p ;  // conversion up class hierarchy
Runnable runp = p ; // conversion to an interface reference
Object obj = p ; // conversion to the root of the hierarchy
MyPanel p2 = (MyPanel) obj ; // conversion with a cast
Runnable runp2 = (Runnable) obj ;
```

Interface Complications

Interfaces can have subinterfaces, just as classes have subclasses. However, you should be aware of one difference: An interface can be defined as extending more than one interface. This follows from the fact that a class can *implement* more than one interface. One example of an interface inheriting from more than one interface is as follows:

```
public interface RunObs extends Runnable, Observer
```

Any class implementing this interface will have to provide methods required by both **Runnable** and **Observer** and, of course, you could cast a reference to an object implementing **RunObs** to either a **Runnable** or **Observer** interface reference. The following expressions using **instanceof** would return **true** if **rx** were a reference to an instance of a class implementing **RunObs**:

```
1. rx instanceof RunObs
2. rx instanceof Runnable
3. rx instanceof Observer
```

The Special Case Of Arrays

Arrays are a special kind of reference type that does not fit in the class hierarchy but can always be cast to an **Object** reference. Arrays also implement the **Cloneable** interface and inherit the **Clone** method from **Object,** so an array reference can be cast to a **Cloneable** interface. Two kinds of arrays exist: arrays of primitives and arrays of references.

Primitive Arrays

Primitive arrays have no hierarchy, and you can cast a primitive array reference only to and from an **Object** reference. Converting and casting primitive array elements follow the same rules as converting and casting simple primitive variables. Although the syntax for casting to an array type, as shown in line 3 in the following code, may look a little strange, it is perfectly legal. As with other runtime casts, if the **obj** reference in line 3 is not to an **int** array, a **ClassCastException** will be thrown:

```
1. int sizes[] = { 4,6,8,10,14,20 };
2. Object obj = sizes ;
3. int x = (( int[] ) obj )[2] ;
```

Arrays Of Reference Types

Casting of arrays of reference types follows the same rules as casting single references. Note that an array reference can be converted independently of whether or not the array has been populated with references to real objects. For example, suppose you have a class named **Extend** that extends a class named **Base.** You could then use the following code to manipulate a reference to an array of **Extend** references:

```
Extend[] exArray = new Extend[ 20 ];
Object[] obj = exArray ;
Base[] bArray = exArray ;
Extend[] temp = ( Extend[] ) bArray ;
```

Summary Of Reference Conversion Rules

The rules for reference conversions that can be coded legally in Java are summarized in the following list. Note that these are conversions that the compiler will not throw out. To pass the runtime check, the actual reference will have to be of the proper type.

- ➤ An **Object** reference can be converted to:
  - ➤ an **Object** reference
  - ➤ any class reference with runtime check
  - ➤ any array reference with runtime check
  - ➤ any interface reference with runtime check

- ➤ A class reference can be converted to:
  - ➤ any superclass type, including **Object**
  - ➤ any class reference with runtime check
  - ➤ an interface reference if the class implements the interface
  - ➤ any interface reference with runtime check

- ➤ An interface reference can be converted to:
  - ➤ an **Object** reference
  - ➤ an interface that it implements
  - ➤ any interface reference with runtime check

- ➤ A primitive array reference can be converted to:
  - ➤ an **Object** reference
  - ➤ a **Cloneable** reference
  - ➤ a primitive array reference of the same type

- ➤ A reference array can be converted to:
  - ➤ an **Object** reference
  - ➤ an **Object** array reference
  - ➤ a **Cloneable** reference
  - ➤ any superclass array reference
  - ➤ any class array with runtime check

Practice Questions

Question 1

What will happen when you try to compile the following code?

```
1. public void printArray( Object x ){
2.   if( x instanceof int[] ){
3.     int[] n = (int[]) x ;
4.     for( int i = 0 ; i < n.length ; i++ ){
5.       System.out.println("integers = " +
           n[i] );}
6.   }
7.   if( x instanceof String[] ){
8.       System.out.println("Array of Strings");
9.   }
10. }
```

○ a. It compiles without error.

○ b. The compiler objects to line 2 comparing an **Object** with an array.

○ c. The compiler objects to line 3 casting an **Object** to an array of **int** primitives.

○ d. The compiler objects to line 7 comparing an **Object** to an array of **Objects**.

Answer a is correct. This is perfectly good code. Answers b, c, and d are incorrect because array references are treated like other **Objects** by the **instanceof** operator.

Question 2

Here are three proposed alternatives to be used in a method to return **false** if the object reference **x** has the **null** value. Which statement will work?

○ a. if(x == null) return false ;

○ b. if(x.equals(null)) return false ;

○ c. if(x instanceof null) return false ;

Answer a is the only correct way to check a reference for the **null** value. Answer b is incorrect because if x is **null**, there will not be an object whose **equals** method can be called. This statement would cause a **NullPointerException** at runtime when x is **null**. Answer c is incorrect because only a reference type, such as a class, interface, or array, can be the right operand of the **instanceof** operator.

Question 3

Here is the class hierarchy showing the **java.awt.event.ActionEvent** class family tree:

```
java.lang.Object
   |-- java.util.EventObject
          |-- java.awt.AWTEvent
                 |-- java.awt.event.ActionEvent
```

Suppose you have the following code to count events and save the most recent event.

```
1. int evtCt = 0 ;
2. AWTEvent lastE ;
3. public void saveEvent( AWTEvent evt ){
4.    lastE = evt ;
5.    evtCt++ ;
6. }
```

Which of the following calls of **saveEvent** would run without causing an exception? [Check all correct answers]

❑   a. an **AWTEvent** object reference

❑   b. an **ActionEvent** object reference

❑   c. an **EventObject** object reference

❑   d. **null** value

Answer a is correct because it matches the method signature. Answer b is correct because a subclass reference can always be cast up the hierarchy. Answer d is also correct because any reference can be set to **null**. Answer c is incorrect because the reference cannot be cast to a subclass down the hierarchy.

Question 4

> Suppose you have two classes defined as follows:
>
> ```
> class ApBase extends Object implements
>     Runnable
> class ApDerived extends ApBase implements
>     Observer
> ```
>
> Given two variables created as follows:
>
> ```
> ApBase aBase = new ApBase() ;
> ApDerived aDer = new ApDerived();
> ```
>
> Which of the following Java statements will compile and execute without error? [Check all correct answers]
>
> ❑ a. Runnable rn = aDer ;
>
> ❑ b. Runnable rn2 = (Runnable) aBase ;
>
> ❑ c. Observer ob = aBase ;
>
> ❑ d. Observer ob2 = (Observer) aBase ;

Answer a is correct because the **ApDerived** class inherits from **ApBase,** which implements **Runnable.** Answer b is also correct because the inserted cast **(Runnable)** is not needed but it does not cause a problem. Answer c fails to compile because the compiler can tell that the **ApBase** class does not implement **Observer.** Answer d compiles, but fails to execute. Because of the specific cast, the compiler thinks you know what you are doing, but the type of the **aBase** reference is checked when the statement executes and a **ClassCastException** is thrown.

Question 5

Suppose you we have an **ApBase** class declared as:

```
class ApBase extends Object implements Runnable
```

The following code fragment takes a reference to an **ApBase** object and assigns it to a variety of variables. What will happen when you try to compile and run this code?

```
1. ApBase aBase = new ApBase();
2. Runnable aR = aBase ;
3. Object obj = aR ;
4. ApBase x = (ApBase)obj ;
```

○ a. The compiler objects to line 2.

○ b. The compiler objects to line 3.

○ c. The code compiles but when run throws a
     ClassCastException in line 4.

○ d. The code compiles and runs without a problem.

Answer d is correct. These casts and assignments are all legal. Answer a is incorrect because an object reference can be assigned to an interface reference as long as the compiler knows that the object implements the interface. Answer b is incorrect because an Interface reference can be assigned to a reference to **Object** because **Object** is the base of the Java class hierarchy. Answer c is incorrect because the object referred to has not lost its identity, so it passes the runtime cast check.

Question 6

> Given that you have a method, **scale,** defined as follows, where
> **scalex** and **scaley** are **int** constants:
>
> ```
> 1. public Point scale( long x, long y ){
> 2.    return new Point((int)(x / scalex),(int)
>          (y / scaley));
> 3. }
> ```
>
> Keeping in mind that the signature of the **scale** method specifies
> **long** integer inputs, what will happen when you call this method
> with **int** primitives as in the following fragment?
>
> ```
> 4. int px = 100 ;
> 5. int py = 2000 ;
> 6. Point thePoint = scale( px, py );
> ```
>
> ○ a. A compiler error is caused.
>
> ○ b. The program compiles but a runtime cast exception
>   is thrown.
>
> ○ c. The program compiles and runs.

Answer c is correct because promotion of the **int** primitives to **long** values is
handled automatically by the compiler. Answer a is incorrect because of this
promotion. Answer b is incorrect both because the promotion is legal and because cast exceptions are thrown only by reference variable casts.

Question 7

Which of the following casts of primitive values will *not* lose information? Keep in mind that **long**s are 8 bytes, **int**s are 4 bytes, and **short**s and **char** are 2 bytes. [Check all correct answers]

❑ a.
```
long lx = 0x05544332211L ; // 366216421905
decimal
int ix = (int) lx ;
```

❑ b.
```
short sx = (short) 0x7654 ; // 30292 decimal
char cx = (char) sx ;
```

❑ c.
```
long lx = 0x0FFFFL ; // 65535 decimal
short sx = (short) lx ;
```

❑ d.
```
int ix = (int) 37 ;
byte bx = (byte) ix ;
```

Answers b and d do not lose information; therefore, they are both correct. In answer a, the bits representing the hex digits 55 are lost. In answer c, the high order bit in sx is set, and because a **short** is a signed integer, this represents -1.

Question 8

Suppose you have two classes defined as follows:

```
class ApBase extends Object implements Runnable
class ApDerived extends ApBase implements
Observer
```

Given two variables created as follows:

```
ApBase aBase = new ApBase() ;
ApDerived aDer = new ApDerived();
```

Which of the following Java code fragments compiles and executes without error?

○ a.
```
Object obj = aBase ;
Runnable rn = obj ;
```

○ b.
```
Object obj = aBase ;
Runnable rn = (Runnable) obj ;
```

○ c.
```
Object obj = aBase ;
Observer ob = (Observer)aBase ;
```

○ d.
```
Object obj = aDer ;
Observer ob2 = obj ;
```

Answer b is correct; it compiles and runs. The compiler assumes you know what you are doing with the cast to **Runnable**. Answer a fails to compile. As far as the compiler is concerned, **obj** is a plain **Object** so it objects to the assignment to a **Runnable** reference. Answer c compiles but fails to run. Because of the specific cast, the compiler thinks you know what you are doing, but the type of the **aBase** reference is checked when the statement executes, and a **ClassCastException** is thrown. Answer d fails to compile. As far as the compiler is concerned, **obj** is a plain **Object** so it objects to the assignment to an **Observer** reference.

Need To Know More?

 Gosling, James, et al. *The Java Language Specification*. Addison-Wesley, Reading, MA, 1996. ISBN: 0-201-63451-1. The most authoritative source on the language. Chapter 5 covers casting and converting.

 Venners, Bill. *Inside the Java Virtual Machine*. McGraw-Hill, New York, NY, 1998. ISBN: 0-07-913248-0. If you want the bit-twiddling details of how the JVM interprets Java bytecodes, this is a good source. Chapter 11 covers the bytecodes which convert numeric primitives.

 ftp://ftp.javasoft.com/docs/tutorial.zip

An excellent tutorial in HTML form can be downloaded from this site. (Although this document is updated frequently, it may not be entirely current with JDK 1.2 information.)

 http://java.sun.com/docs/books/jls/html/index.html

The definitive Java language specification document is maintained in HTML form on the Sun Microsystems Web site.

 http://java.sun.com/products/jdk/1.2/index.html

The Java API documentation in Javadoc-generated form can be downloaded from Sun Microsystems. Although this site changes a lot, it was a good starting point the last time I looked.

Flow Control And Exceptions

7

Terms you'll need to understand:

√ **break**

√ **continue**

√ **throw**

√ **throws**

√ **try**

√ **catch**

√ **finally**

Techniques you'll need to master:

√ Recognizing the legal forms for **if** and **switch** statements

√ Predicting the flow of control through complex nested control structures

√ Using **break** and **continue** with statement labels in loops

√ Understanding when to use **throws** in method declarations

√ Writing code that creates and **throws** exceptions

Many of the aspects of Java flow control are familiar to programmers who have worked with other languages, particularly C. The **if, else, switch, do,** and **while** statements behave the same way in Java as they do in C. The **for** loop in Java is also similar to C. In the exception concept, Java has a highly developed improvement over C for controlling program flow when errors or other exceptional conditions occur. Exceptions vastly simplify the task of designing programs that handle errors and exceptional conditions gracefully.

Basic Flow Control

You should already be familiar with the basics of Java flow control, so the following sections concentrate on areas that have caused people trouble in my online testing of proposed questions for this book.

Boolean Expressions

The first point to stress is that Java requires expressions that evaluate to a **boolean** primitive result in flow control statements. C programmers who are used to using integer values of zero for **false** and nonzero for **true** will have to watch out for this.

Another important point has to do with the sequence of evaluation in complex logical expressions. Although you can control the sequence with parentheses, you should also study the precedence of the various arithmetic and logical operators (as shown in Chapter 3, Tables 3.2 and 3.4). For example, given the following statement

```
if( a + b > aMax | c + d < cMin )
```

you should recognize that operator precedence causes the compiler to evaluate the additions first, followed by the arithmetic comparisons. Finally, the two **boolean** primitive results are ORed together.

No goto In Java Flow Control

Note that although **goto** is a reserved word in Java, it is not currently used. Java does not allow arbitrary jumps to labeled statements. However, statement labels can be used with the **break** and **continue** statements in loops.

The if-else Structure

The **if** statement simply evaluates an arbitrary expression resulting in a boolean primitive value. If the value is **true**, the code block attached to the **if** is executed. This code block can be a single statement, which for simplicity does not have to be enclosed in braces, or it can be an arbitrarily long block of code in braces. The programmer has the option of putting an **else** statement immediately following the **if** code block to provide an alternate block of code that will be executed if the value is **false**.

Whether or not to enclose a single statement in braces is a matter of style. A good reason to always use braces is that debuggers will not let you set breakpoints on a single statement following **if** or **else** unless it is in its own code block. If you have any doubts about which **if** an **else** statement goes with, the rule is that it is considered to go with the innermost **if** it could legally belong to.

 Programming problems frequently involve a complex nested set of **if-else** constructs. The first step in solving one of these is figuring out which code blocks go with which **if** and **else** statements. The questions at the end of the chapter include some examples of nested **if** statements.

The switch-case Structure

Java provides the extremely handy **switch-case** construct to facilitate selecting between multiple alternatives. This is such a common programming situation that the Java Virtual Machine (JVM) has bytecodes designed to speed this operation. Within the block of code controlled by a **switch** statement, the programmer can place **case** statements and (optionally) a **default** statement. In the following example, a **String** variable gets set according to the value of the integer variable x:

```
switch( x ) {
  case 0 : str = "none" ; break ;
  case 1 :
    str = "single" ; break ;
  case 2 :
    str = "pair" ;
    break ;
  default :  str = "many" ;
}
```

Each **case** keyword is followed by an integer constant, followed by a colon. Notice that the code block belonging to each **case** can immediately follow the colon on the same line or on separate lines. If the value of x is not one of the values provided for in **case** statements, the **default** statement code is executed. If there is no **default** statement and no exact match, execution resumes after the **switch** block of code.

The preceding example uses **break** statements, which terminate the code for each **case** and cause execution to continue after the **switch** code block. If a break does not appear, execution "falls through" to execute code in subsequent cases. For example, in the following code fragment, a value of 0 would cause output of "A, B, ":

```
switch( x ){
  case 0 : System.out.print("A, ");
  case 1 : System.out.print("B, "); break ;
  default : System.out.println("huh?");
}
```

The block of code associated with each **case** can be as simple as a single statement or it can be hundreds of lines of code. In addition, this code block can have another **switch** statement. However, for optimum readability, you should consider turning any complex code into a separate method and simply calling that method from the **case** statement.

What A *switch* Must Have

The expression in a **switch** statement must evaluate to one of the 32-bit or smaller integer types: **byte, char, short,** or **int.** The compiler will check that the legal range of the integer type covers all of the constants used in **case** statements in the **switch** code block.

 Apparently, this fact is not well known among Java programmers, so it's probably worth repeating. The compiler will throw an error if the legal range of the integer type in the **switch** statement does not cover all of the constants used in **case** statements.

What A *case* Statement Cannot Have

Each **case** statement must have a constant of an integer type of 32-bit or smaller size. It cannot have a **float** constant, a **long** constant, a variable, an expression, a **String,** or any other object. Furthermore, the compiler checks that the constant is in the range of the integer type in the **switch** statement. In other words, if you are using a **byte** variable in the **switch** statement, the compiler will object if it finds **case** statement constants outside the -128 to 127 range that a **byte** primitive can have.

The code block associated with a **case** must be complete within the **case.** In other words, you can't have an **if-else** or loop structure that spreads across multiple **case** statements.

What A *case* Statement Can Have

Constants in **case** statements can be integer literals, or they can be variables defined as **static** and **final.** For example, the **java.awt.event.KeyEvent** class defines a bunch of "public static final int" variables, such as **VK_F1, VK_F2,** and so on. The compiler is able to use these values in **case** statements because it can look up the integer value at compile time.

Using *break, continue,* And Labeled Statements

In addition to the plain **break** statement that simply causes execution to continue after the **switch** code block, you can use a **break** with a statement label. This is typically done to terminate a loop that encloses the switch code block, as in the following code fragment:

```
1.  int state = 0 ;
2.  lab: for( int x = 0 ; x <100 ; x++ ){
3.        switch( state ){
4.          case 0 :
5.            state = tryX( x ); break ;
6.          case 1 :
7.            state = tryAgain(x); break ;
8.          case 2 :
9.            System.out.println("Found key");
10.           break lab ;
11.       }
12.       System.out.println("tried " + x );
13.    }
```

Think of the label in line 2 as labeling the entire **for** loop. When the **break** in line 10 is executed, execution breaks out of that loop and continues after line 13.

If the statement in line 10 read

```
10.            continue lab ;
```

execution would skip line 12 and resume the loop with the next value of *x*.

Label Rules

Identifiers used for labels on statements do not share the same namespace as the variables, classes, and methods of the rest of a Java program. The naming rules, as far as legal characters, are the same as for variables except that labels are always terminated with a colon. You can reuse the same label name at multiple points in a method as long as one usage is not nested inside another. Labels cannot be freestanding—they must always be associated with a statement.

The for Loop Structure

Java provides the **for** loop to let you repeat blocks of code under control of a loop counter variable. The general form of the **for** loop is a **for** statement followed by a loop body. The **for** statement consists of three sections, as shown in the following code:

```
for( initialization ; logical test ; update )
```

When a **for** statement is executed, the first thing that happens is that the initialization expressions, if any, are executed. Next, the logical test expression, if present, is executed—if the result is false, the loop is exited immediately. If there is no logical test or the result is **true**, the loop body statement(s) is executed. Finally, the update expression(s), if present, is executed and the logical test is repeated.

Initialization

The initialization section can be empty, have a single expression, or have multiple expressions separated by commas. This section is typically used to set the initial value of a loop counter, for example:

```
1.  for( int i = 0 ; i < iMax ; i++ )
2.  for( i = 0, j = 100 ; ; j -= i )
```

If the expression both declares and initializes a variable as in line 1, it must be the only expression in the section. You should be aware that a loop counter declared in the initialization section has a scope restricted to the loop. A common error is to attempt to use a loop counter declared inside the **for** statement outside the loop.

Logical Test

If a logical test is present, it must be a single expression that results in a boolean value. Expressions that don't result in a boolean value will cause a compiler error. If no logical test is present, as in line 2 of the preceding example, the only ways a programmer can stop the loop are by using a **break** statement or by throwing an exception.

Update

The update section can be empty, have a single expression, or have multiple expressions separated by commas. Typically, this section is used to increment or decrement the loop counter.

Using **break** And *continue*

In addition to the logical test, you can control the operation of a loop with **break** and **continue** statements, with and without labels. The plain **break** statement immediately terminates the loop code block, whereas the **continue** statement skips any remaining code in the block and continues with the next loop iteration. The following code fragment illustrates both uses:

```
1. for( int i = 0 ; i < iMax ;i++ ){
2.   if( toDo[i] == null ) continue ;
3.   if( processToDo( toDo[i] ) ) break ;
4.   System.out.println( "Still looking");
5. }
```

The statement in line 2 uses **continue** to skip the code in lines 3 and 4 if the array element is null; the loop continues with the next iteration of the loop counter. In contrast, the **break** statement in line 3 terminates the loop entirely. The limitation of **break** and **continue**, which is that they can only affect the loop they reside in, is overcome with labeled statements. The following example shows the same code embellished with an inner loop. Note that the outer loop now has a label "labA" on the starting statement:

```
1. labA: for( int i = 0 ; i < iMax ;i++ ){
2.         for( int j = 0 ; j < jMax ; j++ ){
3.           if( toDo[i][j] == null ) continue labA ;
4.           if( processToDo( toDo[i][j] ) ) break labA ;
5.         } // end loop over j values
6.         System.out.println( "Still looking");
7.       }
```

Now the **continue** statement in line 3 jumps out of the loop over the values of *j* and continues with the next value for *i* as generated by the **for** statement in line 1. The **break** statement in line 4 terminates the outer loop, and execution resumes after line 7.

Optional Parts Of A for Loop

Actually, just about everything in a **for** loop is optional. The following statement represents the bare minimum **for** loop, with "{}" representing an empty code block:

```
for(;;){}
```

Naturally, any **Thread** starting this loop would never be heard from again. Here are some more practical examples of **for** loops with missing parts:

```
1.   int x ;
2.   for( x = 0 ; testX( x ) ; x++ ){}
```

In the preceding example, all of the work is done in the **testX** method which, of course, has to return a boolean value. The following example skips the initialization section because the variable *x* is already initialized:

```
1.  int x = 199 ;
2.  for( ; x >= 0 ; x-- ) {
3.    // calculations go here
4.  }
```

Common Mistakes With *for* Loops

Here are some common mistakes with **for** loops:

➤ **Variable Scope** Remember that a variable declared in a **for** statement can only be referred to inside the loop. Watch out for accidentally declaring a variable in a loop with the same name as an instance variable. The compiler will let you get away with this and will use the local variable inside the loop. The results can be very confusing.

➤ **Loop Counter Problems** Watch out for paths through the loop that fail to increment or decrement the loop counter.

Using while And do

The other loop constructs in Java are provided by **while** and **do**. The general form of a **while** loop is:

```
while( logical_test ){
    code block
}
```

The logical test is performed first. If the result is **true**, the code block is executed. If the result is **false**, the code block is skipped and execution continues after the closing brace. You can also combine a **while** test with an expression in a single statement, as follows:

```
while( i < ans.length() && ans.charAt( i ) != '*') i++ ;
```

If you want a loop that continues indefinitely, you can use a boolean literal value of **true** in the **while** statement.

The **do** loop construct moves the position of the logical test to the end of the code block; therefore, the code is always executed at least once:

```
do {
    code_block
}while( logical_test );
```

The **break** and **continue** statements with and without labels work with **while** and **do** loops just as they do with **for** loops. The **break** statement exits the loop entirely, and **continue** skips to the end of the loop.

Exceptions

In the best of all possible worlds, nothing would ever go wrong in a Java program. In reality, your program may have to deal with many unexpected problems, such as missing files, bad user input, dropped network connections, and (unfortunately) programming errors. Java provides an elegant approach to handling these problems with the exception mechanism. This mechanism uses exception and error objects to handle everything from an end-of-file condition to an out-of-memory error.

The Hierarchy Of Throwable Things

Java exceptions are objects that are instances of classes derived from the **java.lang.Throwable** class, as shown in the following diagram:

```
java.lang.Object
   +-- java.lang.Throwable
          +---- java.lang.Error
          |         +-- a whole bunch of errors
          |
          +---- java.lang.Exception
                  +---- java.lang.RuntimeException
                  |         +-- various unchecked exceptions
                  +-- various checked exceptions
```

A **Throwable** exception or error is said to be "thrown" at the point where it is generated and "caught" at the point where execution continues. When an exception or error is thrown, the JVM works back through the chain of method calls that led to the error, looking for an appropriate handler to "catch" the object. If no handler is found, the **Thread** that created the error or exception dies.

The **Throwable** class provides methods that can trace the "stack" of method calls that a **Thread** has executed to get to the point at which the error occurred. This provides one of the main tools for debugging Java programs after an error or exception has occurred. **Throwable** objects can also have a **String** attached to them. Typically, this is used to explain the cause of the exception or error.

The Error Classes

As you can see, the first major division in the hierarchy is between errors and exceptions. Subclasses of **Error** are used to signal errors that are usually fatal and are not caught by **catch** statements in the program. Their function is to provide some information before the program has to terminate. As a programmer, you will usually be concerned with the **Exception** branch of the **Throwable** hierarchy only.

Catching Exceptions

The programmer can provide for handling of exceptions using the Java keywords **try** and **catch,** with or without **finally.** We will first consider how exceptions are handled in a method that uses **try** and **catch** only.

How *try* And *catch* Work

A **try** statement is used to enclose a block of code in which an exception may occur. Each **try** statement must have one or more associated **catch** "clauses" that provide for handling exceptions. A **catch** clause declares a variable that must be of the class **Throwable** or a subclass of **Throwable.** This variable can be used in the code block associated with the **catch.** The general form is as follows:

```
1. try {
2.    code_block
3. }catch( ExceptionType varname ){
4.    optional code which can use varname
5. }
```

When an exception is thrown in the code block, the JVM looks at the type of the exception in the first **catch** clause. If the thrown exception can legally be assigned to that variable, it is assigned and the **catch** code block is executed. You can think of the **catch** clause as the *exception handler* for a particular exception type. The scope of the variable named in the **catch** clause is restricted to the **catch** code block.

Multiple *catch* Clauses

A succession of **catch** clauses can be attached to a **try** statement. If the thrown exception cannot be assigned to the variable in the first **catch** clause, the JVM looks at the second, and so on. If the thrown exception cannot be caught by any of the **catch** clauses provided, and there is no **finally** clause, the JVM looks for a handler in the calling method. If the code block in the **try** statement executes without throwing an exception, all of the **catch** clauses are ignored and execution resumes after the last **catch.**

The order of the **catch** clauses must reflect the exception hierarchy, with the most specific exception first. Obviously, if the first **catch** was the most general, none of the others could be reached.

How *try* And *catch* Work With *finally*

The principal idea behind **finally** is that the programmer needs to have a way to correctly dispose of system resources, such as open files, no matter which exceptions are thrown by the code in a **try** block. If a **try** statement has a **finally** clause attached, the code block associated with **finally** is *always* executed unless the **Thread** executing the **try** dies. To illustrate this, consider the following code. The method "someMethod" can throw a **NullPointerException**, which is a subclass of **RuntimeException,** or several other kinds of **RuntimeException,** such as **ArithmeticException.** Note that the **catch** for **NullPointerException** has to come before that for **RuntimeException** because **NullPointerException** is a subclass of **RuntimeException:**

```
public int testX( String x){
  try {
    return someMethod( x );
  }catch( NullPointerException nex ){
    System.out.print("NullPointer, " );
    return -1 ;
  }catch( RuntimeException rex){
    System.out.print("Runtime ");
    return -2;
  }finally{
    System.out.println("Finally");
  }
}
```

Here are some examples of possible results from executing this code:

➤ No exception thrown in **someMethod**. "Finally" is printed, and the method returns the value from **someMethod**.

➤ A **NullPointerException** is thrown in **someMethod**. "NullPointer, Finally" is printed, and -1 is returned.

➤ An **ArithmeticException** is thrown in **someMethod**. "Runtime Finally" is printed, and -2 is returned.

➤ An uncaught exception is thrown in **someMethod**. "Finally" is printed, and nothing is returned because the JVM now treats the exception as if it were thrown directly by the **testX** method.

In my online testing of questions related to exceptions, many errors were made regarding the operation of **try** and **catch** with **finally** clauses. I suggest you experiment with test programs until you are confident that you can predict the program flow under various conditions.

Checked And Unchecked Exceptions

The most important division in the exception branch of the **Throwable** hierarchy is between checked and unchecked exceptions. All classes that descend from **RuntimeException** are called unchecked because the compiler does not require explicit provision in the code for catching them.

All other classes that descend from **Exception** are called "checked" exceptions because the compiler will insist on provisions in the code for catching them. The design philosophy that the Java designers used to place various exceptions in the checked or unchecked categories was an attempt to balance the likelihood of an exception being generated, with a desire to avoid cluttering the code with **try** and **catch** statements. Some overhead is involved in setting up a **try** statement, so considerations of performance also entered into the design decisions.

Using *throws*

The alternative to using **try** and **catch** wherever a checked exception might occur in a method is simply to declare that the method **throws** the exception. For instance, if you have a method that opens a file, reads some data, and closes the file, you will be calling many library methods that **throw IOException** or one of its subclasses. You might declare the method as follows:

```
public int readMyData(String filename) throws IOException
```

Note that the Java keyword **throws** comes after the method parameter list. If the method can throw more than one kind of exception, you simply list them separated by commas after the **throws** keyword. For example:

```
public int readMyData(String filename) throws EOFException,
    FileNotFoundException, InterruptedIOException
```

Because these are checked exceptions, the compiler will insist on them being handled by any method that calls **readMyData**. On the other hand, if you have a method that declares that it throws a list of unchecked exceptions, the compiler will not insist on them being handled.

Throwing An Exception

Throwing an exception involves two things: creating an object from an exception class by calling a constructor and using it in a **throw** statement. In general, exceptions can be constructed with or without an explanatory message. However, nothing prevents you from creating a custom exception class that carries more information than a single **String**. I'll look at a custom exception class in the section "Creating Your Own Exception." Here is an example of a statement to create and **throw** an exception:

```
throw new ArithmeticException("Out of Range");
```

Rethrowing Exceptions

In some cases you may want to catch an exception, do some processing, and then *rethrow* the exception so the calling method can also do some processing. This is accomplished with the **throw** statement as shown in the following code fragment:

```
try {
    readMyData("booklist.txt");
}catch(FileNotFoundException ex){
    System.out.println("book list not found!");
    throw ex ;
}
```

Exceptions In Overriding Methods

When you have a method in a subclass that has the same name, parameter list, and return type as a method in the parent class, the subclass method is said to *override* the parent class method. Let's suppose the parent class method is defined as follows:

```
public boolean readTest( String x) throws IOException
```

The Java compiler will allow the overriding subclass method to be defined as throwing **IOException**, throwing one or more subclasses of **IOException**, or not throwing any exceptions. It will not allow the overriding subclass to be declared as throwing a more general exception or exception from another hierarchy.

Program Design With Exceptions

Designing with exceptions can greatly simplify programming and in some cases speed it up. For example, try the following suggestion for speeding up iteration through a large array.

Because Java performs an array bounds check with every array access, you do not need to use a loop counter when iterating through an array. Instead, just catch the exception that results when the bounds check fails, as in the following code fragment:

```
int i = 0, sum = 0 ;
try {
```

```
for(;;) sum += count[i++] ;
}catch( IndexOutOfBoundsException e ){}
```

Although it is true that this is faster than using a loop counter as long as the array is large enough that the overhead of setting up the **try** is relatively small, this approach is not necessarily a good idea in all situations. For one thing, it prevents the use of "stop on exception" logic in a debugger.

Creating Your Own Exception

In this section, I'll illustrate some of the considerations involved in creating and using your own exception class. The example I'll have chosen has been reinvented a number of times by programmers who miss the "assert" construct in C that is frequently a big help in debugging. The custom exception is **AssertionException**, and the class needed to make use of it is **Assertion**. Both classes are shown in Listing 7.1, but because they are both public, they would have to be defined in separate files.

 To really understand programming with exceptions, you can't beat hands-on experience. I suggest you add the classes in Listing 7.1 to a real Java project and experiment with ways to use them.

Listing 7.1   The two classes needed to implement AssertionExceptions.

```
1. public class AssertionException extends RuntimeException {
2.     // this constructor assures that there will always be a
       // message
3.   public AssertionException(){
4.     super("AssertionException");
5.   }
6.
7.   public AssertionException(String msg ){
8.     super( msg ) ;
9.   }
10. }
11.
12. /* a class with only static methods to check assertions */
13.
14. public class Assertion {
15.   public static boolean ASSERTION_ON = true ;
16.   private Assertion() {} ; // no public constructor
17.   // method without a message
18.   public static void assert( boolean validFlg )
19.        throws AssertionException {
```

```
20.     if( ASSERTION_ON && !validFlg ) {
21.         throw new AssertionException();
22.     }
23.   }
24.   // method with a message
25.   public static void assert( boolean validFlg, String msg )
26.       throws AssertionException {
27.     if( ASSERTION_ON && !validFlg ) {
28.         throw new AssertionException(msg);
29.     }
30.   }
31. }
```

Using The Assertion Class

The idea behind assertions is that at critical points in your program, you can insert a single statement that can check for a required condition and produce a custom informative message if the condition does not exist. For example, suppose you need to ensure that the value of X does not exceed a given maximum. You could use code like this

```
Assertion.assert( X <= xMax, "X too large" );
```

that would throw an **AssertionException** if the test expression evaluated to **false**. The exception will be created with an attached message in the code on line 28 of Listing 7.1. If you had a **catch** clause in a position to catch this exception, such as the following

```
catch(AssertionException ex ){
   System.out.println( ex );
}
```

you would get the following message on the standard output:

```
AssertionException: X too large
```

Exception Vs. RuntimeException

In line 1 of Listing 7.1, you can see that I derived **AssertionException** from the class **RuntimeException**. This means that the compiler will not check for the appropriate exception-handling mechanism in the surrounding code. You can put in the **try-catch** structure to catch an **AssertionException,** but the compiler will not insist on it. The following example would compile without a problem:

```
public void checkName(String tmp){
  Assertion.assert( tmp != null && tmp.length() > 1, "Name");
```

```
    // more code here
}
```

However, if you changed the parent of **AssertionException** from **Runtime-Exception** to **Exception**, the same code would cause the compiler to report the following error: "Exception **AssertionException** must be caught or it must be declared in the **throws** clause of this method." In other words, if **Assertion-Exception** were a checked exception, the compiler would require either an explicit **try-catch** structure in the **checkName** method or a declaration of the method as follows:

```
public void checkName(String tmp) throws AssertionException{
    Assertion.assert( tmp != null && tmp.length() > 1, "Name");
    // more code here
}
```

 Be sure you remember the distinctly different meanings of the two keywords, **throw** and **throws**. **Throw** is used to **throw** an exception object inside a method, whereas **throws** appears in method declarations.

Practice Questions

Question 1

A method to compute the sum of all elements in an array of **int** is needed. The following proposed method is incomplete; select the correct statement for line 3 from the options provided.

```
1. public int total( int[] x ){
2.    int i, t = 0 ;
3.    -select statement to go here
4.    { t += x[ i++ ] ;
5.    }
6.    return t ;
7. }
```

○ a. for(int i = 0 ; i < x.length ;)

○ b. for(i = 0 ; i < x.length ;)

○ c. for(i = 0 ; i < x.length ; i++)

○ d. for(i = 1 ; i <= x.length ; i++)

Answer b is correct because it avoids the errors of the other options. Answer a is incorrect because it will result in a compiler error because *i* is already declared in line 2. Answer c is incorrect because the loop counter *i* is incremented twice, thus skipping alternate array elements. Answer d is incorrect for several reasons: the first element of the array is missed and the final cycle of the loop will cause an **ArrayIndexOutOfBoundsException**; also, the loop counter is incremented twice.

Question 2

The following method takes a **char** input and returns an **int** value.

```
1. public int maze( char d ){
2.   if( d <= 'N' ){
3.     if( d == 'E' ) return 2 ;
4.     return 1 ;
5.   }
6.   else if( d == 'S' ) return 3;
7.   else if( d == 'W' ) return 4;
8.   return 0 ;
9. }
```

Check all of the following statements about this method that are true: [Check all correct answers]

❑ a. Input of 'A' produces output of 1.

❑ b. Input of 'X' produces output of 0.

❑ c. Input of 'D' produces output of 0.

❑ d. The method fails to compile due to syntax errors.

Answers a and b are correct. Answer c is incorrect because with a value of 'D' the statements at lines 3 and 4 are executed. Answer d is incorrect because this code compiles without problems.

Question 3

You want the following method to print a message when the input value is in the range equal to or greater than *xMin* and less than or equal to *xMax*. The options show alternate expressions that could be substituted for *XXXX* in line 2 of the code. [Check all correct answers]

```
1. public void chkRange( int x ){
2.   if( XXXX ) System.out.println("In Range");
3. }
```

❑ a. (x <= xMax) && (x >= xMin)

❑ b. xMin <= x <= xMax

❑ c. !(x < xMin || x > xMax)

Answers a and c are correct. Answer a works fine. Note that the && form "shortcuts" evaluation if the first test fails. Answer c also works fine. Note that the || form "shortcuts" evaluation if the first term is true. The ! (NOT) operator is then applied to the result. Answer b is incorrect because it causes a compiler error because the result of the first test "xMin <= x" is a **boolean** primitive, which cannot be combined with the remaining arithmetic expression.

Question 4

Given the following method that will be called with various input values:

```
1. public void soundOff( int x ){
2.    switch(x){
3.       case 1: System.out.print("One ");
4.       case 2: System.out.print("Two "); break ;
5.       case 3: System.out.print("Three ");
6.       default: System.out.print("Do what?");
7.    }
8. }
```

Which of these input and output pairs will be observed? [Check all correct answers]

❑   a. Input = 1, Output = "One"

❑   b. Input = 0, Output = "One Two"

❑   c. Input = 3, Output = "Three Do What?"

❑   d. Input = 4, Output = "Do What?"

Answer c is correct because case 3 "falls through" to the **default** statement. Answer d is correct because any value not in a **case** statement will execute the **default** statement. Answer a is incorrect because case 1 does not have a **break** statement, so the following case would execute also, producing "One Two". Answer b is incorrect because any value not in a **case** statement executes the default. The **switch-case** structure does not care about the numerical order in which cases appear.

Question 5

Given the following code fragment, choose all of the declarations of *x* that will *not* cause a compiler error. [Check all correct answers]

```
1. switch( x ) {
2.    case 100 : System.out.println(
         "One hundred");break ;
3.    case 200 : System.out.println(
         "Two hundred");break ;
4.    case 300 : System.out.println(
         "Three hundred");break ;
5. }
```

❑ a. byte x = 100 ;

❑ b. short x = 200 ;

❑ c. int x = 300 ;

❑ d. long x = 400 ;

Answer b is correct. The variable *x* can be a **short** because all of the cases can be accommodated. Answer c is also correct. *x* can be an **int** because all of the cases can be accommodated in the **int** range. Answer a is incorrect! The variable *x* cannot be a **byte** type because the values 200 and 300 are not compatible (the byte range is -128 to 127). The type used in the **switch** statement must accommodate all of the values in the **case** statements. Answer d is incorrect because **switch** statements cannot use **long** values. You would have to have a specific **cast** for *x* to be a **long,** as follows:

```
1.   switch((int)x) {
```

Question 6

Given the following code fragment with a break to a labeled statement, predict the printed output.

```
1. int i, j ;
2. lab: for( i = 0 ; i < 6 ; i++ ){
3.          for( j = 5 ; j > 2 ; j-- ){
4.              if( i == j ) {
5.                  System.out.print(" " + j ); break
                       lab ;
6.              }
7.          }
8.      }
```

○ a. Output will be 3 4 5

○ b. Output will be 3 4

○ c. Output will be 3

Answer c is correct. The statement on line 5 executes with a value of 3, and then the **break** terminates the loop started on line 2. Answers a and b are incorrect because the statement on line 5 executes only once, and the **break** terminates the loop started on line 2.

Question 7

The following method is designed to convert an input string to a floating-point number while detecting a bad format.

```
1. public boolean strCvt( String s ){
2.    try {
3.      factor =
            Float.valueOf( s ).floatValue();
4.      return true ;
5.    }catch(NumberFormatException e){
6.      System.out.println("Bad number " + s );
7.      factor = Float.NaN ;
8.    }finally { System.out.println("Finally");
9.    }
10.   return false ;
11. }
```

Which of the following descriptions of the results of various inputs to the method are correct? [Check all correct answers]

❑ a. Input = "0.234" - Result: factor = 0.234, "Finally" is printed, true is returned.

❑ b. Input = "0.234" - Result: factor = 0.234, "Finally" is printed, false is returned.

❑ c. Input = null - Result: factor = NaN, "Finally" is printed, false is returned.

❑ d. Input = null - Result: factor unchanged, "Finally" is printed, NullPointerException is thrown.

Answer a is correct, and b is wrong because the return value in line 4 is used. Answer d is right and c is wrong because a **NullPointerException** is thrown in line 3 and is not caught in the method. Line 7 is never reached.

Question 8

Here is the hierarchy of exceptions related to array index and string index errors:

```
Exception
  +-- RuntimeException
        +-- IndexOutOfBoundsException
              +-- ArrayIndexOutOfBoundsException
              +-- StringIndexOutOfBoundsException
```

Suppose you had a method *X* that could throw both array index and string index exceptions. Assuming that X does not have any **try-catch** statements, which of the following statements are correct? [Check all correct answers]

❑ a. The declaration for *X* must include "throws ArrayIndexOutOfBoundsException, StringIndexOutOfBoundsException".

❑ b. If a method calling *X* catches **IndexOutOfBoundsException**, both array and string index exceptions will be caught.

❑ c. If the declaration for *X* includes "throws IndexOutOfBoundsException", any calling method must use a **try-catch** block.

❑ d. The declaration for *X* does not have to mention exceptions.

Answers b and d are correct. Answer b is correct because exceptions obey a hierarchy just like other objects. Because these exceptions descend from **RuntimeException**, they do not have to be declared. Therefore, answer d is correct. The significant word here is "must." Because these exceptions descend from **RuntimeException**, they do not have to be declared. Therefore, answer a is incorrect. Answer c is incorrect for a similar reason, because these exceptions descend from **RuntimeException**. They do not have to be caught even if declared by method *X*.

Question 9

You are writing a set of classes related to cooking and have created your own exception hierarchy derived from **java.lang.Exception** as follows (note that both **BitterException** and **SourException** descend from **BadTasteException**):

```
Exception
    +-- BadTasteException
            +-- BitterException
            +-- SourException
```

Your base class, **BaseCook**, has a method declared as follows:

```
int rateFlavor(Ingredient[] list) throws
    BadTasteException
```

A class, **TexMexCook**, derived from **BaseCook** has a method that overrides **BaseCook.rateFlavor()**. Which of the following are legal declarations of the overriding method? [Check all correct answers]

❏　a. int rateFlavor(Ingredient[] list) throws BadTasteException

❏　b. int rateFlavor(Ingredient[] list) throws Exception

❏　c. int rateFlavor(Ingredient[] list) throws BitterException

❏　d. int rateFlavor(Ingredient[] list)

Answers a, c, and d are correct. Answer a is correct because overriding methods can throw the same exception. Answer c is correct because the overriding method can throw an exception that is a subclass of the original. Answer d is correct because the overriding method does not have to throw an exception at all. Answer b is incorrect because if the overriding method throws an exception, it must throw the same exception or a subclass.

Question 10

> You are writing a set of classes related to cooking and have created your own exception hierarchy derived from **java.lang.Exception** as follows:
>
> ```
> Exception
>     +-- BadTasteException
>             +-- BitterException
>             +-- SourException
> ```
>
> Your custom exceptions have constructors taking a **String** parameter. You have a method declared as follows:
>
> ```
>  int rateFlavor(Ingredient[] list) throws
> BadTasteException
> ```
>
> Which of the following shows a correct complete statement to throw one of your custom exceptions?
>
> ○ a. new SourException("Ewww!") ;
>
> ○ b. throws new SourException("Ewww!");
>
> ○ c. throw new SourException("Ewww!");
>
> ○ d. throw SourException("Ewww!");

Answer c is correct. This statement creates and throws the exception. Answer a is incorrect because this statement is missing the keyword "throw." Answer b is incorrect because the keyword needed is "throw"; **throws** is used in method declarations. Answer d is incorrect because it does not create an exception object with the "new" keyword.

Question 11

Given the following code for the test method:

```
1.  public int test(String x, int n ){
2.    if( n == 0 ) return n ;
3.    else if( n == 1 ){
4.      if( x != null ) return 5 ;
5.    }
6.    else if( n == 2 && x != null ){
7.      if( x.equals("YES") ) return 3;
8.      else if( x.equals("NO") return 4 ;
9.    }
10.   return -1 ;
11. }
```

Which of the following statements are true? [Check all correct answers]

❑ a. If the input n = 1, line 6 will always be executed.

❑ b. If the input string *x* is "NO" and n is 2, the method returns 4.

❑ c. If the input n is 1 and the input string is "YES", the method returns 3.

❑ d. The **else** on line 6 goes with the **if** on line 3.

Answers b and d are correct. Answer a is incorrect because if *x* is not null, the method returns from line 4. Answer c is incorrect because if n is 1, lines 7 and 8 are not executed.

Need To Know More?

 Flanagan, David. *Java in a Nutshell, 2nd Edition*. O'Reilly & Associates, Inc., Sebastopol, CA, 1997. ISBN: 1-56592-262-X. This is the most compact desktop reference book documenting the Java language. Chapter 2, which emphasizes the differences between C and Java, is useful here.

 Gosling, James, et al. *The Java Language Specification*. Addison-Wesley, Reading, MA, 1996. ISBN: 0-201-63451-1. The most authoritative source on the language. See Chapter 11 for information on Exceptions, Chapter 14 for flow control.

 Venners, Bill. *Inside the Java Virtual Machine*. McGraw-Hill, New York, NY, 1998. ISBN: 0-07-913248-0. If you want the bit-twiddling details of how the JVM interprets Java bytecodes, this is a good source. See Chapters 16 and 17 for the details on how flow control and Exceptions are implemented in bytecodes.

 ftp://ftp.javasoft.com/docs/tutorial.zip

An excellent tutorial in HTML form can be downloaded from this site. (Although this document is updated frequently, it may not be entirely current with JDK 1.2 information.)

 http://java.sun.com/docs/books/jls/html/index.html

The definitive Java language specification document is maintained in HTML form on the Sun Microsystems Web site.

 http://java.sun.com/products/jdk/1.2/index.html

The Java API documentation in Javadoc-generated form can be downloaded from Sun Microsystems. Although this site changes a lot, it was a good starting point the last time I looked.

Working With Java Classes And Objects

8

Terms you'll need to understand:

√ Polymorphism

√ Extending

√ Overloading

√ Overriding

√ Garbage collection

√ Finalize

Techniques you'll need to master:

√ Recognizing the distinction between "is a" and "has a" in Java class design

√ Understanding the difference between overloading and overriding a method, and the limitations on each technique

√ Understanding how Java manages memory recycling with garbage collection

√ Understanding how Java finalizer methods are used

This chapter covers some topics related to programming with Java objects. I will examine some basic aspects of designing classes to fit various programming problems. I will also review Java's built-in mechanisms for freeing and reusing memory and other system resources used by objects after they are no longer needed.

Object-Oriented Design

I am certainly not going to be able to cover all of object-oriented design in a single chapter. It's not a subject you can master overnight. I recommend a combination of studying good object-oriented code—such as the Java standard library classes—and reading books, such as the book *Design Patterns* cited at the end of the chapter.

To gain a complete understanding of object-oriented design, you need to be comfortable with some of the basics, such as the object relationships expressed as the phrases "is a" and "has a". You will also need to be comfortable with the implications of class hierarchies, overloading, and overriding.

A Class Hierarchy

To facilitate this discussion, I'll outline the class hierarchy that you might use to represent a book, such as this one. The parent of our specialized set of classes is **BookElement**, descended directly from **Object**. For simplicity's sake, I'll ignore any consideration of which package these classes should be in. The **BookElement** class has some variables and methods that are common to all parts of a book, and the subclasses have some specialized variables and methods, as shown in the following outline:

```
Object
    +--BookElement
            +--TableOfContents
            +--Introduction
            +--Chapter
            +--Appendix
            +--Index
```

The class declarations for these classes might look like this:

```
public class BookElement extends Object
public class TableOfContents extends BookElement
public class Chapter extends BookElement
...[etc.]
```

In the terminology I want to emphasize, a **BookElement** object "is an" **Object**. A **Chapter** object "is a" **BookElement** and of course, it also "is an" **Object** by virtue of inheritance. Recalling the **instanceof** operator, which was discussed in Chapter 6, you can see that in the following code fragment, the logical test would result in "true" being printed:

```
Chapter chap1 = new Chapter();
if( chap1 instanceof BookElement ) System.out.println("true")
```

A class to represent a book would require member variables to hold each of the possible **BookElement**-related components, as suggested by the following code fragment:

```
public class Book extends Object {
  TableOfContents toc;
  Introduction  intro ;
  Chapter[] chapt ;
...[etc.]
```

I would then say that a **Book** object "has a" **TableOfContents** member variable.

Polymorphism

Looking at the **Book** class described in the preceding section, consider the **TableOfContents** object that **toc** refers to. Because this object can also be referred to as a **BookElement** object or an **Object** class object, it is said to exhibit *polymorphism*. If there were a method that operated on **BookElement** objects, you could call it with an **Introduction** object, a **Chapter** object, or any of the other classes that extend **BookElement**. These objects behave like **BookElement** objects because they inherit from **BookElement**, but they never lose their original identity.

Model, View, And Controller

One of the most useful object-oriented design concepts involves separating the elements of a problem into *model, view,* and *controller* aspects. Model elements are responsible for holding data and performing elementary operations. The **Book** class described in the previous section would be a model of a book and hold the **BookElement** objects that are models of pieces of the book. However, **BookElements** would not display themselves or interact directly with users—that is the responsibility of views and controllers.

You can see the virtue of separating these functions when you consider the number of different views you might want to have of a single model. For example, you might want an outline view, a page layout view, and an editing view.

Controller functions would handle interaction with the user, for example, interpreting a scrollbar movement into a change in a view. The controller aspects of a problem are frequently linked closely with a particular view, so you should not expect a model/view/controller approach to always neatly yield separate classes for each aspect.

 If you have not already done so as part of your Java experience, you should experiment with setting up your own hierarchy of classes to represent something in which you are interested. Reading about object-oriented design is no substitute for experience.

When Inheritance Is Not Possible

Programmers who are new to Java frequently run into the problem of inheritance not being possible. They have planned a class hierarchy but find that Java will not allow them to extend the class they wanted to use as a base. For example, the following class declaration won't compile because **String** is declared as a **final** class:

```
public BookElement extends String
```

In other words, **BookElement** cannot possibly "be a" **String**. The solution is simple: Let the class have a **String** member variable, thus **BookElement** "has a" **String**.

Overloading And Overriding

The terms *overloading* and *overriding* are applied to situations in which you have multiple Java methods with the same name. Within a particular class, you can have more than one method with the same name as long as they have different input parameter types. This is described as *overloading* the method name. To continue the book example, the **BookElement** class might have methods declared as follows:

```
public void addText( String txt )
public void addText( String[] lines )
```

You would say that **addText** has been overloaded. The Java compiler can distinguish between calls to these two methods because they have different *signatures*. The number, type, and order of the input parameters plus the method name determines the signature. The overloaded methods can have different return types and can **throw** different exceptions.

As far as Java is concerned, these are entirely different methods. The duplicate names are really just a convenience for the programmer. If one method was declared in the **BookElement** class and the other in the **Chapter** class, you would still describe these as overloaded method names. The compiler will not allow a class to have two methods with identical signatures but different return types, even if one method is declared in a parent class and is inherited.

Overriding Methods

If a subclass method has the same name, parameter list, and return type as a superclass method, you say that the subclass method overrides the superclass method. Continuing with the book example, if **BookElement** has a method declared as

```
public void addText( String txt )
```

the **Chapter** class could declare a method that would override as follows:

```
public void addText( String s )
```

Now consider the following code fragment in which a **Chapter** object is created but the reference is cast to a **BookElement** variable. The question is: Which method is executed, the one in the **Chapter** class or the one in the **BookElement** class?

```
Chapter ch = new Chapter();
BookElement b = ch ; // casting to the parent class
b.addText("If a subclass has "); // which method is called?
```

The answer is related to the fact that objects always know what type they are; just being cast to a **BookElement** reference does not change the object type. Because the Java Virtual Machine (JVM) resolves method calls at runtime using the actual object, the **Chapter** version of **addText** is executed. The ability to do this is part of what makes Java so flexible, but there is a price to pay in the restrictions you must observe when writing an overriding method. These restrictions can be summarized as follows:

➤ **Access modifiers** An overriding method cannot be made more private than the method in the parent class.

➤ **Return type** The return type must be the same as in the parent class method.

➤ **Exceptions thrown** Any exceptions declared must be of the same class as that thrown by the parent class or of a subclass of that exception.

You should know how to distinguish between overloaded and overridden methods.

Overriding Methods And The *abstract* Keyword

Java allows the class designer to declare a method as **abstract**. This essentially nails down the access, parameter list, and return type for a particular method name but does not provide a code body. Any class with such a method must also be declared **abstract**. This is done so that all classes extending the **abstract** class and overriding the **abstract** method are compatible.

In the example hierarchy, **BookElement** could be declared as follows:

```
public abstract class BookElement extends Object
```

A good candidate for an **abstract** method might be:

```
public abstract void addText( String s );
```

Every class extending **BookElement** must now either override **addText** with a *concrete* definition or itself be declared **abstract**.

When You Can't Override A Method

Methods that are declared **final** cannot be overridden—that's the meaning of the word *final*. Methods that are declared **private** cannot be seen outside the class and therefore cannot be overridden. However, because the private method name cannot be seen, you can reuse the method name in a subclass. This is not the same as overriding because you do not have access to the overridden method.

Calling The Overriden Method

In many cases, a programmer overrides a method in a base class simply to add some embellishments. When doing this, you do not need to repeat code that already exists in the parent class method. You can call that method using the **super** keyword. For example, suppose the **BookElement** class has a **setFont** method declared as follows:

```
public void setFont(Font f, int size)
```

If your **Chapter** class, which extends **BookElement**, needs to do some additional computation every time the **setFont** method is called, the overriding method could follow the following scheme:

```
public void setFont( Font f, int size){
   super.setFont( f, size );
   // more calculations here
}
```

Note that the **super** notation can be used only to execute a method in the immediate superclass. A class derived from **Chapter** could not execute the setFont method in the **BookElement** class. Furthermore, a class outside the **BookElement** hierarchy has no way of using a reference to a **Chapter** object to execute the setFont method in **BookElement**.

 It's important to understand how overriding works, including how to use **super** to execute an overridden method. Another important topic is the restrictions placed on the signature and return type of both overloaded and overridden methods. In my online testing, many programmers were weak on these restrictions, so study up!

Can You Override A Variable?

Yes, you can override a variable. This is the short answer. A subclass can have a variable with the same name as a variable in the parent class. In this case, if the parent class variable is not private, the subclass variable is said to *shadow* the parent class variable. However, there is a significant difference between the way the Java compiler treats methods and the way it treats variables. Because of the way variables are stored in the memory allocated to an object, references to variables can be computed at compile time based on the type of the variable.

Suppose that the **BookElement** class defines a variable named **lineCt** and the subclass **Chapter** defines another variable named **lineCt**. Which value would be printed by the following code fragment?

```
Chapter ch = new Chapter();
BookElement b = ch ; // casting to the parent class
System.out.println( b.lineCt );
```

If you guessed the compiler would use the **lineCt** variable found in the **BookElement** class because b is a **BookElement** reference, you are correct.

 Remember that references to member variables are computed at compile time using the type of the reference. References to member methods are resolved at runtime using the type of the object.

Object Garbage

I looked at the creation of objects using constructors in Chapter 4. Now I'll look at how objects are destroyed. Unlike C, Java does not allow for explicit destruction of objects. Instead, the memory space used by an object that is no longer reachable by the program is reclaimed by a method quaintly called "garbage collection." It could be more appropriately named memory recycling. For an excellent detailed description of how the innerworkings of Java accomplish this, see the book *Inside the Java Virtual Machine* by Bill Venners (see the "Need To Know More" section for more information).

The JVM can maintain control of all available memory because all object creation goes through the same mechanism. The Java programmer cannot pull any sneaky C-like tricks of getting memory directly from the operating system. JVMs typically run the garbage collection as a low priority **Thread**, which is activated when the JVM feels that it is running short of available memory. The programmer can also *suggest* to the JVM that now is a good time to run garbage collection with one of the following method calls, but there is no guarantee that the JVM will do it:

```
System.gc() ;
Runtime.getRuntime().gc();
```

As a programmer, you cannot control when garbage collection is run, which can be annoying because garbage collection is CPU-intensive. You can make delays less obvious by calling one of the **gc** methods when you know the user is unlikely to be demanding instant response, for example, just after your program shows a new data screen.

The design decision to remove object destruction from the control of the programmer and place it under the control of the JVM vastly simplifies the programmer's job, but you still need to know how it works. In spite of automatic garbage collection, you can still write code that runs out of memory when it shouldn't.

How Is Garbage Collected?

Strange as it may seem, the Java language specification does not lay down the law on how garbage is to be collected. It does not even say that every JVM must provide garbage collection. By leaving garbage collection unspecified, every designer implementing the JVM gets to try to come up with the optimum **gc** method for a particular system.

Basically, garbage collection works by locating objects that no longer have references in the current program. To detach an object from your program, just set all references to that object to **null**. For example, in the following code fragment, a **String** object is created with a reference stored in **str**. Assuming that the **System.out** object does not keep a copy of the reference, the **String** object will be eligible for garbage collection after line 3 is executed.

```
1. String str = new String("Size = " + x );
2. System.out.println( str );
3. str = null ;
```

Java operations with text are prolific creators of **String** objects, many of which do not even have a program reference. For example, in the following statement the **substring** method creates a **String** object that is eligible for garbage collection as soon as it is printed:

```
System.out.println( filename.substring( 0,8 ) );
```

Memory Traps For The Unwary

Suppose you had an object representing some data to which you attached a scrollbar as an **AdjustmentListener**. You might set your reference variable to null, but the data object would still be attached to the scrollbar and thus would not be garbage-collected. (That is why Java provides a **removeAdjustment-Listener** method.)

Normally, all objects created for local variables in a method become eligible for garbage collection when the method exits. Exceptions would be if an object was added to a collection somewhere or returned to the calling method.

Garbage Collection And Finalizers

Because Java objects may use other system resources beside memory, Java provides for *finalizer* methods. The **Object** class defines a do-nothing **finalize** method, as shown in the following code:

```
protected void finalize() throws Throwable{
}
```

If your class definition declares an instance method that overrides this, the JVM will run the method after it has decided that an object is eligible for reclamation, but before reclaiming the memory used by the object. This is your last chance (as a programmer) to clean up after yourself! However, because you cannot be sure when the JVM will run the **finalize** method, you should not rely on it to be run at any particular time. Also, you cannot ensure that one object's finalizer is run before another's.

The JVM may identify an object as being available for garbage collection and finalization but not run the **finalize** method at that time. Instead it keeps a list of objects to be finalized. The Java language specification says that the **System.runFinalization** method call "suggests" that the JVM expend effort toward running the finalization methods of objects that have been found to be discarded but whose finalization methods have not yet been run. Other books suggest that the call *will* run the finalization methods. I believe that the major JVM implementations do respond at once to **runFinalization**, but it is not required by the language specification.

You should be concerned with file handles as a system resource. Even if you close all files after you are finished with them as good programming practice, you might be concerned that exceptions or other problems could skip your normal file closing. You could write a **finalize** method that would check to see if a file had been closed and close it if necessary, except that the Java standard library file classes generally already have **finalize** methods that do this, but you get the idea.

 Remember that the Java programmer has no direct control over when garbage collection is done. After you remove the last reference to an object, it is up to the JVM to decide when to recycle the memory involved. You cannot force the JVM to run object **finalize** methods at a particular time or in a particular order.

Practice Questions

Question 1

> You are working on an aquarium simulation class named **Aquarius**.
> You already have a method that adds a **Fish** object to the aquarium
> and returns the remaining fish capacity. This method has the fol-
> lowing declaration:
>
> ```
> public int addFish( Fish f )
> ```
>
> Now you want to provide for adding a whole school of fish at
> once. The proposed method declaration is:
>
> ```
> protected boolean addFish( Fish[] f )
> ```
>
> The idea is that it will return **true** if there is more room in the tank
> or **false** if the tank is now too full. Which of the following state-
> ments about this proposal is true?
>
> ○ a. This technique is called overloading.
>
> ○ b. This technique is called overriding.
>
> ○ c. The compiler will reject the new method because the
> return type is different.
>
> ○ d. The compiler will reject the new method because the
> access modifier is different.

Answer a is correct. This is overloading the method name **addFish**. Answer b
is incorrect. Overriding means that a method with the exact same signature
and return type was created in a subclass. Answer c is incorrect because overloading methods can have any return type. Answer d is incorrect because
overloading methods can have any access modifier.

Question 2

The **GenericFruit** class declares the following method:

```
public void setCalorieContent( float f )
```

You are writing a class **Apple** to extend **GenericFruit** and want to add methods that overload the method in **GenericFruit**. Which of the following would constitute legal declarations of overloading methods? [Check all correct answers]

❑ a. protected float setCalorieContent(String s)

❑ b. protected void setCalorieContent(float x)

❑ c. public void setCalorieContent(double d)

❑ d. public void setCalorieContent(String s) throws NumberFormatException

The correct answers are a, c, and d. Answer a is a valid overloading method declaration because the parameter list differs from the method in **GenericFruit**. Answer c is a valid overloading method declaration because the parameter list differs from the method in **GenericFruit**. Answer d is a valid overloading method declaration because the parameter list differs from the method in **GenericFruit**. Answer b is incorrect. It overrides, not overloads, the parent class method because it has the same parameter list. Note that option b would cause a compiler error because it is more private than the method it overrides.

Question 3

You are designing an application to give dietary advice. To maximize the advantage of working in an object-oriented language, you have created a **GenericFruit** class that will be extended by classes representing different kinds of fruit. The following code fragment shows the class declaration and all of the instance variables in the **GenericFruit** class:

```
1. public class GenericFruit extends Object {
2.    protected float avgWeight ;
3.    protected float caloriesPerGram ;
4.    String varietyName ;
5.    // class definition continues with methods
```

Which of the following would be reasonable variable declarations for the **Apple** class that extends **GenericFruit**?

❍ a. Image picture ;

❍ b. private float avgWeight ;

❍ c. private GenericFruit theFruit ;

Answer a is correct; you would then say that **Apple** "has an" Image. Answer b is incorrect. Shadowing the base class **avgWeight** variable would only cause trouble. Answer c is incorrect. There is no need for **Apple** to "have a" **GenericFruit** because it "is a" **GenericFruit** by inheritance.

Question 4

You are taking over an aquarium simulation project. Your predecessor had created a generic **Fish** class that includes an **oxygenConsumption** method declared as follows:

```
public float oxygenConsumption( float
    temperature )
```

The aquarium simulation sums oxygen consumption for all fish in the tank with the following code fragment, where **fishes** is an array of **Fish** object references:

```
1. float total = 0 ;
2. for( int i =0 ; i < fishes.length ;i++ ){
3.   total += fishes[i].oxygenConsumption( t );
4. }
```

You are writing a subclass for a particular fish species. Your task is to provide a method with species-specific metabolism data that will transparently fit into the simulation. Do you want to overload or override the **oxygenConsumption** method?

○ a. overload

○ b. override

Answer b is correct; by *overriding* the **oxygenConsumption** method, the Java runtime will call the overriding method for all fish where a specific method is provided or the generic method if there is none. Answer a is incorrect. If you *overloaded* the **oxygenConsumption** method using a different method signature, the Java runtime would not call the specific method for **Fish** where a specific method was provided. It would always call the generic method.

Question 5

The **GenericFruit** class declares the following method to return a **float** number of calories in the average serving size:

```
public float aveCalories( )
```

Your **Apple** class, which extends **GenericFruit**, overrides this method. In a **DietSelection** class that extends **Object**, you want to use the **GenericFruit** method on an **Apple** object. Select the correct way to finish the statement in the following code fragment so the **GenericFruit** version of **aveCalories** is called using the **gf** reference, *or* select option d.

```
1. GenericFruit gf = new Apple();
2. float cal = // finish this statement using gf
```

○ a. gf.aveCalories();

○ b. ((GenericFruit)gf).aveCalories();

○ c. gf.super.aveCalories();

○ d. There is no way to call the GenericFruit method.

Answer d is correct. There is no way for a class outside the **GenericFruit** hierarchy to call the **GenericFruit** method using an **Apple** reference. Answer a is incorrect because the runtime resolution of method calls finds the **Apple** method. Answer b is incorrect because this extra cast does not change the object type. Answer c does not create a valid Java statement.

Question 6

You have a **BuildDB** class that has a method for opening a local file declared as:

```
public InputStream openFile(String filename)
    throws FileNotFoundException
```

Now you want to extend **BuildDB** with a new class, **BuildNetDB**, and override **openFile** as follows:

```
public InputStream openFile(String urlstring )
    throws IOException
```

Note that **FileNotFoundException** is a subclass of **IOException**. Which of the following statements are true? [Check all correct answers]

❑ a. The compiler will consider the **BuildNetDB** method to be an overloading of the base class method.

❑ b. The compiler will object to the **BuildNetDB** method because **FileNotFoundException** is a subclass of **IOException**.

❑ c. The compiler will object to the method in **BuildNetDB** because of the different name in the parameter list.

❑ d. Changing the exception thrown by the method in **BuildDB** to **IOException** will make the compiler happy.

Answers b and d are correct. Answer b is correct because an overriding method cannot throw an exception that is more general than the original method. Answer d is correct because if the overriding method and original method throw the same exception, there is no problem. Answer a is incorrect because the name and parameter list match, so the compiler considers this an overriding method. Answer c is incorrect because the compiler considers only the number, type, and order of parameters, not the name used in the parameter list.

Question 7

Here is a method that creates a number of **String** objects in the course of printing a countdown sequence:

```
1. public void countDown(){
2.   for( int i = 10 ; i >= 0 ; i-- ){
3.     String tmp = Integer.toString( i );
4.     System.out.println( tmp );
5.   }
6.   System.out.println("BOOM!");
7. }
```

When the program reaches line 6, how many of the **String** objects created in line 3 are eligible for garbage collection? (Assume that the **System.out** object is not keeping a reference.)

○ a. none

○ b. 1

○ c. 10

○ d. 11

Answer c is correct. Answers a, b, and d are incorrect because only the last **String** object of the 11 created still has a reference. Note that d is incorrect also because even though the **tmp** variable is out of scope in line 6, the local variable still has a reference to the last **String** created.

Question 8

Which of the following statements about Java garbage collection are true statements? [Check all correct answers]

❑ a. The following code will start the garbage collection mechanism:

```
Runtime.getRuntime().gc();
Thread.yield();
```

❑ b. The following code will start the garbage collection mechanism:

```
System.gc();
Thread.sleep(1000);
```

❑ c. The garbage collection **Thread** has a low priority.

❑ d. The method by which Java tracks unused objects is specified in the language definition.

❑ e. The method by which Java determines that a chunk of memory is garbage is up to the implementor of the JVM.

Answers c and e are correct. Answer c is correct because the JVM assigns a low priority to the garbage collection thread. Answer e is also correct because picking the best garbage collection method is left up to the individual JVM implementor. Answers a and b are incorrect. The key phrase here is *will* start: these code fragments *may* start the garbage collector, but there is no guarantee. Answer d is incorrect because the language specification does not prescribe a method.

Question 9

Which of the following statements about **finalize** methods is true?

- ○ a. The purpose of a **finalize** method is to recover system resources other than memory.
- ○ b. The purpose of a **finalize** method is to recover memory and other system resources.
- ○ c. You should always write a **finalize** method for every class.
- ○ d. The order in which objects are created controls the order in which their **finalize** methods are called.

Answer a is correct. Answer b is incorrect because memory is recovered by garbage collection; finalizers are for other resources. Answer c is incorrect because objects that do not use system resources other than memory do not need finalizers. Answer d is incorrect because there is no guarantee about the order of object finalization.

Question 10

The **GenericFruit** class declares the following method to return a **float** calculated from a serving size:

```
protected float calories( float serving )
```

In writing the **Apple** class that extends **GenericFruit**, you propose to declare an overriding method with the same parameter list and return type. Which access modifiers could you use with this overriding method? [Check all correct answers]

- ❑ a. private
- ❑ b. protected
- ❑ c. public
- ❑ d. "package"; that is, a blank access modifier

Answers b and c are correct. Answer b would work because the access does not change from the overridden method, and answer c would work because there is no problem with a more public access. Answer a is incorrect because the overriding method cannot be made more private than the method it is overriding. Answer d is incorrect because package access is more private than protected.

Need To Know More?

 Flanagan, David. *Java in a Nutshell, 2nd Edition*. O'Reilly & Associates, Inc., Sebastopol, CA, 1997. ISBN: 1-56592-262-X. This is the most compact desktop reference book documenting the Java language. Chapter 3 has good material on working with Java classes.

 Gamma, Erich, et al. *Design Patterns: Elements of Reusable Object-Oriented Software*, Addison-Wesley, Menlo Park, California, 1994. ISBN: 0-201-63361-2. Often humorously referred to as "Design Patterns by the Gang of Four," this book is a resource for inspiration when trying to figure out how to apply object-oriented design to a problem.

 Venners, Bill. *Inside the Java Virtual Machine*. McGraw-Hill, New York, NY, 1998. ISBN: 0-07-913248-0. If you want the bit-twiddling details of how the JVM interprets Java bytecodes, this is a good source. See Chapter 9 for details on Java garbage collection.

 ftp://ftp.javasoft.com/docs/tutorial.zip

An excellent tutorial in HTML form can be downloaded from this site (although this document is updated frequently, it may not be entirely current with JDK 1.2 information).

 http://java.sun.com/products/jdk/1.2/index.html

The Java API documentation in Javadoc-generated form can be downloaded from Sun Microsystems. Although this site changes a lot, it was a good starting point the last time I looked.

 http://www.bruceeckel.com/javabook.html

This online version of the book *Thinking in Java* is highly recommended for object-oriented programming in Java.

9

Java Threads

Terms you'll need to understand:

- √ **Thread**
- √ **Runnable**
- √ **Synchronized**
- √ Monitor
- √ Lock
- √ **InterruptedException**
- √ Deadlock

Techniques you'll need to master:

- √ Writing code that starts a new thread of execution
- √ Understanding the requirements of the **Runnable** interface
- √ Knowing all the states a **Thread** object can exist in and the transitions it can undergo
- √ Writing code that uses the **synchronized** keyword
- √ Writing code that uses **wait** and **notify** or **notifyAll** to coordinate access to objects by **Thread**s

Everything that happens in a Java program is the result of a thread executing a method associated with an object. Although Java provides many tools for manipulating threads, Java's portability has limitations because of variations in the underlying operating systems. It is essential for a Java programmer to understand both the power and limitations of Java threads.

Thread Background

One of the most striking features of Java is the ease with which a programmer can use multiple threads of execution. In C or C++, implementing multiple threads may involve you in a proprietary and platform-specific toolkit, using concepts that have been tacked on to the original language. Java, by contrast, was designed from the start to accommodate multiple threads.

Multithreading Vs. Multitasking

In modern operating systems, such as Windows 95, each program appears to run independently of all other programs. Although the CPU can do only one thing at a time, the operating system accomplishes *multitasking* by switching its attention so rapidly between the different applications that the applications appear to be running simultaneously. The operating system also prevents conflicts in the use of memory and other resources by the various programs.

In *multithreading*, multiple processes exist within a single program. If you use a modern Web browser, you have probably seen multithreading in action as the browser appears to load text and multiple images simultaneously. In the browser, each thread of execution tries to load a separate resource, so the overall loading process does not have to wait for a slow server response.

In the Java multithreaded environment, the Java Virtual Machine (JVM) objects and resources can be accessed by many separate threads. Each thread has its own path of execution but can potentially access any object in the program. It is up to the programmer to ensure that the threads do not interfere with each other. The Java language has built-in constructs that make this relatively easy, but you will need to put some effort into becoming comfortable with multithreading.

The Java language specification does not say how the JVM should implement multithreading. Because there is so much variation among the various operating systems and hardware on which Java is expected to run, the language specification leaves the specific implementation up to JVM designers. The Java **Thread** class describes the required behavior of **Thread** objects.

The **Thread** Class

Thread objects are used to encapsulate and conceal the details of a particular operating system's approach to multithreading. The JVM creates and runs several **Thread**s to support even the simplest Java program. The **Thread**s are used to load class files, interpret operating system events, and start the execution of your program.

The Life Of A Thread

Thread objects have a distinct life cycle with four basic states: new, runnable, blocked, and dead (see Figure 9.1). The transitions from new to runnable and from runnable to dead are simple and permanent; the transitions between runnable and blocked occupy most of the Java programmer's attention.

A **Thread** in the runnable state can resume execution at the whim of the **Thread** scheduler in the JVM. Moving a **Thread** from the running to the ready state is also up to the **Thread** scheduler. Java also uses the term **Runnable** when referring to the **Runnable** interface. When referring to the interface, I will show the word in bold with the first letter capitalized. Running **Thread**s can be moved to and from the blocked state by various circumstances.

Thread Creation

Thread objects are created by constructor methods, just like any other object. A **Thread** just created by **new** is essentially an empty object; it does not yet have any operating system resources and can only be started. When a **Thread**

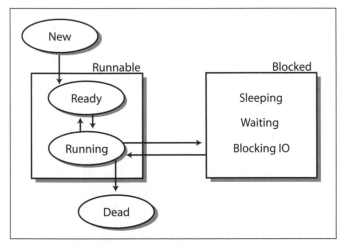

Figure 9.1   The possible states in the life of a thread.

is started, it gets connected to the JVM scheduling mechanism and executes a method declared as follows:

```
public void run()
```

This method can be the **run** method of the **Thread** class, the overriding **run** method of a class extending **Thread**, or the **run** method of a class that implements the **Runnable** interface.

A number of different **Thread** constructors exist, including some that let you create named **Thread**s and assign **Thread**s to **ThreadGroup** objects. However, the use of names and **ThreadGroup** objects is not among the objectives for the exam, so the interested student will have to investigate other sources. Here are the two types of constructors to consider:

```
1. Thread myT = new Thread();
2. Thread myT = new Thread( Runnable r );
```

Line 1 shows the construction of a plain **Thread**. Actually, plain **Thread**s are not useful for anything because the **run** method in the **Thread** class is empty, but classes extending **Thread** can be quite useful. Line 2 shows the creation of a **Thread** with a reference to an object that implements the **Runnable** interface. When started, this **Thread** will execute the **run** method in the **Runnable** object.

The *Runnable* Interface

The **Runnable** interface is simple. A class implementing **Runnable** need only provide a method declared as:

```
public void run()
```

Any **Thread** attached to an object implementing **Runnable** will execute the **run** method of that object. It is possible to attach more than one **Thread** to a **Runnable** object.

Starting A Thread

A **Thread** does not do anything until its **start** method is executed. When a **Thread** is started, the JVM sets up some resources and puts the **Thread** in the list of runnable **Thread**s. Exactly when a **Thread** gets to execute depends on its priority, the activity of other **Thread**s, and the characteristics of the particular JVM.

You can simultaneously create and start a **Thread** as in the following method:

```
public void startThread() {
  new Thread(this).start();
}
```

You might think that the new **Thread** in the preceding example would be garbage-collected because no reference to it is being kept, but the JVM created a reference in its list of **Thread**s. After **Thread** A has called **Thread** B's **start** method, you have no way of knowing whether A will continue to execute or B will start immediately. Make sure you have set up everything for **Thread** B before calling its **start** method.

Thread Priorities

Thread objects have an instance variable, **priority**, that has integer values from 1 to 10, with 10 being the most urgent. The JVM **Thread** scheduler always attempts to allow the highest priority available **Thread** to execute, but this is not guaranteed. The constants **MIN_PRIORITY, MAX_PRIORITY,** and **NORM_PRIORITY** are defined in the **Thread** class with values 1, 10, and 5. It is considered good form to use these constants rather than integer literals when using the **setPriority** method.

 A newly created **Thread** inherits the priority of the **Thread** that creates it, not **NORM_PRIORITY**. If you want to have a particular priority, you should call **setPriority** before starting the **Thread**.

The JVM may adjust the priority downward to match the underlying operating system, so don't be surprised if the **getPriority** method returns a value different from the one you requested.

Death Of A Thread

When a **Thread** exits the **run** method to which it is attached, it becomes a dead **Thread**. This may occur because of a normal return from the **run** method or from an exception that is not caught. A dead **Thread** cannot be restarted.

Killing A *Thread*

In the first version of the Java language, the instance method **stop** was used to cause a **Thread** to stop what it was doing and die. In JDK 1.2, using **stop** is no longer recommended. (See the discussion later in the "Some Deprecated Methods" section.)

Static Methods Of The Thread Class

The **Thread** class has a number of methods affecting the operation of individual **Thread**s that are implemented as **static** (class) methods instead of instance methods. The methods of greatest interest are **sleep** and **yield**.

Sleeping For A While

The **Thread** that calls the **sleep** method is put to sleep for a number of milli-seconds at least equal to the input parameter. This method has two forms:

```
1. Thread.sleep(long millisecs)
2. Thread.sleep(long millisecs, int nanosecs )
```

The inclusion of form 2 in the Java language specification is rather ambitious because no current computer provides software timers of that precision. Because **sleep** is a **static** method, you can also call it with a reference to a **Thread** object, as in the following example where **myT** is a **Thread** reference variable:

```
1. try {
2.   myT.sleep( 500 );
3. }catch (InterruptedException e ){ }
```

I don't recommend this approach because it misrepresents what is happening. It is the currently executing **Thread** that sleeps, not necessarily the one referred to.

Notice that in the preceding code fragment, I had to enclose the **sleep** call in a **try-catch** structure to catch an **InterruptedException**. A sleeping **Thread** can be rudely awakened before its time by calling the **interrupt** method of the particular **Thread** instance, which generates an **InterruptedException**.

 Sleep is not a high-precision timing operation because it depends on the clock of the underlying operating system. In addition, there is no guarantee that the **Thread** will immediately begin to execute after the time delay is up; that is up to the JVM **Thread** scheduler. Be sure to keep this in mind.

Yielding To Other **Threads**

The static method **yield** simply suspends operation of the current **Thread** and allows the **Thread** scheduler to choose another runnable **Thread** to execute, which may be the same **Thread** that yielded. If you have a **Thread** that is carrying out a complex computation, you should insert an occasional call to **yield** in the code to ensure that other **Threads** get a chance to run.

The Java language specification does not require any particular method for **Thread** scheduling. A computationally intensive program that appears to run fine without using **yield** calls on systems using a time-slicing method of **Thread** scheduling may show unacceptable delays on systems that use a different method of scheduling.

Blocking Input/Output

Java classes that deal with transferring data to and from the world outside the JVM are generally in the **java.io** package. Many of the methods in these classes are expected to read or write a certain amount of data before the **Thread** executing them returns. Because there may be a considerable delay before the underlying operating system and hardware can accomplish this, these methods put the **Thread** in a blocked state until the operation is finished. This allows the **Thread** scheduler to choose another **Thread** to run.

Deadlocks

A moment's reflection will suggest many ways in which two or more **Thread**s could be put into a condition where none of them can proceed until some locked object is released. For example, suppose **Thread** A locks object B in a method that must access object Z. However, **Thread** X has already locked object Z and is trying to access object B. This is called a *deadlock* condition, the bane of multithreaded programming. Although Java provides many tools for managing multiple **Thread**s, the programmer is ultimately responsible for avoiding deadlocks.

Synchronizing **Threads**

The major problem in designing a multithreaded language is preventing collisions in which more than one **Thread** attempts to modify the same object at the same time. Naturally, the CPU cannot actually do two things at once, but a **Thread** might be halted in midcalculation and another allowed to use the same data, resulting in a disaster.

Java provides the foundation for solving this problem in the **Object** class, the ultimate parent of all Java objects. Each object has an associated *lock* variable that can be manipulated only by the JVM. This lock provides a *monitor* mechanism that can be used to allow only one **Thread** at a time to have access to an object.

In various Java books, *monitor* and *lock* are used interchangeably. Some language purists, however, feel that monitor has a specific formal definition. I will use monitor to mean the mechanism and lock in the context of a **Thread** obtaining the lock on an object.

Because it would take additional time for the JVM to check the lock condition of an object every time it is accessed, the lock is ignored by default. The keyword **synchronized** is used to indicate a method or block of code that needs to be guarded by the lock mechanism. Here is the syntax used with **synchronized** and a block of code, where **obj** must be an object reference:

```
synchronized( obj ) {
   balance += payment ;
   // any amount of code
}
```

When **synchronized** is used as a statement, it requires a reference to the object to be locked. For convenience, **synchronized** can be used as a method modifier, in which case the entire method is the block of code, and **this** is automatically the object reference.

Once obtained, a **Thread's** lock on an object is not released until the **Thread** exits the **synchronized** code block or uses the special **wait** method in the **Object** class that I will discuss shortly.

Overriding Methods And synchronized *Methods*

If you have a **synchronized** method in a class, a subclass with an overriding method does not have to declare it as **synchronized**. The **synchronized** keyword affects only the code block in the original class.

synchronized Methods And Speed

A **synchronized** method consumes extra CPU cycles on entry and exit, so you should not synchronize without good cause. For example, the initial releases of the Java standard library made the access methods in the **java.util.Vector** class **synchronized**. Although this ensured that only one **Thread** at a time could modify a **Vector** object, it did not give the programmer any flexibility. Java 1.2 adds new collection types, including **ArrayList,** which can be used in place of **Vector** and does not use **synchronized** methods. With these new classes, the programmer can use synchronization as needed.

How Not To Synchronize

Don't synchronize on a local variable as shown in the following fragment, which attempts to prevent interference with addition of a new **String** to the **active** array:

```
1. String[] active ;
2. public int addActive( String name, int id ){
3.    String tmp = name + " ID= " + id ;
4.    synchronized( tmp ){
5.       for( int i = 0 ; i < active.length ; i++ ){
6.          if(active[i] == null ) { active[i] = tmp ;
7.             return i ;
8.          }
9.       }
10       return -1 ;
```

```
11.  } // end synchronized block
12. }
```

The statement in line 4 in the preceding code accomplishes nothing because every **Thread** has its own copy of local variables, such as **tmp** in the preceding code. To accomplish the desired protection, line 4 should use the instance variable, **active**, as follows:

```
4.   synchronized( active ) {
```

 Remember that **synchronized** has to be used with an object reference because only objects can have locks. It does no good to synchronize on a local variable. Be sure that the object chosen really protects the data you want to protect.

How Many Locks? How Many Threads?

A single **Thread** can obtain locks on many objects and/or multiple locks on the same object. A new lock is obtained for each entry into a **synchronized** code block. The JVM ensures that the lock is removed when a **Thread** exits the code block, whether or not the exit is normal.

Any number of **Thread**s can be ready to execute a **synchronized** code block. The first one the **Thread** scheduler allows to run after the lock is released will establish a lock and prevent the rest from executing.

Coordinating Threads With wait And notify

Some applications require coordination of **Thread**s beyond that provided by **synchronized** code blocks. A classic example is that of an animated scene in which an object contains a collection of the parts of the scene. One **Thread** can generate an image of the current position of the changing scene. However, because of the way the JVM organizes operating system events, displaying the current image on the screen is best left to the system event thread that calls the **paint** method of a screen component. If both **Thread**s did not coordinate, the screen could show incomplete images.

What you want is a way for the **Thread** that is generating animation to wait after each animation step until the scene has been shown on the screen and for the painting **Thread** to wait until the animation **Thread** has completed a step before showing the image. In addition, you want the painting **Thread** to be able to tell the animation **Thread** that it can start work on the next step.

The following code fragment shows the **run** method executed by the animation **Thread**. The entire method is **synchronized**, so the animation **Thread** has a lock on the object. The only time the lock is released is when the animation

Thread calls **wait**. The **wait** method, which is defined in the **Object** class, puts the **Thread** that executes it into a special state. Any locks that the **Thread** has are released, and it is put in a "wait set" list of waiting **Thread**s that is attached to the object:

```
1. public void synchronized run(){
2.    while( true ){
3.        createNextScene() ;
4.        repaint();
5.        try{ wait() ;
6.        }catch( InterruptedException e){}
7.    }
8. }
```

After creating the next scene, the **repaint** method is called in line 4 just before the animation **Thread** calls **wait**. A call to **repaint** essentially is a request to the JVM to refresh the screen display for this component. When the JVM gets around to it, the **paint** method of the component will be called by the **Thread** that the JVM devotes to handling screen events. As shown in the following code fragment, the **paint** method draws the image to the screen and calls **notify**:

```
1. public void paint(Graphics g ){
2.    if( sceneImage == null ) return ;
3.    synchronized( this ) {
4.      g.drawImage( sceneImage, 0, 0, null )
5.      notify();
6.    }
7. }
```

Before painting to the screen, the painting **Thread** has to enter the **synchronized** block starting at line 3. If the animation **Thread** has a lock on the object, the painting **Thread** will be stopped at this point. When the painting **Thread** is allowed to proceed, the animation **Thread** must have called **wait**, so the **sceneImage** must be complete.

When **notify** is called, a **Thread** is removed from the wait set and returned to the list of runnable **Thread**s. If more than one **Thread** is waiting, you cannot control or predict which one it will be. However, in this example, only the animation **Thread** is waiting. As soon as the painting **Thread** exits the **synchronized** code block, the animation **Thread** can lock the object and run again.

More About notify And notifyAll

If more than one **Thread** is waiting for an object lock, the programmer cannot control or predict which one will be returned to the runnable set when **notify** is called. If there is a chance that more than one **Thread** is waiting, you can use **notifyAll.**

The **notifyAll** call removes all waiting **Thread**s from the wait list. Only one of these will actually get a lock on the object and be allowed to execute the **synchronized** method; the others will run and find that the object is still locked. If a **Thread** that has a lock on one or more objects dies, the JVM removes the locks and does the equivalent of **notifyAll** for each object locked.

More About *wait*

There is a **wait** method with a timeout in milliseconds. After the time is exhausted, the **Thread** will attempt to proceed but will be allowed to do so only if no other **Thread** has a lock on the object. This method is handy when you are not sure that another **Thread** will be able to call **notify**, because it guarantees that the **Thread** will not be stuck in the wait state forever.

The *IllegalMonitorStateException*

If a **Thread** that does not have a lock on an object attempts to call the object's **wait** or **notify** method, an **IllegalMonitorStateException** is thrown—typically with the message "current thread not owner." To ensure that this never happens, your calls to **wait** or **notify** or **notifyAll** should be in **synchronized** code blocks.

Some Deprecated Methods

The first version of Java used some **Thread** methods that are now considered unsafe and are *deprecated*. These methods are still in the Java standard library and may be used; however, programmers are advised to find substitutes because deprecated methods may not appear in future versions of the language. I discuss them here because they are used in example programs from earlier versions of Java and because they illustrate some important points. The use of these methods should not appear in the test.

The *suspend* And *resume* Methods

The idea behind these methods was that you could temporarily halt a **Thread** by calling its **suspend** method and later allow it to proceed by calling **resume**. The problem with this is that if the **Thread** has a lock on an object, it retains the lock while suspended. If that locked object happens to be important for the progress of the rest of the program, a deadlock can result.

The *stop* Method

You would think that it ought to be possible to stop a **Thread** without causing any harm, but the designers now feel that arbitrarily stopping a **Thread** can leave an object in a damaged or inconsistent state that might then cause unpredictable program behavior. The suggested alternatives to using **stop** include using a flag variable in the **run** method. For a **Thread** blocked while waiting for input, the use of the **interrupt** method is suggested.

Keeping The Methods Straight

Let's review the classes and methods that you are likely to be using when working with **Thread**s. When I tested questions online for this chapter, many people made mistakes in this material.

Table 9.1 summarizes the methods in the **Thread** and **Object** classes with which you need to be particularly familiar. Many more methods exist in the **Thread** class, but these are the ones you must be able to recognize and use correctly in programming. Naturally, because **Thread** descends from **Object**, it also has the **wait** and **notify** methods, but these are not used directly in **Thread** programming.

 Take particular note of which methods are static and which are instance methods as shown in the "Type" column in Table 9.1. Also note which methods need to be enclosed in **synchronized** code blocks and/or **try-catch** structures to catch the **Interrupted-Exception**, as shown in the "Needs" column. In the "Timeout Form" column, note that **sleep** is always used with a timeout and that **wait** has forms with and without timeouts.

Table 9.1   A summary of methods used with Threads.

Class	Method	Type	Needs	Timeout Form
Thread	yield()	static		no
Thread	sleep(#)	static	try-catch	always
Thread	start()	instance		no
Thread	run()	instance		no
Thread	interrupt()	instance		no
Object	wait()	instance	synchronized, try-catch	optional
Object	notify()	instance	synchronized	no
Object	notifyAll()	instance	synchronized	no

Practice Questions

Question 1

You are creating a class that extends **Object** and implements **Runnable**. You have already written a **run** method for this class, and you need a way to create a **Thread** and have it execute the **run** method. Which of these **start** methods should you use?

⭕ a.
```
public void start(){
    new Thread( this ).start();
 }
```

⭕ b.
```
 public void start(){
    Thread myT = new Thread();
    myT.start();
 }
```

⭕ c.
```
 public void start(){
    Thread myT = new Thread(this);
    myT.run();
 }
```

Answer a correctly creates a new **Thread** attached to the **Runnable** object and starts it. It does not matter that there is no reference to the **Thread** in the **start** method. Answer b is incorrect because the new **Thread** is not attached to the **Runnable** object so it cannot find the **run** method. Instead, the default **run** in the **Thread** class will be executed. Answer c is incorrect because the **Thread** that is executing the **start** method calls **run** in the **Thread** class. The **myT Thread** is not started.

Question 2

> Which of the following methods are **static** methods of the **Thread** class? [Check all correct answers]
>
> ❑ a. sleep(long msec);
>
> ❑ b. yield();
>
> ❑ c. wait();
>
> ❑ d. notifyAll();

Answer a is correct. The **sleep** method is a static method of the **Thread** class. A typical call would be:

```
Thread.sleep( 1000 );
```

Answer b is also correct. The **yield** method is a static method of the **Thread** class. A typical call would be:

```
Thread.yield();
```

Answer c is incorrect because **wait** is an instance method of the **Object** class and thus an instance method of **Thread** by inheritance. Answer d is incorrect because **notifyAll** is also an instance method of the **Object** class.

Question 3

> You have an application that executes the following line:
>
> ```
> Thread myT = new Thread();
> ```
>
> Which of the following statements are true?
>
> ○ a. The **Thread myT** is now in a runnable state.
>
> ○ b. The **Thread myT** has the NORM_PRIORITY priority.
>
> ○ c. If **myT.start()** is called, the **run** method in the **Thread** class will be executed.
>
> ○ d. If **myT.start()** is called, the **run** method in the calling class will be executed.

Answer c is true because **myT** is a **Thread** object created without a reference to a **Runnable** object, so the **run** method in the **Thread** class will be executed.

Answer a is false because the **Thread** is in the "new" state; **start()** must be called to put it in the runnable state. Answer b is false because the priority will be that inherited from the **Thread** that called the constructor, which may or may not be NORM_PRIORITY. Answer d is false because the **Thread** constructor method used did not connect the new **Thread** to a **Runnable** object.

Question 4

You have written a class extending **Thread** that does time-consuming computations. In the first use of this class in an application, the system locked up for extended periods of time. Obviously, you need to provide a chance for other **Thread**s to run. The following is the **run** method that needs to be modified. Select all of the statements that could be inserted at line 5 to allow other **Thread**s a chance to run. [Check all correct answers]

```
1. public void run(){
2.    boolean runFlg = true ;
3.    while( runFlg ){
4.       runFlg = doStuff();
5.
6.    }
7. }
```

❏ a. yield();

❏ b. try{ sleep(100); }catch(InterruptedException e){}

❏ c. suspend(100);

❏ d. wait(100);

Answers a and b are correct. Answer a is correct because **yield** will let the thread-scheduling mechanism run another **Thread**. Answer b is correct because **sleep** will allow time for other **Thread**s to run. Answer c is incorrect because there is no such method as **suspend** with a time delay. The **suspend()** method would permanently suspend your **Thread** and, of course, **suspend** is a deprecated method. Answer d is incorrect because it would not compile as written; calls to **wait** must provide for catching an **InterruptedException**. Furthermore, the call to **wait** would have to be in a **synchronized** code block.

Question 5

> The **Object** class has a **wait** method that is used to coordinate access to an object by multiple **Thread**s. Which of the following statements about the **wait** method are true? [Check all correct answers]
>
> ☐ a. The **wait** method is an instance method of the **Object** class.
>
> ☐ b. The **wait** method is a static method of the **Object** class.
>
> ☐ c. To call **wait**, a **Thread** must have a lock on the object involved.
>
> ☐ d. An object can have only one **Thread** in a waiting state at a time.

Answers a and c are correct. Answer a is correct because **wait** is indeed an instance method. Answer c is correct because if a **Thread** that does not have a lock on an object attempts to **wait**, an **IllegalMonitorStateException** results. Answer b is incorrect because the idea of **wait** is to control access to each individual object; therefore, each object must have its own **wait** method. Answer d is incorrect because any number of **Thread**s can be waiting for an object.

Question 6

> Java **Thread** A is attached to an object, **B**, which is responsible for writing data to a file. After writing data, **Thread** A calls the following method in object **B**, where it waits until more data is available.
>
> ```
> 1. private void synchronized waitForData(){
> 2.    try{ wait();
> 3.    }catch(InterruptedException e) {}
> 4. }
> ```
>
> Another **Thread**, executing a method in another object (**C**), needs to wake up **Thread** A. Assuming that object **C** has references to both **A** and **B**, select all of the following code fragments that would cause **Thread** A to exit the **waitForData** method. [Check all correct answers]
>
> ☐ a. A.interrupt();
>
> ☐ b. synchronized(A){ A.notifyAll() ; }
>
> ☐ c. synchronized(B){ B.notifyAll() ; }
>
> ☐ d. A.resume();

Answers a and c are correct. Answer a is correct because this would generate an **InterruptedException**, bringing **Thread** A out of the **wait**. Because line 3 catches this exception, the **Thread** exits the **waitForData** method normally. Answer c is correct because it removes all **Threads** waiting for object B from the wait list, including **Thread** A. Answer b is incorrect because it refers to the **Thread** A, not to the object **B** for which the **Thread** is waiting. Answer d is incorrect because the **resume** method works only with suspended **Threads** and is a deprecated method.

Question 7

Here is part of the code for a class that implements the **Runnable** interface:

```
1. public class Whiffler extends Object
      implements Runnable {
2.    Thread myT ;
3.    public void start(){
4.      myT = new Thread( this );
5.    }
6.    public void run(){
7.      while( true ){
8.        doStuff();
9.      }
10.     System.out.println("Exiting run");
11.   }
12. // more class code follows....
```

Assume that the rest of the class defines **doStuff**, and so on, and that the class compiles without error. Also assume that a Java application creates a **Whiffler** object and calls the **Whiffler start** method, that no other direct calls to **Whiffler** methods are made, and that the **Thread** in this object is the only one the application creates.

Which of the following are correct statements? [Check all correct answers]

❑   a. The **doStuff** method will be called repeatedly.

❑   b. The **doStuff** method will never be executed.

❑   c. The **doStuff** method will execute at least one time.

❑   d. The statement in line 10 will never be reached.

Answers b and d are correct. Answer b is correct because **myT.start()** is never called, the **Thread** never runs. Answer d is correct because **myT.start()** is never called. Answer a is incorrect. The **Thread** is never started, so **run** is never executed. Answer c is incorrect because the **Thread** is never started, so **run** is never executed.

Question 8

Which of the following methods are instance methods of the **Thread** class, excluding any methods deprecated in Java 1.2? [Check all correct answers]

❑ a. start()

❑ b. stop()

❑ c. run()

❑ d. suspend()

❑ e. sleep(long msec)

❑ f. toString()

Answers a, c, and f are correct. Answer a is correct because **start** is an instance method of Thread that makes a new **Thread** runnable. Answer c is also correct because the **run** method is the key to **Thread** operation. Answer f is correct because all Java objects have a **toString** method. Answer b is incorrect because **stop** is a deprecated method. Answer d is incorrect because **suspend** is a deprecated method because a suspended **Thread** may retain a lock on an important system object. Answer e is incorrect because **sleep** is a **static** (class) method, not an instance method.

Question 9

You have written an application that can accept orders from multiple sources, each one of which runs in a separate **Thread**. One object in the application is allowed to record orders in a file. This object uses the **recordOrder** method, which is **synchronized** to prevent conflict between **Thread**s.

While **Thread** A is executing **recordOrder**, **Thread**s B and C, in that order, attempt to execute the **recordOrder method**. What happens when **Thread** A exits the **synchronized** method?

○ a. **Thread** B, as the first waiting **Thread**, is allowed to execute the method.

○ b. **Thread** C, as the last waiting **Thread**, is allowed to execute the method.

○ c. One of the waiting **Thread**s will be allowed to execute the method, but you can't be sure which one it will be.

Answer c is correct. You cannot determine which **Thread** will be allowed to execute next. Answers a and b are incorrect because the JVM does not track the order in which **Thread**s attempt to access a locked object.

Question 10

You have created a **TimeOut** class as an extension of **Thread**, the purpose of which is to print a "Time's Up" message if the **Thread** is not interrupted within 10 seconds of being started.
Here is the **run** method that you have coded:

```
1. public void run(){
2.    System.out.println("Start!");
3.    try { Thread.sleep(10000 );
4.      System.out.println("Time's Up!");
5.    }catch(InterruptedException e){
6.      System.out.println("Interrupted!");
7.    }
8. }
```

Given that a program creates and starts a **TimeOut** object, which of the following statements is true?

❍ a. Exactly 10 seconds after the start method is called, "Time's Up!" will be printed.

❍ b. Exactly 10 seconds after "Start!" is printed, "Time's Up!" will be printed.

❍ c. The delay between "Start!" being printed and "Time's Up!" will be 10 seconds plus or minus one tick of the system clock.

❍ d. If "Time's Up!" is printed, you can be sure that at least 10 seconds have elapsed since "Start!" was printed.

Answer d is correct, it is the only statement that can be made with confidence. Answers a, b, and c are all incorrect because the expiration of a sleep timer does not guarantee that a **Thread** *will* run—only that it *can* run.

Need To Know More?

Flanagan, David. *Java in a Nutshell, 2ⁿᵈ Edition*. O'Reilly & Associates, Inc., Sebastopol, CA, 1997. ISBN: 1-56592-262-X. This is the most compact desktop reference book documenting the Java language. Documentation of the Thread class is in Chapter 25.

Gamma, Erich, et al. *Design Patterns: Elements of Reusable Object-Oriented Software*, Addison-Wesley, Menlo Park, CA, 1994. ISBN: 0-201-63361-2. Often humorously referred to as "Design Patterns by the Gang of Four," this entire book is a resource for inspiration when trying to figure out how to apply object orientation to a problem.

Oaks, Scott, and Henry Wong. *Java Threads*. O'Reilly & Associates, Inc., Sebastopol, CA, 1997. ISBN: 1-56592-216-6. Although written for Java version 1.02, this entire book is still useful. Just watch out for methods that are now deprecated.

ftp://ftp.javasoft.com/docs/tutorial.zip

An excellent tutorial in HTML form can be downloaded from this site (although this document is updated frequently, it may not be entirely current with JDK 1.2 information).

http://java.sun.com/products/jdk/1.2/index.html

The Java API documentation in Javadoc-generated form can be downloaded from Sun Microsystems. Although this site changes a lot, it was a good starting point the last time I looked.

Standard Library Utility Classes

Terms you'll need to understand:

➤ Collection

➤ Enumeration

➤ Iterator

➤ List

➤ Map

➤ Set

➤ Wrapper class

Techniques you'll need to master:

➤ Using the **Math** methods

➤ Using the **Wrapper** classes

➤ Converting numeric values to and from **String** objects

➤ Understanding the Collections API interfaces:
Collection, **Set**, **List**, **Map**, **SortedMap,** and **SortedSet**

➤ Understanding what the Reflection API does

In this chapter, we will review some of the many utility classes that are in the Java standard library. As Java has developed from version 1.0 to 1.2, there has been an enormous increase in the number of classes and methods that are considered part of the standard programming library. I can't cover everything, but I will attempt to touch on those topics likely to be on the exam.

Utility Classes In The java.lang Package

The Java standard library places a large number of useful classes in the **java.lang** package. This package is automatically imported by the Java compiler for all programs. Because a working knowledge of these classes is essential for any Java programmer, you have probably used many of them already, so the purpose of this section is to review the most important aspects.

The Math Class

The **Math** class provides the usual mathematical functions and defines the commonly used constants, *e* and *pi*, as the **static double** variables **Math.E** and **Math.PI**. All elements of the **Math** class are **static**, so you never create an instance of **Math**. Here are some important points to remember about some of the more commonly used methods:

➤ **Trig functions** The trigonometric functions take **double** primitive arguments and return **double** results. Angles are always expressed in radians.

➤ **The max, min, and abs functions** These methods are overloaded, with separate versions for **int, long, float,** and **double** arguments. Remember that integer inputs smaller than 32 bits will be automatically promoted to **int**.

➤ **The random function** This method returns a **double** primitive randomly distributed between 0.0 and 1.0.

String And StringBuffer

The **String** class occupies a special position in the Java standard library in recognition of the fact that typical programs use text strings extensively. For example, as discussed in Chapter 3, the Java compiler allows the use of the operators "+" and "+=" in connection with **String** objects. In terms of programming problems, you should always remember that once created, a **String** can't be changed.

You should use the **StringBuffer** class when you need to manipulate character strings efficiently. **StringBuffer** objects automatically expand as necessary, and the contents can be efficiently turned into a **String** when desired.

 Remember, **String** and **StringBuffer** objects deal with 16-bit Unicode characters to support international alphabets. Although you create **String** literals with 8-bit ASCII code, Java automatically converts them to 16-bit Unicode.

Wrapper Classes

Java uses "wrapper" classes to provide a variety of functions related to primitives. The **static** methods of these classes provide many convenient utility functions, such as conversion to and from **String** representation. The **static final** variables of these classes provide useful constants, such as the **MAX_VALUE** constant of the **Integer** class. Table 10.1 shows the Java wrapper classes along with their corresponding primitive variables.

 Because so many of these wrapper classes have only an upper-case initial letter to distinguish them from Java primitives, it is easy to make a mistake. Read carefully to ensure that you are not treating an object as a primitive or vice versa.

General Uses For Wrapper Objects

The wrapper classes let you use the many Java utility classes that manipulate objects for manipulating primitive values. For example, if you are creating a calculator application, you can store intermediate numeric results as **Double**

Table 10.1	Wrapper classes and their corresponding primitive variables.	
Wrapper Class	**Corresponding Java Primitive**	**Values**
Byte	byte	8-bit signed integer
Short	short	16-bit signed integer
Character	char	16-bit unsigned Unicode integer
Integer	int	32-bit signed integer
Long	long	64-bit signed integer
Float	float	32-bit floating point number
Double	double	64-bit floating point number
Boolean	boolean	true or false

objects on a **Stack**. The operation of Java **Stack** objects is considered later in this chapter.

The *Integer* Class

Frequently used methods include the following static methods that are typically used to turn user input **Strings** into **int** primitive values, as shown in the following code:

```
public static int parseInt( String s )
public static int parseInt( String s, int radix )
```

Both of these methods will throw a **NumberFormatException** if the input **String** contains any non-numeric characters. It is easy to confuse these methods with the following, which returns **Integer** objects. When in doubt, check the documentation.

```
public static Integer valueOf( String s )
public static Integer valueOf( String s, int radix )
```

Handy constants for use with integers are provided as final static variables. **Integer.MAX_VALUE** is the largest (positive) value and **Integer.MIN_VALUE** is the smallest (most negative) value that an **int** primitive can contain.

Other Integer Wrapper Classes

Classes similar to **Integer** are provided to wrap **byte, short,** and **long** integer primitives. As you would expect, these classes are named **Byte, Short,** and **Long**. Each class provides constants for the largest and smallest value they can contain.

The *Character* Class

The **Character** class provides many handy character classification static methods, such as **isDigit, isLetter,** and **isJavaIdentifierStart,** which take a **char** primitive and return a **boolean** result depending on the type of character represented.

The *Float* And *Double* Classes

These classes provide wrapper objects for the **float** and **double** primitive values. They also define constants for the special **NEGATIVE_INFINITY, POSITIVE_INFINITY,** and NaN (Not a Number) values that can be created by floating-point arithmetic, as discussed in Chapter 3. Whereas in the integer classes, **MIN_VALUE** was the most negative number that could be represented, in the floating-point classes, it is the smallest (nonzero) value.

The *Boolean* Class

The **Boolean** class simply provides an object to wrap a **boolean true** or **false** primitive value. To find out the value contained in a **Boolean** object, use the **booleanValue** method.

The System And Runtime Classes

The intent of the designers of the Java language was to make Java as platform-independent as possible. To that end, the **System** and **Runtime** classes were designed to encapsulate the necessary connections to the underlying operating system. All methods and variables in the **System** class are static—you can't create a **System** object. The methods described in the following sections are some of the more useful **System** and **Runtime** methods.

Input And Output With The *System* Class

The **System** class automatically creates a standard input, standard output, and standard error output stream, named **System.in**, **System.out**, and **System.err**. The **out** and **err** streams normally go to the Java console in a Web browser or a "DOS Window" for an application on a Windows system. The **in** stream gets data from the keyboard in applications that do not use a graphical interface. These streams can be redirected but only if the security settings allow it.

A Timing Utility

The **System.currentTimeMillis** method returns a **long** primitive representing the number of milliseconds since 00:00:00 GMT January 1, 1970, a base time commonly used with Unix systems. This is the method to use if you want to time a particular routine, because the **java.util.Date** class is rather clumsy to use.

The Fast *arraycopy* Method

Java operators for working with arrays are inherently slowed by the fact that each array access is checked against the known size of the array. Suppose you needed to make a copy of an array, **myX**, of **int** primitives, known to be **mxX** in size. Doing it this way

```
1. int[] aX = new int[ mxX ];
2. for(int i = 0 ; i < mxX ; i++){ aX[i] = myX[i] ; }
```

would perform array bounds checks in both **aX** and **myX** for every *i* value. Obviously, if a method could first check whether the highest index is legal, all of the other bounds checks would be unnecessary. The **System.arraycopy** method does exactly that and uses optimized native code to do the actual copying. Here is the way the **arraycopy** method would replace line 2 in the preceding example:

```
2. System.arraycopy( myX, 0, aX, 0, mxX ) ;
```

All of the Java classes, such as **StringBuffer** and **Vector**, which expand as needed to hold more elements, use **System.arraycopy** to copy their current contents into enlarged arrays.

Stopping An Application

The **System** class provides the **exit** method to stop the Java Virtual Machine (JVM). It is called with an **int** status code that is returned to the operating system. By convention, a nonzero status indicates that an error has occurred:

```
System.exit( status );
```

The **exit** method should not be called in a Java applet. It is the Web browser's responsibility to halt the JVM as needed.

Getting A *Runtime* Reference

A single **Runtime** object is automatically created when a program starts. You can get a reference to it as follows:

```
Runtime rt = Runtime.getRuntime();
```

Many of the **Runtime** methods, such as the garbage collector request (**gc**) are frequently called through the **System** class. **System.gc** actually calls the **Runtime** object's **gc** method. Other handy methods in the **Runtime** class include **total-Memory** and **freeMemory,** which return the total number of bytes the JVM has access to and the amount that is available for new object construction.

The **java.math** Package

The 1.1 release of Java added a **java.math** package with the **BigDecimal** and **BigInteger** classes for arbitrary precision arithmetic. Objects created from these classes can represent numbers with any desired degree of precision, and the methods can conduct any of Java's normal arithmetic operations. The **BigDecimal** methods are used primarily for financial calculations in which the rounding method needs to be specified exactly. **BigInteger** is mostly of interest to programmers doing cryptography.

The Reflection Package

An important innovation that first appeared in Java 1.1 is the Reflection API. Classes in the **java.lang.reflect** package allow a program to discover the variables, methods, and constructors available in any class, and the interfaces implemented. This capability is essential to the JavaBeans concept and to the Serialization API.

Access to class information starts with getting a **Class** object using the static **forName** method in the **java.lang.Class** class, which takes a **String** input:

```
1.   Class c = Class.forName( namestr );
```

This object is then used to get instances of the classes in the **java.lang.reflect** package that are specialized for providing information about the individual variables, methods, interfaces, and constructors:

```
2.   Field[] fields = c.getDeclaredFields();
3.   Method[] methods = c.getDeclaredMethods();
4.   Class[] interfaces = c.getInterfaces();
5.   Constructor[] constructors = c.getDeclaredConstructors();
```

In line 4, the interfaces that a class implements are represented as **Class** objects because interface specifications are compiled to class files. Most programmers will not have to work with the Reflection API directly. The important thing for you is that Reflection permits JavaBeans and object serialization.

JavaBeans

The JavaBeans API allows the creation of reusable "software components" that can be manipulated in a visual development tool. The usefulness of the "plugging components together to make a program" model of software development is shown by the great success of Visual Basic. With JavaBeans, you can have a rapid development environment and the virtue of Java's true object orientation.

The Reflection API classes and methods permit a development tool to present the programmer with a list of the properties of a JavaBean component without having access to the source code. This in turn makes it feasible for developers to create and sell toolkits of JavaBean components.

Serialization

Object serialization, which was introduced with Java 1.1, refers to the ability to write out the complete state of an object to a file or over a network connection to another computer. To recreate the object, the receiving computer takes the class file for the class that the object belongs to and uses the Reflection API to understand how to rebuild the object. The classes **ObjectOutputStream** and **ObjectInputStream,** which perform serialization, are discussed in Chapter 14.

The *Serializable* Interface

Only objects that implement the **java.io.Serializable** interface can be serialized with the **ObjectOutputStream** and **ObjectInputStream** standard classes. This interface does not define any methods or constants. It just exists to tag an object as being serializable. For Java 2 (JDK 1.2), a surprisingly large number of classes in the standard library have been made serializable.

Utility Classes In The java.util Package

The **java.util** package has been greatly expanded for JDK 1.2. In this section, I will review the most commonly used interfaces and classes.

The Arrays Class

The new **java.util.Arrays** class is similar in purpose to the **java.lang.Math** class. It contains many static methods for sorting and searching arrays of the Java primitives and arrays of objects. This class can also be used to create array objects and manipulate individual elements.

The **Arrays** class also provides a method for creating a **List** object from the data in an array of objects (but not an array of primitives). **List** is a new interface for collections of objects (which is discussed in a later section titled "The New Collections"). Here is an example of this transformation in action:

```
String[] days = { "Mon","Tue","Wed","Thu","Fri","Sat","Sun"};
List dayList = Arrays.asList ( days );
```

However, the **List** that is created simply provides methods for accessing the array as a **List**; it does not create a separate copy of the data.

The Comparator Interface

The new **Comparator** interface in the **java.util** package allows the programmer to define principles for ordering and comparing custom objects. This means that your custom objects will automatically be able to use all of the sorting and searching methods in the new **Arrays** class. All you have to provide is a method named **compare,** which takes two object references, **oA** and **oB,** and returns an integer that is negative, zero, or positive (if **oA** is less than, equal to, or greater than **oB**).

The Original Collections

These classes in the **java.util** package were the only ones for dealing with collections of objects in the initial release of Java. Although simple, they are very powerful, and you will undoubtedly find them used in many code examples. The new Collections API will supplement rather than supplant these original collection classes.

Vector

The **Vector** class holds an array of **Object** references that can automatically grow in size as needed. Because all Java classes inherit from **Object,** you can add any reference to a **Vector.** Various methods provide for retrieving objects by index and for searching. The internal storage order retains the order in which objects are added. All of the **Vector** methods that alter the contents are **synchronized** to coordinate access by multiple threads.

For the JDK 1.2 release of Java, several changes were made to the **Vector** class. These changes do not break existing code but add functions to make **Vector** compatible with the new Collections API. In particular, **Vector** now implements the **List** interface (discussed later in this chapter).

The *Hashtable* Object

A **Hashtable** object can store and retrieve "value" objects indexed by "key" objects. Originally, this class was derived from the abstract **Dictionary** class, but this approach was made obsolete by the new Collections API. **Hashtable** still extends **Dictionary,** but for JDK 1.2, **Hashtable** implements the new **Map** interface. **Hashtable** objects are used extensively in Java to associate objects with names efficiently.

For example, this code fragment creates a **Hashtable** and stores a URL **String** with a short **String** as a key:

```
1. Hashtable pageTable = new Hashtable();
2. String page = "http://www.coriolis.com" ;
3. String key = "coriolis";
4. pageTable.put( key, page );
```

Because the methods that retrieve objects from **Hashtable**s are defined as returning an **Object** reference, you have to provide a specific cast, as in the following line, that would retrieve the **String** stored in the **Hashtable:**

```
String val = (String)pageTable.get("coriolis");
```

A **Hashtable** can only store one "value" per "key"—if you add a new reference with a duplicate key, the old reference is dropped. The **contains** and **containsKey** methods let you discover whether a given object or key is present. Internally, **Hashtables** store object references according to hashcodes, so if you get an **Enumeration** of all of the stored "value" or "key" objects, the order is not predictable.

The *Stack* Class

This class, which extends **Vector**, lets you store objects in a last-in/first-out (LIFO) stack. In addition to the **Vector** methods, **push** and **pop** methods let you manipulate the objects on the top of the stack. The following code fragment illustrates the use of a **Stack** of numeric operands (**opStack**) with **Double** wrapper objects in a calculator application. The method puts the result back on the **Stack** and also returns the value. In this case, we know that **opStack** has only **Double** objects and that at least two objects are on the **Stack**:

```
1. double addTopTwo(){
2.    double d1 = ((Double)opStack.pop()).doubleValue() ;
3.    double d2 = ((Double)opStack.pop()).doubleValue()  + d1 ;
4.    opStack.push( new Double( d2 ) );
5.    return d2 ;
6. }
```

The *Enumeration* Interface

The **Enumeration** interface provides a way to iterate over all of the objects contained in a **Vector, Hashtable,** or **Stack.** For example, if **v** is a **Vector,** the following code would do a **println** for every object contained in the **Vector:**

```
1. for (Enumeration e = v.elements(); e.hasMoreElements(); ){
2.    System.out.println( e.nextElement() ) ;
3. }
```

While an **Enumeration** is in use, nothing can be allowed to modify the underlying **Vector** data because the **Enumeration** is still using it. If you need to continue using the **Vector,** create the **Enumeration** from a clone of the **Vector** as in the following code fragment:

```
1. Vector clonev = (Vector)v.clone();
2. for (Enumeration e = clonev.elements(); e.hasMoreElements(); ){
3.    System.out.println( e.nextElement() ) ;
4. }
```

The new Collections API provides the **Iterator** interface that is expected to supplant the **Enumeration** interface in most applications. The **Vector, Stack,** and **Hashtable** classes have been modified for JDK 1.2 to support both the **Enumeration** and **Iterator** interfaces.

The New Collections

One of the biggest changes in the Java standard library with the JDK 1.2 release is the introduction of a totally new set of classes and interfaces for dealing with collections of objects. This new Collections API has many benefits for the programmer, primarily as a standard for communication between unrelated toolkits. For example, a database query that results in a **Collection** can cooperate seamlessly with an interface toolkit that expects a **Collection**.

The new classes also cooperate well with each other and with Java arrays. For example, **Collections** can be converted into arrays of objects.

Collections API Interfaces

The basis for the new Collections API is a set of six interfaces that define the basic types. These are supplemented by a set of "Abstract Implementation" classes that implement the interfaces to provide root classes suitable for extension by the programmer.

Although there are a huge number of classes that implement these interfaces, the intent of the designers is that most programmers will use the interface methods as much as possible; therefore, you should concentrate on learning the interfaces first.

The *Collection Interface*

This interface is the root of the Collections API hierarchy and defines the basic functions that all **Collection** classes must provide. The **AbstractCollection** class provides a skeleton set of the interface methods to serve as a starting point for concrete classes. Among other things, the **Collection** interface requires methods for adding, removing, locating, and selecting objects. Classes implementing **Collection** may contain duplicates and null values.

The *Set Interface*

A class implementing this interface holds objects in an order that is fixed when the set is created. No duplicates are allowed, and at most, one element can have the **null** value. The **Set** interface extends the **Collection** interface, so any class implementing **Set** also implements **Collection**.

The *List Interface*

A class implementing this interface holds an ordered collection of objects. The **Vector** class as revised for JDK 1.2 implements the **List** interface. The AWT graphics package also contains a **List** class used for presenting a list of choices. This means you may have to specify the full name **java.awt.List** or **java.util.List** to avoid confusing the compiler. The **List** interface extends the **Collection** interface.

The *Map* Interface

A class implementing **Map** associates "key" objects with "value" objects. Each key must be unique. The **Hashtable** class as modified for JDK 1.2 implements the **Map** interface. The actual order of the keys and values is not specified.

The *SortedSet* Interface

This interface extends the **Set** interface by adding the requirement that the contents be ordered. Only objects that implement the **Comparator** interface or can be compared by an external **Comparator** object can be held by a **SortedSet**.

The *SortedMap* Interface

This interface extends the **Map** interface by adding the requirement that the collection will be ordered according to key values.

The Iterator Interface

This interface replaces the **Enumeration** interface that was used in Java 1.0. An object implementing **Iterator** lets the programmer examine every object in a **Collection** in a fixed order. All classes implementing **Collection** must have an **iterator** method that returns an **Iterator** object. The main changes from **Enumeration** are more compact names, and a method that allows the removal of an object from the underlying **Collection**. Table 10.2 summarizes the **Iterator** methods.

The Collections API Classes

The JDK 1.2 standard library has a large number of classes that implement the new Collections API interfaces. It is unlikely that you will need to have detailed knowledge of these classes for the exam. For details on these classes, consult the JDK documentation.

Table 10.2 Iterator interface methods.		
Iterator Method	**Returns**	**Replaces Enumeration Method**
hasNext	boolean	hasMoreElements
next	Object	nextElement
remove	void	(no equivalent)

The *Abstract* Classes

These classes provide a barebones implementation of most of the methods required by the various interfaces to make it easier for the programmer to extend in concrete implementations:

➤ **AbstractCollection** This class implements all of the methods of the **Collection** interface except **iterator** and **size**. It is extended by **AbstractList** and **AbstractSet**.

➤ **AbstractList** This class extends **AbstractCollection** and implements the **List** interface.

➤ **AbstractMap** This class implements the **Map** interface.

➤ **AbstractSequentialList** This class extends the **AbstractList** class, and provides the basis for the **LinkedList** class.

➤ **AbstractSet** This class extends **AbstractCollection** and implements the **Set** interface.

Some Concrete Classes

Finally, it's time for some non-abstract classes. Here is a quick survey of the classes most likely to be useful to the programmer:

➤ **ArrayList** This class, which extends **AbstractList**, is roughly equivalent to the **Vector** class in the original library. It can expand as needed just like **Vector**, but does not use **synchronized** methods, so it is somewhat faster.

➤ **HashMap** This class extends **AbstractMap** and is similar to **Hashtable** in the original library.

➤ **LinkedList** An implementation of the classic linked list data structure.

➤ **TreeMap** Extending **AbstractMap** and implementing the **SortedMap** interface, a **TreeMap** object keeps entries in ascending key order.

The *Collections* Class

Now here is a source of potential confusion! The **java.util.Collections** class, not to be confused with the **java.util.Collection** interface, implements a number of utility methods that can be applied to objects implementing the various interfaces in the Collections API. For example, there are methods for sorting objects contained in a **List** and for searching for an object in an ordered collection.

Probably the most significant methods in the **Collections** class are used to wrap objects implementing the various Collections API interfaces in code that enforces **synchronized** access to the data. For example, if you had an object implementing **Map**, named **myMap**, the following code would give you a reference to a new **Map** that accesses the existing data but with **synchronized** methods:

```
Map safeMap = Collections.synchronizedMap( myMap );
```

Performance Considerations

In Java 1.1 and earlier versions, most of the methods in the **Vector, Hashtable,** and **Stack** classes were **synchronized** to prevent "simultaneous" modification by more than one **Thread,** which would lead to unpredictable results. The disadvantage of synchronization is the extra overhead imposed by the process that obtains and releases object locks. The new **Collections** classes do not use synchronization; instead, they throw a **ConcurrentModificationException** if more than one **Thread** tries to modify a **Collection.**

Thus, it is up to the programmer to decide whether a risk exists and make provisions for preventing simultaneous modification. As previously described, the **Collections** class provides a set of methods that "wrap" the unsynchronized collections in an object that synchronizes all of the access methods. There is one of each of these methods for each interface. However, an **Iterator** derived from the synchronized collection has to be protected separately by the programmer's code:

```
// In the following, List syncL is a local reference used to get an
  Iterator
// and L is a reference to an object implementing the List
  interface
// The reference that is returned is to a static nested in the
// Collections class, name SynchronizedList but that class only has
  package
// visibility so we have to refer to it by the List interface
List syncL = Collections.synchronizedList( L )
// now all normal list methods should use syncL to be safe
// except that if you need an Iterator, it should be synchronized
// on the list separately as follows
  synchronized( syncL ) {
      Iterator isL = syncL.iterator();
      while( isL.hasNext() ) doSomething( isL.next() );
  } // end synchronized access
```

Practice Questions

Question 1

> You need a method to take a **double** primitive value and return
> the square root, ignoring the sign. Which one of these options
> is correct?
>
> ○ a.
> ```
> double mySqrt( double val ){
>       return Math.sqrt( val );
>    }
> ```
>
> ○ b.
> ```
> double mySqrt( double val ){
>       return Math.sqrt( Math.abs( val ) ) ;
>    }
> ```
>
> ○ c.
> ```
> double mySqrt( double val ){
>       Math myM = new Math();
>       return myM.sqrt( myM.abs( val )) ;
>    }
> ```

Answer b correctly uses the **Math static** methods to take the absolute value of
the input before passing it to the square root function. Answer a is incorrect
because it does not take into account the possibility of a negative input. Answer c is incorrect because it attempts to create and use a **Math** object, which is
not possible.

Question 2

> Trying to compile the following method causes an error:
>
> ```
> 1. public void status( Boolean flag ){
> 2.    if( flag ) {
> 3.        System.out.println("TRUE!");
> 4.    }
> 5.    else System.out.println("FALSE!");
> 6. }
> ```
>
> Which of the following suggested changes will allow the method to compile? [Check all correct answers]
>
> ❑ a. Change line 2 to read:
>
> ```
> 2.    if( flag.equals( true ) ){
> ```
>
> ❑ b. Change line 1 to read:
>
> ```
> 1. public void status( boolean flag ){
> ```
>
> ❑ c. Change line 2 to read:
>
> ```
> 2.    if( flag.booleanValue()){
> ```

Answers b and c are correct. Answer b is correct because it changes the input parameter to the primitive **boolean** type expected by the **if** statement. Answer c is also correct because it gets the **boolean** value contained in the **Boolean** object. Answer a is incorrect because the **equals** method requires an object reference, and **true** is a **boolean** primitive value.

Question 3

> Here are some statements about the **java.lang.System** class. Which of the following statements is correct?
>
> ○ a. You must initialize **System** with a path and filename if you want to use the **System.err** output.
>
> ○ b. The **System.timer** method allows timing processes to the nearest microsecond.
>
> ○ c. The **System.arraycopy** method works only with arrays of primitives.
>
> ○ d. The **System.exit** method takes an **int** primitive parameter.

Only answer d is correct. The **exit** method expects an **int** primitive, which by convention is 0 if no error has occurred. Answer a is incorrect. **System.err** is automatically created when your program starts. Answer b is incorrect—no such method exists. Answer c is incorrect because **arraycopy** can copy arrays of primitives or object references.

Question 4

Which of the following statements about the **java.lang.Runtime** class is incorrect?

○ a. A **Runtime** object is created by the following code:

```
Runtime rt = Runtime.getRuntime();
```

○ b. There is a **Runtime** method to request that the JVM start garbage collection.

○ c. The following **Runtime** method call returns the approximate amount of free memory available to the JVM:

```
long avail = Runtime.getRuntime().freeMemory();
```

Answer a is correct because the statement is in error: a **Runtime** object is created when the program is started, and the **getRuntime** method simply returns a reference to it. Answer b is incorrect because the statement is correct. Answer c is incorrect because the statement shows the correct way to call the **Runtime** **freeMemory** method.

Question 5

Which of the following statements about the **java.util.Vector** and **java.util.Hashtable** classes are correct? [Check all correct answers]

❑ a. A **Vector** can hold object references or primitive values.

❑ b. A **Vector** maintains object references in the order they were added.

❑ c. A **Hashtable** requires **String** objects as keys.

❑ d. A **Hashtable** maintains object references in the order they were added.

❑ e. Both **Vector** and **Hashtable** use **synchronized** methods to avoid problems due to more than one **Thread** trying to access the same collection.

Answers b and e are correct. Answer b is correct because **Vector** objects maintain the order in which objects are added. Answer e is correct because this is one of the major distinctions between the original and new Collections API classes. Answer a is incorrect. Only object references can be held in a **Vector**. If you need to store primitive values, you have to use the wrapper classes to create objects. Answer c is incorrect. Although keys are frequently **Strings**, they can be any object. Answer d is incorrect because the order of items in a **Hashtable** is not predictable.

Question 6

In a celestial navigation application, you need a method to take a sextant reading in degrees and return the tangent of the angle. Which of the following options will do the job?

○ a.
```
double calcTan( double angle ){
    return Math.tan( angle * Math.PI /180.0 );
   }
```

○ b.
```
double calcTan( double angle ){
    return Math.tan( angle * PI /180.0 ) ;
   }
```

○ c.
```
double calcTan( double angle ){
    return Math.tan( angle );
   }
```

○ d.
```
double calcTan( double angle ){
    Math myM = new Math( );
    return myM.tan( angle * (myM.PI /180.0));
   }
```

Answer a is correct because it recognizes that all **Math** trig functions take angle inputs in radians and uses the **PI** constant to convert. Answer b is incorrect because it does not address the **PI** constant correctly. Answer c is incorrect because the question specified that the angle was in degrees and the trig functions require radians. Answer d is incorrect because it attempts to create a **Math** object, which is not possible.

Question 7

The new Collections API introduces a number of new interfaces and classes to the Java standard library. From the following options, select the names that represent interfaces. [Check all correct answers]

- ❑ a. **java.util.List**
- ❑ b. **java.util.TreeMap**
- ❑ c. **java.util.AbstractList**
- ❑ d. **java.util.SortedMap**
- ❑ e. **java.util.Iterator**
- ❑ f. **java.util.Collections**

Answers a, d, and e are correct. These are the names of interfaces. Answer b is incorrect because **TreeMap** is a class that implements the **SortedMap** interface. Answer c is incorrect because **AbstractList** is an abstract class implementing the **List** interface. Answer f is incorrect because **Collections** (with a final s) is a utility class that you must distinguish from the **Collection** (no final s) interface.

Question 8

The **java.lang.reflect.Method** class is used to obtain information on the methods available in a given class. How do you get a **Method** object?

- ○ a. From any instance of the class to be examined
- ○ b. From a **Class** object created using the name of the class to be examined
- ○ c. From a **Reflect** object created using the name of the class to be examined

Answer b is correct. You obtain an array of **Method** objects from the **Class** object representing the class to be examined. Answer a is incorrect because there is no method in the **Object** class to obtain a **Method** object. Answer c is incorrect because there is no such thing as a **Reflect** object.

Question 9

> Which of the following classes in the new Collections API is most similar to the **Vector** class?
>
> ○ a. **LinkedList**
> ○ b. **TreeSet**
> ○ c. **AbstractCollection**
> ○ d. **ArrayList**
> ○ e. **Collections**

Answer d is correct. The **ArrayList** is similar in function to the **Vector** class. Answer a is incorrect because the **LinkedList** provides many functions in excess of those in **Vector**. Answer b is incorrect because a **TreeSet** has restrictions on duplicated items that do not occur in **Vector**. Answer c is incorrect because **AbstractCollection** is an abstract class. Answer e is incorrect because the **Collections** class is a utility class used, among other things, for sorting and transforming collections.

Question 10

> An object of the **Hashtable** class can store and retrieve object references based on associated "key" objects. Which of the following interfaces does **Hashtable** implement?
>
> ○ a. **SortedMap**
> ○ b. **Map**
> ○ c. **List**
> ○ d. **SortedSet**

Answer b is correct. **Hashtable** implements the **Map** interface. Answer a is incorrect because the **SortedMap** would require that **Hashtable** impose a sorting order on keys, which it does not. Answer c is incorrect because the **List** interface does not require keys to recover stored objects. Answer d is incorrect because a **SortedSet** is a completely different kind of collection.

Need To Know More?

 Flanagan, David: *Java in a Nutshell, 2nd edition*. O'Reilly & Associates, Inc., Sebastopol, CA, 1997. ISBN: 1-56592-262-X. This is the most compact desktop reference book documenting the Java language. Chapter 30 addresses the utility classes, but only those in Java 1.1.

 ftp://ftp.javasoft.com/docs/tutorial.zip

An excellent tutorial in HTML form can be downloaded from this site (although this document is updated frequently, it may not be entirely current with JDK 1.2 information).

 http://java.sun.com:80/beans/software/bdk_download.html

The Bean Development Kit (BDK) provides a testing environment for JavaBean development and a number of sample beans which you can use as a basis for your own bean development. You can download the BDK from this site.

 http://java.sun.com/products/jdk/1.2/index.html

The Java API documentation in Javadoc-generated form can be downloaded from Sun Microsystems. Although this site changes a lot, it was a good starting point the last time I looked.

The Java AWT Components

11

Terms you'll need to understand:

- √ **Component** class
- √ **Container** class
- √ **Frame** class
- √ **Panel** class
- √ **MenuItem** class
- √ **Graphics** class
- √ **Font** class
- √ **FontMetrics** class
- √ **Color** class

Techniques you'll need to master:

- √ Controlling user access to interface elements
- √ Understanding the AWT class hierarchy
- √ Understanding how to control the appearance of text
- √ Understanding how to control the placement and appearance of user controls

The Abstract Windowing Toolkit (AWT) library is the essential basis for creating graphical user interfaces (GUIs) in Java. It will take several chapters to cover the topics you need to understand when building graphical user interfaces in Java. This chapter concentrates on the AWT component library. Chapter 12 covers layout managers and interface building topics, and Chapter 13 covers handling user events.

Overview Of The AWT Packages

The original release of Java used a relatively simple set of classes to create user interfaces. As people tried developing more complex user interfaces, the deficiencies in these classes became apparent. The 1.1 release of Java fixed some of the problems, especially those stemming from the crude interface event handling of the 1.0 release. This improved event handling is used in the Java 1.2 (JDK) release.

The main additions to the AWT library for the Java JDK 1.2 are designed to provide much greater flexibility and power, but they still rely on basic AWT concepts. There are now 11 related **java.awt** packages; the following list gives a short description of each:

➤ **java.awt** The set of classes used to create user interfaces in the original release of Java. Although many simple concepts in the original AWT now have more advanced capabilities in additional packages, the original classes still work.

➤ **java.awt.color** Advanced color manipulation classes that provide for representing and converting colors in a variety of standard forms.

➤ **java.awt.datatransfer** Classes that facilitate cut-and-paste operations between Java components and with native applications. Note that MIME types play an important role.

➤ **java.awt.dnd** Classes to support a drag-and-drop user interface.

➤ **java.awt.event** Classes that encapsulate and process the huge variety of events that can occur in a program with a graphical user interface.

➤ **java.awt.font** Classes providing advanced text layout and rendering with techniques much more powerful than the original AWT. These techniques provide better support for international alphabets and symbol systems.

➤ **java.awt.geom** Advanced 2D drawing capabilities are supported by classes in this package.

➤ **java.awt.im** Contains the **InputContext** class, which manages communication between user input events and text editing components, and the **InputMethodHighlight** class, which handles text highlighting in a variety of languages.

➤ **java.awt.image** This package, which was in the original Java release, has been greatly expanded with a variety of image manipulation classes.

➤ **java.awt.renderable** A group of classes to make image rendering more flexible.

➤ **java.awt.print** This group of classes supports flexible printing from Java applications.

The Basic AWT Classes

One of the reasons for the rise in popularity of object-oriented programming is the ease with which screen objects can have corresponding software objects. The AWT classes illustrate very clearly the virtues of object-oriented programming. By basing almost all of the display classes on the **Component** class, the designers greatly simplified the interface designer's task. All of the graphical objects that inherit from **Component** can use the same method calls for basic functions.

Component Class

Objects derived from **Component** have a graphical representation on the screen and can interact with the user. **Component** is an **abstract** class, which is extended by a large number of classes in various packages.

To rapidly get Java 1.0 available on several different operating systems, the designers used the facilities of the underlying operating system as much as possible. Thus, to show a **Button** on the screen, Java has the operating system create a corresponding object. These native operating system objects that correspond to Java objects are called *peers*, and the resulting combination of a Java object and an operating system object is called a *heavyweight* component.

There are many more methods in the **Component** class than I have room to discuss here. The following are the methods you are most likely to be using, arranged in functional groups. In general, if you need a way to control the appearance or behavior of a screen object in the **java.awt** package, start your search by looking at the methods in the **Component** class.

In the following discussion, I'll show the method return type, name, and parameter list as it appears in the javadoc documentation. I use the word component to refer to any graphical object having **Component** as an ancestor.

Controlling Position And Size

Component objects always occupy a rectangle on the screen. Position is always relative to the containing object, not to the overall screen. Note that if a layout manager is controlling a container, these methods may be ineffective. Layout managers are discussed in Chapter 12. The following list shows the commonly used methods related to component position and size:

➤ **void setBounds(int x, int y, int width, int height)** This method sets the location of the upper-left corner of the component and its width and height in pixels. Another version takes a **Rectangle** as input.

➤ **setLocation(int x, int y)** Moves the component. Another version takes a **Point** as input.

➤ **setSize(int width, int height)** Resizes the component.

➤ **Rectangle getBounds()** Returns a **Rectangle** object with the component's location and size.

➤ **boolean contains(int x, int y)** Returns **true** if this point is inside the component.

 Screen positions are always measured in pixels from the upper-left corner of the container. The upper-left pixel is at x = 0 and y = 0, with x increasing to the right and y increasing downward. For an independent window, the measurement is from the upper-left corner of the screen.

Controlling Appearance

Each component has a set of defaults for background and foreground colors and for the font to be used. If you don't set these, the default values of the container this component is in will be used when a font or color is required. If you don't specify any appearance factors, the JVM will provide defaults. Not all components will use the background color you set because the appearance of these heavyweight components depends on the operating system peer.

➤ **void setBackground(Color c)** When the component is repainted, this is the default background color. The **Color** object is discussed later.

➤ **void setForeground(Color c)** Sets the default color to be used to draw lines or text in this component.

➤ **void setFont(Font f)** This method sets the default font to be used when drawing text.

➤ **void setCursor(Cursor cr)** This method establishes the cursor image that will be displayed when the cursor is over the component.

The size of a component can be set with one of the following methods:

➤ **setSize(int width, int height)** Sets the size; width and height are in pixels.

➤ **setBounds(int x, int y, int width, int height)** This sets both size and position of the upper-left corner relative to the container.

However, the size you set with one of these methods may be overridden by a layout manager. Layout managers are discussed in Chapter 12.

Control Of User Access And Visibility

In user interface design, you will frequently want to permit use of **Button** objects and other controls according to the program state. For example, you might want to enable a Save button only when data has been modified.

➤ **void setEnabled(boolean flag)** By default, components are enabled when created, but you can use this method to disable and re-enable them. An enabled component can respond to user input and generate events. For components such as buttons, the enabled state is reflected in the way they are displayed.

➤ **void setVisible(boolean flag)** If the flag is **true,** the component is shown; if **false,** it is not displayed. This replaces the **show** method used in Java 1.0.

Figure 11.1 shows **java.awt.Label** and **java.awt.Button** objects in their enabled and disabled states on a Windows NT system. On another operating system, the appearance might be different.

Event Generation

Component objects can generate a variety of events based on the user's actions with mouse and keyboard. Event handling is discussed in detail in Chapter 13. The important thing to note here is that the programmer has control over which events a **Component** will generate. The **AWTEvent** class defines "event mask" constants for each of the various types of events that can be generated by a **Component.** You can combine these into a single **long** primitive that has a bit set for each type of event to be generated, for example:

```
long mask = AWTEvent.ACTION_EVENT_MASK | AWTEvent.FOCUS_EVENT_MASK;
```

Figure 11.1   The appearance of enabled and disabled **Label** and **Button** objects.

The methods that use this mask are:

➤ **void disableEvents(long bitmask)** Generation of the events specified in the bitmask is turned off.

➤ **void enableEvents(long bitmask)** Generation of the events specified in the bitmask is turned on.

The Subclasses Of Component

These are the most commonly used of the classes in the **java.awt** package that extend **Component**. The Swing classes that are in other packages also extend **Component**, but they are not covered in the exam.

➤ **Button** This class creates a labeled button in the style of the underlying operating system. Clicking on a **Button** creates an **ActionEvent**.

➤ **Canvas** This class is typically extended to create a screen component with a custom **paint** method to generate a display.

➤ **Checkbox** This class creates the typical checkbox, which displays an on or off state. **Checkbox** objects controlled by a **CheckboxGroup** will appear as radio buttons.

➤ **Choice** A **Choice** object presents a pop-up style menu of choices.

➤ **Container** This class is the parent of a range of AWT components that can hold a number of components and control their display. See the following **Container** class section for an extended discussion.

➤ **Label** A **Label** object displays a single line of noneditable text.

➤ **List** A **List** object presents a scrollable list of items that the user can select. The programmer can control whether multiple selections are allowed.

➤ **Scrollbar** This class can be used to create a vertical or horizontal scroll bar in the style of the underlying operating system.

➤ **TextComponent** This class is extended by **TextField** and **TextArea**, which are the classes actually used in interface design. A **TextField** object allows editing of a single line of text, whereas a **TextArea** handles multiple line input.

Text Entry Classes

There are two AWT components designed for user text entry: **TextField** for a single line and **TextArea** for multiple lines. Both of these are extensions of the

TextComponent class, which contains many of the methods you will need to control user text input. Some of the most useful are as follows:

➤ **void setEditable(boolean flag)** Use this method to allow or prevent user editing of the displayed text.

➤ **void setText(String s)** The present contents of the field are replaced with this **String**. To clear the field, set the text to "" (the empty **String**).

➤ **String getText()** This method returns a **String** representing the entire contents of the component. The size of the largest **String** a **TextComponent** can hold depends on the underlying operating system.

➤ **String getSelectedText()** This method returns the text that the user has highlighted.

Don't confuse the **setEditable** method with the **setEnabled** method in the **Component** class. A **TextComponent** can be *enabled,* but not *editable,* in which case the user can select text and move the cursor around in the field but cannot change the text. Figure 11.2 shows two **TextField** objects, both of which are enabled. The right field shows an editing cursor that can be moved through the text with the keyboard arrow keys, but the text can't be changed.

Interfaces Implemented By Component

The following interfaces are implemented by the **java.awt.Component** class and thus by all subclasses of **Component**:

➤ **ImageObserver** This interface provides for notifying a component about changes in **Image** information. This is necessary because Java can accomplish image loading as a background process that may not have a complete image ready when a component is ready to be painted. The method that is required by this interface is **imageUpdate**; this method is called by the process loading an image to report status changes.

➤ **MenuContainer** This interface provides methods used to coordinate with menu-related classes. You are not likely to have to deal with these methods directly.

➤ **Serializable** This interface serves to tag objects that can be saved to a file or other output stream. The significance for programmers is that the

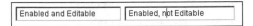

Figure 11.2   Two apparently identical text fields, only one of which is editable.

entire collection of objects that make up a user interface can be written to a file with all of their state data intact and later read back in to reconstruct the interface.

The **Container** Class

The **Container** class adds to **Component** the capability of containing other AWT graphical components. **Container** is an **abstract** class, but you can create a **java.awt.Container** object.

The main function of a **Container** is to maintain and control a list of the components it contains. The order of components in the list is determined by the order of addition unless you use one of the **add** methods that specifies an absolute list position.

Be sure you can distinguish between the functions provided by a **Container** and those provided by a **LayoutManager** object. **LayoutManager**s are covered in Chapter 12.

Container Methods

The methods that **Container** adds to **Component** generally have to do with adding, removing, positioning, and locating components. Here are some of the most frequently used:

➤ **void add(Component c)** Adds this component to the internal list. Alternate forms of this method provide for specifying various constraints on the layout affecting this component.

➤ **void remove(Component c)** Removes this component from the list.

➤ **void setLayout(LayoutManager m)** Puts this **LayoutManger** object in charge of laying out the contained components. **LayoutManager** objects are discussed in Chapter 12.

➤ **void validate()** Causes the **Container** to lay out all of the contained components. Usually called after components have been added or removed.

➤ **int getComponentCount()** Returns the number of components in this container.

➤ **Component getComponentAt(int x, int y)** Returns a reference to the component located at this position relative to the container.

The Subclasses Of Container

Container was an **abstract** class in Java 1.0 and 1.1, but for the Java JDK 1.2 it is no longer declared **abstract**. Nevertheless, you are more likely to be using one of the following classes in an actual program. Note that a *top-level* container is one that can create an independent window.

➤ **java.awt.Panel** The **Panel** class provides the simplest AWT container.

➤ **java.awt.ScrollPane** A **ScrollPane** object provides scrolling action for the display of a single component that is larger than the available display area.

➤ **java.applet.Applet** The **Applet** class is an extension of **Panel** with provision for interacting with a Web browser so that it can be a top-level container.

➤ **java.awt.Window** A **Window** object is a top-level window with no borders and no menu bar or window controls.

➤ **java.awt.Dialog** A top-level window with a title bar typically used to get user input. Although a **Dialog** forms an independent window, it must have a **Frame** as its owner.

➤ **java.awt.Frame** This extension of **Window** adds a title bar, menu bar, and window control widgets. A **Frame** must be the top-level container for applications.

The Container-Contents Relationship

The relationship of a **Container** to its contents forms a sort of hierarchy of relationships that may lead to some confusion. For example, if you have a **Button** object in a **Panel**, the following code

```
Container c = myButton.getParent() ;
```

returns a reference to the **Panel**, not the parent class of **myButton**. You may also see this relationship referred to as the **Panel** *owning* **myButton**. This terminology of *owner* extends to independent windows, such as **Dialog** objects. If an application based on **Frame** creates a **Dialog**, it is said that the owner of the **Dialog** is the **Frame**, in spite of the fact that they are two separate windows.

By default, **Component** objects inherit the colors and **Font** properties of the container they are in. This means that you don't have to set the font style for every component in an application—just set it for the primary container and the rest of the interface will use that font.

The **Window**-Related Classes

The **Window** class extends **Container** and creates top-level window objects that do not have a menu bar or window controls. The classes in the **java.awt** package that extend **Window** are **Frame** and **Dialog**. Although a **Window** is an independent top-level window, to properly interface with the operating system, it must be constructed from a **Frame** or another **Window**. The constructors for a **Window** are:

➤ **Window(Frame owner)** Creates a new **Window** "owned" by the **Frame**. The new **Window** is not initially visible. When you are ready for the **Window** to be displayed, call the **show** method.

➤ **Window(Window owner)** Creates a new **Window** "owned" by another **Window**.

Window objects can be sized and moved with the basic **Component** methods, but note that the positioning will be relative to the upper-left corner of the screen.

Creating A Frame

The **java.awt.Frame** class is the starting point for creating a graphical application using the AWT components. Listing 11.1 shows the minimum code for creating a **Frame**, and Figure 11.3 shows the resulting window.

Listing 11.1   Source code for a simple Frame.

```
1. import java.awt.* ;
2. import java.awt.event.* ;
3. class FrameDemo extends Frame {
4.  public static void main(String[] args ){
5.     new FrameDemo().show();
6.  }
7.  // constructor for FrameDemo
8.  FrameDemo(){
9.    super("Example Frame");
10.   setBounds( 10, 10, 200, 150 );
11.   addWindowListener( new WindowAdapter(){
12.      public void  windowClosing( WindowEvent e ){
13.           setVisible( false );
14.           dispose();
15.           System.exit(0);
16.      }
17.   } ); // end statement starting on line 11
18.  } // end constructor
19. } // end class
```

Figure 11.3   The appearance of a **FrameDemo** application on a Windows NT system.

Here are the important points to note about the **FrameDemo** code:

➤ The constructor in line 9 sets the title for the **Frame**. There is also a constructor without a title, in which case the title bar is empty.

➤ The call to **setBounds** in line 10 establishes the size and position of the **Frame** relative to the upper-left corner of the screen. Without this call, a **Frame** barely large enough to show the window controls would show at the upper-left corner of the screen.

➤ The statement that starts in line 11 and continues to line 17 creates an anonymous inner class extending **WindowAdapter** and installing it as a **WindowListener**. Event listeners will be discussed in Chapter 13; for right now, note that this listener is what allows the window to be closed when the user clicks on the close control. The **windowClosing** method is the last chance for the programmer to warn the user to save modified data, close open databases, and generally ensure correct termination of the program.

Creating A Dialog

The **java.awt** package provides only one standard dialog, the **FileDialog** class. This class creates a file selection dialog in the style of the underlying operating system. A **FileDialog** is always *modal*—while it is being shown, the remainder of the application cannot receive user events.

The **java.awt.Dialog** class can be used to create either a modal or nonmodal dialog. The main limitation on uses of a **Dialog** is that all constructors must have a **Frame** or another **Dialog**, so an application cannot be based on the **Dialog** class. You might think that this restriction prevents you from using a **Dialog** from a Java **Applet** because an **Applet** is not a descendent of **Frame**, but for **Applets**, the Web browser constitutes a **Frame**. You can use code similar to the following to locate that **Frame** and use it to construct a **Dialog**:

```
public void showDlg(){
  Container c = getParent();
  while( c != null ){
    if( c instanceof Frame ){
      myDlg = new TestDialog((Frame) c );
      myDlg.show(); return ;
    }
    c = c.getParent(); // try next parent
  }
}
```

The **Menu**-Related Classes

Adding menus to an application requires a class that implements the
MenuContainer interface. The classes in the **java.awt** package that implement
MenuContainer are **Component, Frame, Menu,** and **MenuBar,** so practically
anything on the screen can host a menu.

The classes that create menus are the only screen display classes that do not
extend **java.awt.Component.** Here is the hierarchy of the menu-related classes:

```
java.lang.Object
  |
  +-- java.awt.MenuShortcut
  |
  +-- java.awt.MenuComponent
        |
        +-- java.awt.MenuBar
        |
        +-- java.awt.MenuItem
              |
              +-- java.awt.CheckboxMenuItem
              |
              +-- java.awt.Menu
                    |
                    +-- java.awt.PopupMenu
```

To create a traditional pull-down menu attached to a frame, you create a
MenuBar object and add **Menu** objects that contain **MenuItem** objects. It is
the **MenuItem** object that registers a mouse click and creates an **ActionEvent.**
The following code fragment, when inserted in the **FrameDemo** constructor
after line 10 in Listing 11.1, creates a pull-down menu system as shown in
Figure 11.4. Note that I have indented the statements to indicate how the
objects created are related to the menu structure.

```
MenuBar mb = new MenuBar();
  Menu fileMenu = new Menu("File");
    fileMenu.add( new MenuItem("New") );
    fileMenu.addSeparator();
    fileMenu.add( new MenuItem("Exit") );
mb.add( fileMenu );
  Menu helpMenu = new Menu("Help");
    helpMenu.add( new MenuItem("About") );
mb.add( helpMenu );
setMenuBar( mb );
```

Here is a quick summary of the menu-related classes in the **java.awt** package:

➤ **MenuBar** A **MenuBar** organizes **Menu** objects to create the familiar drop-down menu interface.

➤ **PopUpMenu** You can have a **PopUpMenu** attached to any screen component.

➤ **Menu** A **Menu** object creates a single drop-down menu such as the File menu in Figure 11.4. Everything in a **Menu** must be a **MenuItem** or **CheckboxMenuItem**.

➤ **MenuItem** This object represents the thing that is selected in a **Menu**.

➤ **CheckboxMenuItem** This descendent of **MenuItem** has a checked or unchecked state.

➤ **MenuShortcut** **MenuShortcut** objects represent keyboard alternatives to activate a **MenuItem**.

Figure 11.4   A Frame with added **MenuBar** containing two drop-down menus.

Geometric Utility Classes

The **java.awt** package provides several utility classes that encapsulate geometric data related to screen displays. In earlier versions of Java, all of these classes used only 32-bit integers. With the expanded graphics capabilities of Java 1.2, some methods that set or get floating-point dimensions were added. However, the constructors expect **int** values.

➤ **Dimension** **Dimension** objects are typically used to encapsulate the width and height of components. These measurements are always in pixels.

➤ **Point** **Point** objects encapsulate the x and y axis positions of a point in 2D space.

➤ **Rectangle** A **Rectangle** object has an x and y position for the upper-left corner plus a width and height.

➤ **Polygon** A **Polygon** object represents a closed two-dimensional region composed of an arbitrary number of lines connecting points in a list of coordinates. The first and final points in the list are joined to complete the polygon. **Polygon** objects can be constructed from arrays of x and y point coordinates or by adding individual points to an existing object. **Polygon** objects are used to define arbitrary regions in display space.

AWT Classes Related To Graphics

The **java.awt** package has a large number of classes related to creating a graphical display. Here is a quick tour of the classes you are most likely to be using:

➤ **java.awt.Color** A **Color** object represents a screen color with red, green, and blue intensity values plus an opacity, or alpha component. The **Color** class also provides common colors as constants.

➤ **java.awt.Cursor** This class can be used to create either a custom or standard cursor bitmap object. You can define an image source and active point, but only in the format used by the underlying operating system. Any **Component** can have a **Cursor** assigned for use when the cursor is over the **Component**.

➤ **java.awt.Font** A **Font** object encapsulates a single font face and size. A **Font** is attached to a **Graphics** object to draw text in a particular style and size.

➤ **java.awt.FontMetrics** This class is used to generate information about how a particular **Font** will appear on the screen, for example, in determining the number of pixels a given **String** will consume.

➤ **java.awt.Graphics** The base class for all graphics contexts that allow a program to draw on the screen. A subclass of the **abstract Graphics** class will be provided by the JVM for a particular operating system.

➤ **java.awt.Graphics2D** This extension of the **Graphics** class adds a number of drawing methods that are a substantial advance over the original Java capabilities. Various methods provide for rendering two-dimensional shapes and greater control over display of text and images.

➤ **java.awt.GraphicsEnvironment** Contains information on the fonts and graphics devices available to a Java program in a particular operating system environment.

The Font Class

Fonts are characterized by a font family name, such as Helvetica or Times Roman; a style, such as bold or italic; and a point size. In earlier releases of Java, font selection was restricted to a few standard fonts, but in the JDK 1.2 release, the programmer has access to all of the fonts on the host operating system. Taking full advantage of these new capabilities is beyond the scope of this book. You create a new **Font** object with a constructor that takes a font name, a style constant and a point size, as in the following example:

```
Font myFont = new Font( "Serif", Font.BOLD, 50 ) ;
```

In Java 1.0, the font names used included "TimesRoman", "Helvetica", and "Courier", but to avoid copyright problems, Java 1.1 preferred to use "Serif", "SansSerif", and "Monospaced" respectively.

To control the drawing of text on the screen, it is necessary to get a **FontMetrics** object for the **Font** in use. Use of a **FontMetrics** object is illustrated in the following discussion.

The Graphics Class

To understand how the **Graphics** class is used, the following looks at the sequence of events that occurs when for some reason a screen object derived from the **Component** class must be redrawn. First, the JVM generates a **Graphics** object that contains the following information:

➤ The **Component** to draw on and its screen location.

➤ A "clipping" **Rectangle,** which limits the area to be drawn in. This is never larger than the **Component,** so a **Component** can never draw out of its own screen area. If part of the **Component** is covered by another window, the clipping rectangle will reflect that.

➤ The current drawing **Color,** set to the default foreground color of the **Component.** A **Graphics** object only knows about one **Color** at a time.

➤ The current **Font** attached to the **Component.** If you have not specified a **Font** for a **Component,** the **Font** attached to its container is used, so there is never a situation in which a **Graphics** does not have a **Font.**

Next, the JVM calls the **update** method of the **Component** to be redrawn. The default functionality of this method is to clear the rectangle occupied by the **Component** using the **Component**'s background **Color,** and then to call the **paint** method:

```
public void update(Graphics g) {
  g.clearRect(0, 0, width, height);
  paint(g);
}
```

The **paint** method is responsible for drawing the rest of the **Component** using the **Graphics** object. Some of the methods provided by the **Graphics** class are illustrated by the code in Listing 11.2.

Listing 11.2   An example paint method demonstrating text drawing.

```
public void paint(Graphics g ){
  String str = "Joy of Java!" ;
  FontMetrics fm = g.getFontMetrics() ;
  int ascent = fm.getAscent();
  int descent = fm.getDescent();
  int length = fm.stringWidth( str );
  int X = 30, Y = 120 ;
  g.setColor( Color.darkGray );
  g.drawString( str , X, Y );
  g.setColor( Color.black );
  g.drawLine( X, Y, X + length, Y ); // baseline
  g.drawLine( X, Y - ascent, X + length, Y - ascent ); // top
  g.drawLine( X, Y - ascent, X, Y + descent );
  g.drawLine( X, Y + descent, X + length, Y + descent );
}
```

This **paint** method was used in a class derived from **Frame** to create the display shown in Figure 11.5. The lines and text on the left side were drawn by the **paint** method, whereas the annotation on the right indicates the various **FontMetrics** parameters. The X and Y positions used in the **drawString** method call refer to a point at the left end of the baseline. Note how a portion of the "y" character descends below the baseline.

Figure 11.5   The result of the **paint** method used in Listing 11.2 (with annotatations added).

The programmer can request that the JVM execute the **update-paint** sequence on a component by calling the **repaint** method in the **Component** class. This is a request, not a command—the JVM repaints the **Component** when it gets around to it. Therefore, you must be sure that your program **Thread** does not hog all the CPU time. Here is a simple example of a **run** method used to create an animated display on a **Canvas**-derived object named **animCanvas**:

```
public void run(){
  while( true ){
    doAnimationMoves();
    animCanvas.repaint();
    try {
      Thread.yield();
    }catch(InterruptedException ex){
    }
  }
}
```

Note that because it is the **animCanvas repaint** method that is called, the JVM will call the **update** method belonging to the **animCanvas** object. An alternative to calling the **yield** method would be to have the **Thread sleep** for a fixed amount of time, this would make the animation run at a more nearly constant rate on different systems.

More About Drawing

The logical coordinates for drawing on the screen are considered to lie between the pixels of the output device. When drawing a real pixel, the "pen" fills in the pixel below and to the right of the logical pixel coordinates. Here are some of the line drawing methods in the **Graphics** class:

➤ **drawLine(int x1, int y1, int x2, int y2)** This draws a single pixel wide line from point (x1, y1) to point (x2, y2).

➤ **drawRect(int x, int y, int wide, int high)** This draws a rectangle based on the upper-left corner at point (x, y) with the prescribed width and height.

➤ **fillRect(int x, int y, int wide, int high)** This draws a filled-in rectangle using the current **Color**.

➤ **drawOval(int x, int y, int wide, int high)** A single pixel-wide line is drawn to create an oval that just fits the rectangle that the parameters describe.

➤ **fillOval(int x, int y, int wide, int high)** This draws a filled-in oval.

➤ **drawArc(int x, int y, int wide, int high, int startAngle, int endAngle)** This draws the outline of an arc just fitting the rectangle described by the first four parameters. The start and end angles are in degrees measured counterclockwise from the 3 o'clock position.

➤ **fillArc(int x, int y, int wide, int high, int startAngle, int endAngle)** Similar to **drawArc** except the entire figure is filled. This is an ideal routine for drawing pie charts.

➤ **drawPolygon(Polygon p)** Outlines the polygon with a single pixel-wide line. If the first and last points are not identical, they are automatically connected with a line.

➤ **fillPolygon(Polygon p)** As with **drawPolygon** but filled in with the current **Color**. This is an ideal routine for drawing special controls.

Listing 11.3 shows some of these methods as they were used to create Figure 11.6. Note how the **fillArc** method starts at 0 degrees in the 3 o'clock position with the end point at 45 degrees measured counterclockwise.

Listing 11.3 The paint method used to create Figure 11.6.

```
public void paint(Graphics g ){
   g.drawRect( 30,40,200, 160);
   g.setColor( Color.cyan );
   g.fillOval( 30,40,200, 160);
   g.setColor( Color.black );
   g.fillArc( 40, 50, 180, 140, 0, 45 );
   g.setColor( Color.black );
   g.fillPolygon( arrow );
}
```

Figure 11.6   A demonstration of drawing geometric figures with the code in Listing 11.3.

Displaying Images On Screen

Java has extensive image manipulation features. The **java.awt.Image** class creates objects that represent images, and the **java.awt.image** package has a number of classes that can be used to manipulate images. Here are some of the methods in the **Graphics** class that can be used to draw an **Image**.

```
1. boolean drawImage( Image img, int x, int y,
      ImageObserver obs )
2. boolean drawImage( Image img, int x, int y, int wide,
      int high, Color bkg, ImageObserver obs )
```

The method in line 2 scales the **Image** to fit in the rectangle defined by the parameters. The **ImageObserver** reference may be **null** or a reference to an object such as a **Component** that implements the **ImageObserver** interface. The **bkg Color** will be used wherever a transparent pixel appears in the **Image**. There are a large number of variations of **drawImage** in the **Graphics** and **Graphics2D** classes, but these are beyond the scope of this book.

Off-Screen Images

You can create off-screen or memory images that can be used to create complex images that are then drawn to the screen. You will frequently see the technique of working with an off-screen image that can be rapidly drawn to the screen referred to as *double buffering*. This technique is used to avoid the flicker that can result when an **update** method clears the component and the **paint** method does a lot of time-consuming drawing.

An off-screen **Image** can supply a **Graphics** object so you can use all of the **Graphics** methods to modify the **Image**. The following code fragment, from a custom **Component**, creates an off-screen image and gets the associated **Graphics** object.

```
Image imgA = createImage( 200, 150 ); // method in Component
Graphic gr = imgA.getGraphics();
// gr can now be used to draw in the off-screen image
```

The Component getGraphics Method

So far I have talked about drawing on the screen with the **paint** method, which is called by the JVM with a **Graphics** object. You can also use this **Component** method

```
public Graphics getGraphics()
```

to get a **Graphics** object for any **Component** currently displayed on the screen. One danger of this approach is that the operating system may have limits on the number of graphics context objects that can exist simultaneously. So, if you use **getGraphics**, be sure to use the

```
public void dispose()
```

method of the **Graphics** class to properly dispose of any system resources. You don't need to dispose of the **Graphics** object provided in the JVM calls to **update** and **paint** methods because that is handled by the JVM.

> *Note: Do not try to get a **Graphics** reference in a method that runs before something is shown on the screen. The JVM does not determine the characteristics of the display until the first window is shown. Any call to getGraphics before then will return **null** and cause you endless trouble.*

Practice Questions

Question 1

> You want to use a particular color for text in an **Applet**, but you have forgotten the syntax for the method that sets the color for drawing. Which class do you look in first?
>
> ○ a. java.applet.Applet
>
> ○ b. java.awt.Panel
>
> ○ c. java.applet.Applet
>
> ○ d. java.awt.Component
>
> ○ e. java.lang.Object

Answer d, **Component**, should always be your first stop when looking for AWT methods that affect appearance. **Applet** inherits from **Panel,** which inherits container methods from **Container,** but the common appearance-changing methods and event-related methods are all in **Component**.

Question 2

> Which of the following AWT components can have a menu, either as a menu bar or pop-up menu, attached to it? [Check all correct answers]
>
> ❑ a. java.awt.Frame
>
> ❑ b. java.awt.Window
>
> ❑ c. java.awt.Applet
>
> ❑ d. java.awt.Panel

Answers a, b, c, and d are correct. All of these components may have an attached menu because the **Component** class implements the **MenuContainer** interface, and all of these classes have **Component** in their ancestry.

Question 3

> The **Component** methods for setting the position and size of a
> screen object use which Java primitive?
>
> ○ a. byte
>
> ○ b. short
>
> ○ c. char
>
> ○ d. int
>
> ○ e. long
>
> ○ f. float

Answer d is correct. All of the **Component** methods expect an **int** primitive
for screen position and dimension values.

Question 4

> Which of the following describes how the angle parameters in the
> **Graphics** class **drawArc** method are used?
>
> ○ a. Angles are interpreted as radians, with zero at the
> 12 o'clock position and positive angles in a clockwise
> direction.
>
> ○ b. Angles are interpreted as degrees, with zero at the
> 3 o'clock position and positive angles in a counterclock-
> wise direction.
>
> ○ c. Angles are interpreted as radians, with zero at the
> 3 o'clock position and positive angles in a counterclock-
> wise direction.
>
> ○ d. Angles are interpreted as degrees, with zero at the
> 12 o'clock position and positive angles in a clockwise
> direction.

Answer b is correct, although measuring angles in integer degrees obviously
limits the method to crude screen graphics. The Graphics2D class has much
more flexible drawing methods.

Question 5

A Java application based on the **Frame** class contains a **Panel**, which in turn contains a **Label**. The only statements in the entire application that have to do with color or font settings are:

```
// in the Frame
setFont( new Font("Serif", Font.ITALIC, 18 );
setBackground( Color.cyan );

// in the Panel
setBackground( Color.white );
setForeground( Color.magenta );
```

What colors and font will the Label display?

○ a. background = white, foreground = magenta, Font = Serif Italic style, 18 point

○ b. background = cyan, foreground = black, Font = Serif Italic style, 18 point.

○ c. background = cyan, foreground = black, Font = System default style for labels

○ d. background = white, foreground = magenta, Font = System default style for labels.

Answer a is correct. The **Font** is inherited from the **Frame** and the colors from the **Panel**. Note that there is a JVM default for colors and **Font** that is characteristic of the JVM, not the operating system.

Question 6

Which of the following statements about the ancestry of the class **java.applet.Applet** is correct?

○ a. An **Applet** is a kind of **Container**.

○ b. An **Applet** is a kind of **Window**.

○ c. An **Applet** is a kind of **Component**.

○ d. An **Applet** is a kind of **Panel**.

Answer b is an incorrect statement, and thus the correct answer. **Window** extends **Container** directly, whereas **Applet** extends **Panel**, which extends **Container**, which extends **Component**.

Question 7

In which category does **java.awt.Container** belong?

- ○ a. interface
- ○ b. **abstract** class
- ○ c. normal class
- ○ d. none of the above

Answer c is correct. **Container** was an **abstract** class in JDK 1.1 but is now a regular class. **Container** is not an interface, but it does inherit implementation of several interfaces from **Component**.

Question 8

Which of the following does not inherit from **java.awt.MenuItem**? [Check all correct answers]

- ❑ a. java.awt.MenuComponent
- ❑ b. java.awt.Menu
- ❑ c. java.awt.CheckboxMenuItem
- ❑ d. java.awt.MenuSeparator

Answers a and d are correct. **MenuItem** inherits from **MenuComponent**, not the other way around. There is no such class as **MenuSeparator**; separators are added to menus with the **addSeparator** method. **Menu** and **CheckboxMenuItem** are direct descendents of **MenuItem**.

Question 9

Of the three classes **TextField**, **TextArea**, and **TextComponent**, which is the parent of the other two?

- ○ a. TextField
- ○ b. TextArea
- ○ c. TextComponent

Answer c is correct. Both **TextField** (for single lines) and **TextArea** (for multiple lines) are extensions of **TextComponent**.

Question 10

You want to show a single line of text in a component that the user can select but not edit. Which of the following would be the way to create this component?

○ a.
```
msgTx = new TextField( 60 );
    msgTx.setEditable( false );
```

○ b.
```
msgTx = new TextArea( 60 );
    msgTx.setEnabled( false );
    msgTx.setEditable( false );
```

○ c.
```
msgTx = new TextField( 60 );
    msgTx.setEnabled( true )
```

Answer a is correct. The **setEditable** method controls whether or not a text field can be edited. Answer b is wrong because **setEnabled(false)** prevents the user from selecting the field. Answer c is wrong because the default for **TextField** components is to be editable.

Need To Know More?

 Flanagan, David. *Java in a Nutshell, 2nd Edition*. O'Reilly & Associates, Inc, Sebastopol, CA, 1997. ISBN: 1-56592-262-X. This is the most compact desktop reference book documenting the Java language. See Chapter 18 for the **java.awt** package. This issue is for Java JDK 1.1 but contains much that is applicable to Java 2—as soon as the Java 2 version comes out, grab it!

 Zukowski, John. *Java AWT Reference*. O'Reilly & Associates, Inc, Sebastopol, CA, 1997. ISBN: 1-56592-240-9. Over 1,000 pages of details on the AWT classes. This version is for JDK 1.1, but almost all of the material is applicable to Java 2.

Building GUIs With The AWT Components

12

Terms you'll need to understand:

√ **LayoutManager**

√ **LayoutManager2**

√ Constraints

√ Insets

√ **preferredSize**

√ **minimumSize**

√ **maximumSize**

Techniques you'll need to master:

√ Choosing the right layout manager for a particular design problem

√ Predicting the result of resizing containers with different layout managers

Creating a graphical user interface (GUI) using the Java AWT library is a matter of choosing the right components and placing them on the screen under the control of layout managers. Layout managers are essential in creating GUIs that have similar behavior on all hardware. The capabilities of a layout manager are specified in two interfaces. **java.awt.LayoutManager** is part of the original Java 1.0 language release. The 1.1 release of Java includes the **java.awt.LayoutManager2** interface, which adds some additional refinements to **LayoutManager**.

The LayoutManager Interface

All Java AWT containers can have an attached **LayoutManager** object added with the

```
public void set setLayout(LayoutManager m )
```

method. The object controls the size and position of all components in the container. You should add the **LayoutManager** to the container before you add any components. Some layout managers let you get away with adding the manager after the components, but others produce very odd results if this is done.

Some containers have a constructor that takes a **LayoutManager** so you can combine creation of the container with setting the **LayoutManager**, as in the following:

```
Panel p2 = new Panel( new BorderLayout() );
```

In general, you do not need to deal with the **LayoutManager** directly after it has been created. However, if you do, the **java.awt.Container** class has the following method:

```
LayoutManager getLayout();
```

The **LayoutManager** interface calls for the methods in the following list. Generally speaking, a programmer never needs to call these methods directly. The **Container** to which the **LayoutManager** is attached calls them as needed:

➤ **void addLayoutComponent(String name, Component c)** This method is called when a component is added to the container. Some layout managers ignore the name.

➤ **void layoutContainer(Container parent)** This method performs the actual positioning and sizing of all of the contained **Component** objects.

➤ **Dimension minimumLayoutSize(Container parent)** This is the method that a **Container** uses to calculate its minimum size requirements.

➤ **Dimension preferredLayoutSize(Container parent)** This method calculates a preferred size based on the preferred size of the components and the layout rules.

➤ **void removeLayoutComponent(Component c)** This removes the component from the list of components controlled by the **LayoutManager**.

The LayoutManager2 Interface

The release of Java 1.1 brought an extension to the **LayoutManager** interface named **LayoutManager2**. This interface adds a general method for attaching constraints to a component in a more general form:

```
void addLayoutComponent( Component c, Object constraints )
```

The **BorderLayout, CardLayout,** and **GridBagLayout** classes implement **LayoutManager2** because they all can use constraints. The other new methods in **LayoutManager2** are as follows:

➤ **float getLayoutAlignmentX(Container parent)** These methods related to alignment are apparently used only in Swing classes and are not on the exam.

➤ **float getLayoutAlignmentY(Container parent)** See previous entry.

➤ **void invalidateLayout(Container parent)** This method forces the layout manager to completely recalculate the layout, discarding any intermediate results it may have cached.

➤ **Dimension maximumLayoutSize(Container target)** This returns a **Dimension** based on the maximum sizes of the contained components, similar to the **getPreferredSize** method of **LayoutManager**.

Review Of The AWT Containers

Before looking at specific layout managers, I'll review some facts about AWT container classes. The size of a container as returned in a **Dimension** object by the **getSize** method reflects the amount of space the container occupies, *not* the space available inside the container. This distinction is not noticeable unless the container has a significant border, as in the case of **Frame** and **Dialog** containers.

A **java.awt.Container** maintains an internal list of **Component** references. Five different methods are used to add a component to a container. The following lists the method signatures (note that the last two **add** methods were introduced with Java 1.1):

➤ **Component add(Component c)** The component is added to the end of the list and the **c** reference is returned.

➤ **Component add(String name, Component c)** The component is added to the end of the list and the **name** is associated with it in case the layout manager uses the **name** as a constraint. Sun suggests that you not use this method. Use the more general **add** with a constraint, making the name **String** the constraint.

➤ **Component add(Component c, int index)** Adds the component at the index position in the internal list, bumping up any existing components at this position or higher.

➤ **void add(Component c, Object constraints)** Adds the component with this **constraints** object. Whether or not the constraint is used depends on the layout manager.

➤ **void add(Component c, Object constraints, int index)** Adds the component with this constraints object at the specified index.

The methods that specify an index can throw an **IllegalArgumentException** if the index is out of range. All methods throw an **IllegalArgumentException** if you try to add a container to itself or if you try to add a **Window** object to the container.

Here are some of the important characteristics of various AWT containers:

➤ **Panel** The basic utility container. **Panel** and its subclass, **java.applet.Applet**, have a **FlowLayout** by default.

➤ **Window** This is the simplest container that can exist as an independent window. **Window** and its descendents have a **BorderLayout** by default. A **Window** has no borders and no menu bar.

➤ **Frame** This extension of **java.awt.Window** has a border and can host a **MenuBar**. If you replace the default **BorderLayout** with a **null** layout, be sure to take into account the **Insets** when positioning components. Unfortunately, because the border and **MenuBar** size are platform-dependent, you can't evaluate the **Insets** until the **Frame** has been shown.

➤ **Dialog** **Dialog** is also an extension of **Window** and thus has a default **BorderLayout**. You must also take **Insets** into account with a **Dialog**.

Working With BorderLayout

A **BorderLayout** can manage up to five components that are placed in named positions: North, South, East, West, and Center. The **BorderLayout** class has these five **String** objects as constants named **NORTH, SOUTH, EAST, WEST,** and **CENTER.** Here is an example of the code to add some elements to a **java.awt.Frame,** which, as you will no doubt recall, has a **BorderLayout** by default:

```
add( new Button( "North" ), BorderLayout.NORTH );
add( new Button( "South" ), BorderLayout.SOUTH );
add( new Button( "East" ), BorderLayout.EAST );
add( new Button( "West" ), BorderLayout.WEST );
add( new Button( "Center" ), BorderLayout.CENTER );
```

This code results in the display shown in Figure 12.1. On the left is the **Frame,** sized so all **Buttons** are visible, whereas the right image shows how the layout manager compensates for a smaller window by compressing the center component.

BorderLayout Defaults

Here are some important facts to remember about the default behavior of AWT components with respect to **BorderLayout:**

➤ **BorderLayout** is the default layout manager for **java.awt.Frame, java.awt.Window,** and **java.awt.Dialog** containers.

➤ If you don't specify a constraint when you add a component to a container with a **BorderLayout,** a constraint of **CENTER** is assumed. If you add more than one component without a constraint, only the last one will be kept and the others will not be shown in any position.

➤ None of the border positions in a **BorderLayout** show up at all if no component has been added. If nothing is added to the center position, it is painted in the container's background color.

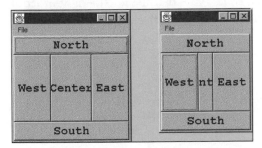

Figure 12.1 A **Frame** containing five **Button** objects at two different sizes.

A **BorderLayout** tries to preserve the preferred width of the **EAST** and **WEST** components and the preferred height of the **NORTH** and **SOUTH** components. The **CENTER** component gets the leftovers.

Working With FlowLayout

The most important characteristics of a **FlowLayout** are as follows:

➤ **FlowLayout** gives every component its preferred size and does not resize components.

➤ **FlowLayout** adds components from left to right and starts a new row when the first one is filled.

➤ Components that don't fit are simply not shown.

Using one of the constants in the **FlowLayout** class, you can specify how the components will be aligned within rows when you create a **FlowLayout**. These constants are **LEFT**, **CENTER**, and **RIGHT**. The following are statements illustrating the three constructors for **FlowLayout**:

```
1. FlowLayout f1 = new FlowLayout( );
2. FlowLayout f2 = new FlowLayout( FlowLayout.LEFT );
3. FlowLayout f3 = new FlowLayout( FlowLayout.RIGHT, 10, 2 );
```

The code in line 1 will result in **f1** having a center alignment and the default gap of five pixels between components horizontally and vertically. The **f2** layout will have the default gap and will align the components on the left, whereas **f3** will align the components on the right with a horizontal gap of 10 and a vertical gap of two pixels.

Figure 12.2 shows a **Frame** containing six buttons, using a layout constructed as in the **f3** layout in the preceding code. Note that the left-to-right order of the buttons is preserved when buttons 5 and 6 overflow the first row and are aligned on the next.

Figure 12.2 A set of six **Button** objects managed by a **FlowLayout**.

Working With **GridLayout**

The **GridLayout** follows very simple rules. The available space is divided into a grid of equal-sized cells and the components are forced to fit. The order of addition defines where each component goes, with rows being filled from left to right starting at the top left. The following code illustrates the three constructors for a **GridLayout**:

```
1. GridLayout g1 = new GridLayout();
2. GridLayout g2 = new GridLayout( int rows, int cols );
3. GridLayout g3 = new GridLayout( int rows, int cols, int hgap,
   int vgap );
```

The constructor in line 1 results in a grid with only one row that will be divided equally among all components and will have the default gap of zero pixels between components. The constructor in line 2 creates an initial grid with the specified rows and columns and the default gap of zero pixels between components. The constructor in line 3 lets you specify the horizontal and vertical gap between components.

Figure 12.3 illustrates the result of placing six buttons in a **GridLayout** created with the following code:

```
new Gridlayout( 2, 3, 10, 15 )
```

Note that the specified gap is inserted only between components, not between components and the container border. To control this gap, you have to create a custom container having an implementation of **getInsets**, as in the following example:

```
class XPanel extends Panel {
    public Insets getInsets(){return new Insets( 25, 15, 10, 5 ) ;}
}
```

Figure 12.3   A **Frame** holding six **Button** objects in a **GridLayout**.

When a container with a **GridLayout** has fewer components than the number of grid positions, the unoccupied grid areas are painted in the container's background color. When a container with a full **GridLayout** has another component added, the **GridLayout** will automatically add an additional column and recompute the layout.

Working With CardLayout

The **CardLayout** is an extremely handy way to organize a potentially complex display into understandable pieces. A **CardLayout** can manage a large number of components (cards), but only one is shown at a time. The program switches the view between components either by addressing it by name or by methods that "flip" through the cards in the order they were added.

To control a **CardLayout,** your program must keep a reference to it. This is in contrast with the other layout managers that a program never calls directly. Here are the **CardLayout** constructors:

```
1. CardLayout card1 = new CardLayout();
2. CardLayout card2 = new CardLayout( int hborder, int vborder );
```

The constructor in line 1 creates a **CardLayout** that does not show a border around the contained components. The constructor in line 2 shows a gap painted in the container background color with **hborder** pixels on left and right and **vborder** pixels on top and bottom around the displayed component.

Because a container with a **CardLayout** shows only one component at a time, it is rather boring to look at. To demonstrate how one is used, you need at least the skeleton of an application, such as the **CardTest** class, shown in Listing 12.1, that creates the skeleton based on the **Frame** class (**BorderLayout** by default). This **Frame** has a **Panel** in the Center position and one in the North position. The center **Panel** uses a **CardLayout** that controls three different components, whereas the north **Panel** has three **Button** objects that are used to control the CardLayout. This is a pretty typical design for applications and dialogs.

Listing 12.1   Source for the **CardTest** class.

```
import java.awt.* ;
import java.awt.event.* ;

public class CardTest extends Frame{

 public static void main( String[] args ){
   new CardTest().show();
 }
```

```
Button b1, b2, b3;
CardLayout cards;
TextArea cmt1;
Label lbl2;
Panel pc, pn, pnl3;

CardTest(){
  super( "Card Test" );
  setSize( 280, 200 );
  addWindowListener( new WindowAdapter(){
    public void windowClosing(WindowEvent e){System.exit(0);}
    } );
  pc = new Panel();
  pc.setLayout( cards = new CardLayout() );
  add( pc, BorderLayout.CENTER );
  cmt1 = new TextArea( "Comments" );
  pc.add( cmt1 , "comments" );
  lbl2 = new Label( "Card # 2" );
  pc.add( lbl2 , "label" );
  pnl3 = new Panel();
  pc.add( pnl3 , "panel" );
  // now to create a control panel
  pn = new Panel();
  add( pn, BorderLayout.NORTH );
  b1 = new Button( "Card 1" );
  b2 = new Button( "Card 2" );
  b3 = new Button( "Card 3" );
  pn.add( b1 ); pn.add( b2 ); pn.add( b3 );
  // now to connect the buttons to an actionlistener
  ActionListener alisten = new CardListen();
  b1.addActionListener( alisten );
  b2.addActionListener( alisten );
  b3.addActionListener( alisten );
}

class CardListen implements ActionListener{
  public void actionPerformed(ActionEvent evt ){
    Object source = evt.getSource();
    if( source == b1 ) cards.show( pc,"comments" );
    if( source == b2 ) cards.show( pc,"label" );
    if( source == b3 ) cards.show( pc,"panel" );
  }
} // end inner class
}
```

One important thing to note in the previous listing is the way the **CardLayout show** method is called in the **actionPerformed** method using the name associated with each component when it was added to the container and a reference to the container. Other methods for switching between cards use the order in which the components were added; they also must have a reference to the container:

➤ **public void next(Container parent)** Displays the next component, going back to the first when the last one is reached.

➤ **public void previous(Container parent)** Displays the previous component, going to the last when the starting one is reached.

Figure 12.4 shows the **CardTest** application with the **TextArea** component displayed by the **CardLayout**.

Working With GridBagLayout

Think of **GridBagLayout** as an extremely flexible version of **GridLayout**. Whereas in **GridLayout** each grid row and column is the same size and each component exactly fills a grid location, in **GridBagLayout** these restrictions are relaxed. Rows and columns can be of different sizes and a component can use more than one grid location. The extent to which a component fills an area is under the programmer's control.

Unfortunately, this flexibility can be obtained only with a very complex programming interface. Basically, each component that goes into a **GridBagLayout** has to be tagged with a **GridBagConstraints** object that carries a number of parameters. The **GridBagLayout** object looks at the constraints of all the components it manages and tries to come up with a layout that satisfies all of them.

Even experienced Java programmers have trouble getting a **GridBagLayout** to do exactly what they want because of the parameters' interaction. For our purposes here, you need to be familiar only with the basic parameters as they affect the positioning of a single component.

The GridBagConstraints Class

Each component in a container controlled by a **GridBagLayout** gets an associated **GridBagConstraints** object. It is the parameters this object carries that

Figure 12.4 The **CardTest** application in action.

the **GridBagLayout** uses to decide on a position and size for each component. The class also defines a number of constants related to various defaults, including the following:

➤ **Positioning** The **gridx** and **gridy** parameters are indexes to the grid position in which the component originates, with 0,0 being the upper-left corner. If the constant **RELATIVE** is used, the component is placed relative to the previous addition. Within the cell or cells that the component occupies, the **anchor** parameter can be used to place the component in the **CENTER** or one of eight "compass" directions such as **NORTHEAST**.

➤ **Sizing** The **gridwidth** and **gridheight** parameters indicate the number of cells allotted to the component horizontally and vertically. The constant **REMAINDER** can be used to indicate that the component takes up the remainder of the row or column. The amount of space the component actually occupies depends on several other parameters. The fill parameter can be set to **NONE, HORIZONTAL, VERTICAL,** or **BOTH**. You can set the **ipadx** and **ipady** parameters that specify the number of pixels to be added to the component's minimum size as an alternative to stretching the component with the **fill** parameter.

➤ **Padding** The **insets** parameter takes an **Insets** object that defines the amount of space to leave clear on each side of the component.

➤ **Distributing extra space** The **weightx** and **weighty** parameters control how extra space is distributed among rows and columns. If you leave these parameters at the default value of zero, all extra space gets distributed around the edges of the whole layout so the components do not expand when the total area is enlarged. The **GridBagLayout** looks at a row or column of components and finds the largest weight for each row (**weighty**) and each column (**weightx**). Extra space is distributed to rows and columns in proportion to the weight.

These parameters interact with each other so getting the effect you want can involve a lot of experimentation. Java development environments such as Symantec's Visual Café and IBM's Visual Age provide a dynamic display that allows you to experiment to find satisfactory settings for **GridBagConstraints** parameters.

A GridBagLayout Example

Fully exploring the possibilities of **GridBagLayout** would take a large chapter. For *Exam Cram* purposes, I show a single example. In this example, three **Button** objects are placed in a **GridBagLayout** using the code in Listing 12.2, which results in the display shown in Figure 12.5.

Figure 12.5 Three **Button** objects in a **GridBagLayout**. The anchor for A is SOUTH and the anchor for B is CENTER.

Listing 12.2 The constructor used to create the Frame shown in Figure 12.5.

```
public GridBagDemo() {
  super( "GridBagLayout" ); // Frame with title
  setFont( new Font("Helvetica", Font.BOLD, 18 ));
  addWindowListener( new WindowAdapter( ){
    public void windowClosing(WindowEvent evt){System.exit(0);}
  } );
  setSize( 220, 200 );
  Button button;
  GridBagLayout gridbag = new GridBagLayout();
  GridBagConstraints c = new GridBagConstraints();
  setLayout(gridbag);
  button = new Button( "Button A" );
  c.insets = new Insets( 5,5,5,5 );
  c.fill = GridBagConstraints.HORIZONTAL;
  c.gridx = 0;
  c.gridy = 0;
  c.gridwidth = 2; // occupy 2 columns
  c.gridheight = 2; // and 2 rows
  c.weightx = 0.5;
  c.weighty = 0.5;
  c.anchor = GridBagConstraints.SOUTH;
  gridbag.setConstraints(button, c);
  // that call clones the constraints object so you can continue to
  // use it, making minor modifications for subsequent uses.
  add(button);
  //
  button = new Button( "B" );
  c.fill  = GridBagConstraints.NONE;
  c.gridx = 2; // because A occupies 2 columns
  c.gridy = 1;
  c.gridwidth = 1;
  c.gridheight =1;
```

```
c.anchor = GridBagConstraints.CENTER;
gridbag.setConstraints(button, c);
add(button);
 //
button = new Button("Button C");
c.gridx = 0;
c.gridy = 2; // because A occupies 2 rows
c.gridwidth =1;
c.gridheight =1;
gridbag.setConstraints(button, c);
add( button );
}
```

It is important to note that the **setConstraints** call clones the **GridBagConstraints** object. This means that you don't have to create a new **GridBagConstraints** and set all the parameters for each component. Instead, after the basic **GridBagConstraints** object has been set up, you only need to modify a few parameters for each new component. Changing the anchor parameter for the "A" button results in the change shown in Figure 12.6.

Working Without A Layout Manager

For many simple applications, some programmers prefer to lay out components in absolute pixel terms using the general **Component** positioning methods. To do this, you simply set the layout manager to null, as shown in the following code:

```
setLayout( null )
```

Many of the methods used for layout purposes in Java 1.0 were renamed in Java 1.1 for consistency. The original methods are still in the library but are deprecated. The following list reviews these methods:

Figure 12.6   The same components as in Figure 12.5 with the anchor for A now NORTH.

➤ **void setLocation(int x, int y)** This sets the location of the upper-left corner of the **Component** relative to the upper-left corner of the container. This method replaces the deprecated **move** method.

➤ **void setLocation(Point p)** This sets the location using an object of the **Point** class.

➤ **void setBounds(int x, int y, int width, int height)** This sets both location and size. This method replaces the deprecated **reshape** method.

➤ **void setBounds(Rectangle r)** This method uses an object of the geometric utility **Rectangle** class.

➤ **void setSize(int width, int height)** This sets size without changing the location. It replaces the deprecated **resize** method.

➤ **void setSize(Dimension d)** This sets size using an object of the geometric utility **Dimension** class. There is also a deprecated **resize** method taking a Dimension.

Practice Questions

Question 1

> Which of the following layout managers can be used to display nine **Button** objects at one time? [Check all correct answers]
>
> ❑ a. BorderLayout
>
> ❑ b. GridLayout
>
> ❑ c. CardLayout
>
> ❑ d. GridBagLayout

Answers b and d are correct. A **GridLayout** or **GridBagLayout** can show nine objects at once. A **BorderLayout** can manage only five objects. Therefore, answer a is incorrect. A **CardLayout** shows only one object at a time, although it can manage more than one. Therefore, answer c is incorrect.

Question 2

> Which of the following is the correct way to create a **Panel** with a **BorderLayout**? Note: The **Panel** is to be used for a central **Canvas** and two **Scrollbar** objects.
>
> ○ a.
> ```
>   Panel p = new Panel();
>        p.setLayout( new BorderLayout() );
> ```
>
> ○ b.
> ```
>   Panel p = new Panel();
>        p.addLayoutManager( new BorderLayout()
> );
> ```
>
> ○ c.
> ```
>   Panel p = new Panel();
>        p.setLayout( new BorderLayout( 3 ) );
> ```
>
> ○ d.
> ```
>   Panel p = new Panel();
>        p.addLayoutManager( new BorderLayout( 3
> ) );
> ```

Answer a is correct. The **addLayoutManager** method does not exist. Therefore, answer b is incorrect. There is no **BorderLayout** constructor that takes a single numeric parameter. Therefore, answer c is incorrect. Answer d combines the errors of b and c.

Question 3

> You need a container to hold six equal-sized buttons in three columns of two. This arrangement must persist when the container is resized. Which of the following will create that container?
>
> ○ a. Canvas c = new Canvas(new GridLayout(2, 3));
>
> ○ b. Panel p = new Panel(new GridLayout(2, 3));
>
> ○ c. Window w = new Window(new GridLayout(2, 3));
>
> ○ d. Panel p = new Panel(new GridLayout(3, 2));

Answer b correctly constructs a **Panel** container with a **LayoutManager** for two rows and three columns. **Canvas** is not a container. Therefore, answer a is incorrect. Although **Window** is a container, it does not have a constructor that takes a **LayoutManager**. Therefore, answer c is incorrect. The **LayoutManager** constructed here has three rows and two columns. Therefore, answer d is incorrect.

Question 4

> You construct a **Panel** with a **GridLayout** and add **Button** objects to it as follows:
>
> ```
> Panel p = new Panel();
> p.setLayout( new GridLayout() );
> for( int i = 1 ; i <= 6 ; i++ ){
>   p.add( new Button( Integer.toString(  i  ) )
> );
> }
> ```
>
> What is the result when the **Panel** is resized to 200x200 and is shown?
>
> ○ a. Only the **Button** "6" would be showing, filling the **Panel**.
>
> ○ b. Six narrow buttons in a row.
>
> ○ c. Six thin buttons in a column.
>
> ○ d. The number showing would depend on the font size.

Answer b is correct and the rest are incorrect because without a specified number of rows and columns, **GridLayout** arranges components in a row with equal space for each.

Question 5

Assume you have created a **Panel** named **cnt** with a **CardLayout** named **card** using the following code:

```
card = new CardLayout();
cnt = new Panel( card );
```

How do you cause a specific component to be shown in the container?

○ a. card.show(cnt, name);

    Where **cnt** is the container and **name** is the **String** used as a constraint for that component when it was added.

○ b. card.show(cnt, n);

    Where **cnt** is the container and **n** is an integer reflecting the order in which the component was added to the container.

○ c. card.show(name);

    Where **name** is the **String** used as a constraint for that component when it was added.

○ d. card.show(n);

    Where **n** is an integer reflecting the order in which the component was added to the container.

Answer a is correct. You have to call the **CardLayout show** method with a **Container** reference and a **String** name. **CardLayout** uses a **String**, not an integer to select a component. Therefore, answers b and d are incorrect. The **CardLayout show** method also requires a reference to the container. Therefore, answer c is incorrect.

Question 6

> Which of the following is a valid alignment parameter for a **FlowLayout**? [Check all correct answers]
>
> ❑ a. FlowLayout.TOP
>
> ❑ b. FlowLayout.LEFT
>
> ❑ c. FlowLayout.BOTTOM
>
> ❑ d. FlowLayout.CENTER
>
> ❑ e. FlowLayout.RIGHT

Answers b, d, and e are correct. **FlowLayout** uses a left-to-right flow and always starts at the top of a container. TOP and BOTTOM are not constants in the **FlowLayout** class. Therefore, answers a and d are incorrect.

Question 7

> Which of the following layout managers does not alter the height of a component?
>
> ○ a. BorderLayout
>
> ○ b. GridBagLayout
>
> ○ c. CardLayout
>
> ○ d. FlowLayout

Answer d, **FlowLayout,** is correct. A **FlowLayout** attempts to fit in components without changing their height. The **EAST, WEST,** and **CENTER** components of a **BorderLayout** have their height changed. Therefore, answer a is incorrect. A **GridBagLayout** typically alters both height and width of components. Therefore, answer b is incorrect. Components in a **CardLayout** are resized to fit the container exactly. Therefore, answer c is incorrect.

Question 8

The component in the East position of a **BorderLayout** cannot be wider than a **Scrollbar**.

○ a. True

○ b. False

Answer b is correct; this statement is false. **BorderLayout** attempts to use the preferred width of the component. Although the East position is typically used for a **Scrollbar**, it can contain any component.

Question 9

Suppose you have a working program that has a **Panel**, **p1**, with a **BorderLayout** that already has components in the North, South, East, West, and Center positions. Now you add the following statement to the end of the method that creates the **Panel**:

```
p1.add( new Button("Help") );
```

What happens when you try to compile and run the program?

○ a. The compiler objects to the statement because **p1** is already full.

○ b. The **Button** labeled "Help" is shown in the Center position of the **Panel**.

○ c. The original **CENTER** component is shown in the Center position of the **Panel**.

○ d. The first component added to the container is discarded and all components move up one position. The "Help" button ends up in the **CENTER**.

Answer b is correct because a component added to a **BorderLayout** without a constraint is assigned the center position by default. The compiler does not have any way to track the eventual contents of containers. Therefore, answer a is incorrect. Only the original **CENTER** component is displaced. Therefore, answers c and d are incorrect.

Question 10

You create a calculator application that has a **Panel** with a **GridLayout** to hold 16 **Button** objects for numerals and operators, using the following constructor for the **Panel**:

```
Panel p = new Panel( new GridLayout( 4, 4, 5,
8 ) );
```

Which of the following statements about the resulting display are true? [Check all correct answers]

- ❑ a. The horizontal space between buttons will be five pixels.

- ❑ b. The gap between the buttons and the edge of the **Panel** will be five pixels on the sides and eight on the top and the bottom.

- ❑ c. The order in which the **Button** objects are added controls their position, filling a row first, from left to right.

- ❑ d. The order in which the **Button** objects are added controls their position, filling a column first, from top to bottom.

Answers a and c are correct. The **GridLayout** is constructed with a **hgap** = 5. The **hgap** and **vgap** parameters control only spacing between components. Container insets control the gap between components and the edge of the container. Therefore, answer b is incorrect. The normal filling order for a **GridLayout** is to fill a row first, from left to right. Therefore, answer d is incorrect.

Need To Know More?

The **GridBagLayout** has always given Java programmers a lot of trouble. Various Java enthusiasts have set up sites on the Web with extensive tutorials and applets with which you can experiment. Here are two I found in a recent search for **GridBagLayout**:

http://links.math.rpi.edu/~finant/GBL/index.html

This site has an Introduction to the AWT **GridBagLayout**.

www.austria.eu.net/java/programs/applets/missgable/index.htm

This site has an applet that lets you experiment with the various parameters online and see the results immediately.

The Java Event Model

Terms you'll need to understand:

√ Adapter

√ Listener

√ **ActionEvent**

√ **AdjustmentEvent**

√ **KeyEvent**

√ **TextEvent**

√ **ItemEvent**

√ **MouseEvent**

Techniques you'll need to master:

√ Attaching the appropriate listener to a component

√ Interpreting mouse events

√ Processing key events

√ Enabling events

√ Implementing listener interface methods

√ Extending event adapters

Communication between the user and your program occurs entirely in the form of events. The Java Virtual Machine (JVM) gets raw event data from the operating system and creates event objects for your program to process. In this chapter, I'll look at the content of these objects and how they are processed in Java 2. I'll start with a quick survey of how events were handled in Java 1.0 to give you a historical perspective.

The Java 1.0 Event Model

In the original event model, all operating system events are turned into **java.awt.Event** objects. The JVM then searches the containment hierarchy and graphical component hierarchy trying to locate a method that can handle the event. The first method to get a chance at the event is the **handleEvent** method in the container of the component that generated the event. If this method returns a **true** value, the JVM assumes the event is taken care of; otherwise, it continues searching.

One of the more notable problems with this model is that the JVM spends a lot of time looking for a method to handle events that are not of interest to anything in the program. For example, just moving the mouse across the display area of a window can generate dozens of events. Each event object must be created with mouse position information and a timestamp, which is a total waste of processing power if no part of the program is interested. The more complex the user interface, the more processing power is wasted.

Another problem is that the Java 1.0 JVM looks for an event handler only in the containment and **java.awt** hierarchy. This forces the programmer to do event processing in a custom version of one of the **java.awt** components even if that is not the most logical place for it. Furthermore, if more than one object is interested in an event, the programmer must add specific code to distribute it. All of these problems were addressed in the major redesign that resulted in Java 1.1 and is continued in Java 2.

Events In Java 2

The redesigned event model is often referred to as the *delegation* model. Java 2 handles events that are generated in a graphical component by delegating to objects that have registered an interest in that type of event. This is an example of the *observer-observable* design pattern, in which the observable is the component that generates events, and the observer is the object that has registered to receive events. In Java 2, event observer objects are called *listeners* and implement listener interfaces.

Instead of the single all-purpose **Event** class of Java 1.0, there is now a hierarchy of classes with specialized variables and methods to suit various purposes. In Java 2, event handling is more flexible and efficient than in Java 1.0, by far. However, nothing in programming is free; this flexibility and efficiency comes at the cost of a large number of new classes and interfaces.

Features Of The Event Hierarchy

The root of the Java 2 event hierarchy is the **EventObject** class in the **java.util** package. An **EventObject** has only one variable, a reference to the object that generated it, which you can get with the following method:

```
public Object getSource()
```

Normally this reference will be to a graphical interface component such as a **Button**, but any object can be the source of an event.

A number of classes are derived from **EventObject**, but I am going to study only the **AWTEvent** branch of this hierarchy. The **java.awt.AWTEvent** class is the base class for all events that deal with user interface components, both in the **java.awt** package and in the Swing classes. **AWTEvent** adds the **int** variable **id** and the **boolean** variable **consumed**, plus the following method that returns the **id** of an **AWTEvent**:

```
public int getID()
```

AWTEvent is an **abstract** class having subclasses as shown in the following diagram:

```
java.util.EventObject
   |
  +-- java.awt.AWTEvent
        |
        +-- java.awt.event.ActionEvent
        |
        +-- java.awt.event.AdjustmentEvent
        |
        +-- java.awt.event.AncestorEvent
        |
        +-- java.awt.event.ComponentEvent
        |
        +-- java.awt.event.InputMethodEvent
        |
        +-- java.awt.event.InternalFrameEvent
        |
        +-- java.awt.event.InvocationEvent
```

```
   |
 +-- java.awt.event.ItemEvent
   |
 +-- java.awt.event.TextEvent
```

Each one of these event classes adds only the variables and methods needed to carry out a particular task. For instance, **Scrollbar** objects generate **AdjustmentEvent** events so they carry the current **Scrollbar** value setting. Each class also provides constants for various types of a particular event. For example, six different constants for different kinds of **AdjustmentEvent** are defined in the **AdjustmentEvent** class. The **getID** method, which is inherited from **AWTEvent**, returns these values.

For typical programming of graphical interfaces, you will probably be working with only a few of the events in this group, along with some events that descend from **ComponentEvent**, as follows:

```
java.awt.event.ComponentEvent
   |
 +-- java.awt.event.ContainerEvent
   |
 +-- java.awt.event.FocusEvent
   |
 +-- java.awt.event.PaintEvent
   |
 +-- java.awt.event.WindowEvent
   |
 +-- java.awt.event.InputEvent
        |
      +-- java.awt.event.MouseEvent
        |
      +-- java.awt.event.KeyEvent
```

Here is a quick summary of how some common events are generated:

➤ **ActionEvent** A button has been selected or a menu item has been double-clicked. This is considered a "high-level" or "semantic" event because additional processing logic was applied to mouse or keyboard primitive events.

➤ **AdjustmentEvent** The setting of a scrollbar has changed.

➤ **ItemEvent** The status of an item in a list, checkbox, or checkable menu item has changed. This is also considered a high-level event because of the additional processing logic.

➤ **FocusEvent** A component has gained or lost focus.

➤ **WindowEvent** The status of a window has changed. Not all changes to a window generate this event.

➤ **MouseEvent** The user has moved, clicked, or dragged the mouse within the area of a Java component.

➤ **KeyEvent** Depressing or releasing any key creates a **KeyEvent**. A separate **KeyEvent** is created for any key sequence that generates a character.

➤ **TextEvent** The text in an object such as a **TextField** or **TextArea** has changed. This is also considered a high-level event because it can result from a combination of mouse movements and keypress events.

Enabling Events

Events are generated by a Java component only if they have been specifically enabled. Every graphical entity carries an event mask variable that is a 64-bit **long** primitive. Each bit enables a particular kind of event. The JVM checks this event mask when processing an operating system event and continues to process event objects only for events that have been enabled.

Enabling events is done with constants defined in the **java.awt.AWTEvent** class. There are only 12 constants at present, so the use of a 64-bit **long** leaves plenty of room for expansion. The **java.awt.Component** class defines **enableEvents** and **disableEvents** methods that take a **long** primitive input that can combine several event mask constants. For example, if you want **object1** to generate keyboard and focus events, you execute this statement in which two constants are ORed together:

```
object1.enableEvents( AWTEvent.KEY_EVENT_MASK |
                      AWTEvent.FOCUS_EVENT_MASK );
```

Processing Events

The first method for getting a newly created event is the **processEvent** method in the originating component. This method is defined in **java.awt.Component**, but it is frequently overridden to provide custom event processing:

```
public void processEvent( AWTEvent e )
```

The default behavior of **processEvent** is to determine the event type and call one of the following:

```
public void processFocusEvent( FocusEvent e)
public void processMouseEvent( MouseEvent e)
```

```
public void processMouseMotionEvent( MouseEvent e)
public void processKeyEvent( KeyEvent e )
public void processComponentEvent( ComponentEvent e )
public void processInputMethodEvent( InputMethodEvent e )
```

The normal behavior of these methods is to send the event to the correct method of any listener that has registered with the component. If you build a custom component class that overrides one of these methods, you should also call the method in the parent class to ensure that listeners are notified:

```
public void processMouseEvent( MouseEvent evt ){
  if( evt.getID() == MouseEvent.MOUSE_PRESSED ){
    doMousePressStuff( evt ) ;
  }
  super.processMouseEvent( evt );
}
```

If the call to the parent class is not used, listeners will not get the event.

Listeners And Adapters

The **java.awt.event** package defines a number of listener interfaces that are named according to the events they process. For programmer convenience, **java.awt.event** also includes classes called *adapters* that provide empty methods for the more complex interfaces. Table 13.1 summarizes the relationship between some common events and the interfaces and adapter classes in the **java.awt.event** package.

 You must be familiar with the listener interfaces and adapter classes that are associated with these events.

The keen-eyed student will observe that this table has two lines for **MouseEvent** events. Events that are generated by the mouse being moved over a component are generated in great profusion but frequently are not of interest to the programmer. For greater efficiency, the distinction between mouse movement and all other mouse events is made as early as possible in event processing. Processing mouse events is discussed in detail in the section titled "The **MouseEvent** Class" later in this chapter.

Each class that can generate one of these events has a method to add a listener for that event. This method is always named by combining "add" with the name of a listener, so the **Button** class has an **addActionListener** method:

```
public void addActionListener( ActionListener a )
```

Table 13.1	Events, listener interfaces, and adapter classes.	
Event Class	**Interface**	**Adapter Class**
ActionEvent	ActionListener	(none)
AdjustmentEvent	AdjustmentListener	(none)
AWTEvent	AWTEventListener	(none)
ComponentEvent	ComponentListener	ComponentAdapter
ContainerEvent	ContainerListener	ContainerAdapter
FocusEvent	FocusListener	FocusAdapter
InputMethodEvent	InputMethodListener	(none)
ItemEvent	ItemListener	(none)
KeyEvent	KeyListener	KeyAdapter
MouseEvent	MouseListener	MouseAdapter
MouseEvent	MouseMotionListener	MouseMotionAdapter
TextEvent	TextListener	(none)
WindowEvent	WindowListener	WindowAdapter

The **Component** class has a system for keeping an unlimited number of listeners for every event descended from **AWTEvent**. The order in which listeners get called is *not* guaranteed.

Controls And ActionEvent Events

Controls that can generate **ActionEvent** events include (but are not limited to) **java.awt.Button, java.awt.MenuItem, java.awt.TextField**, and their Swing equivalents. A **TextField** object generates an **ActionEvent** when the user presses the Enter key.

The **ActionListener** interface has only one method:

```
public void actionPerformed( ActionEvent e )
```

To demonstrate how to work with **ActionEvent** events, I'll suppose you have an application with two **Button** objects and a **TextField**. One way to handle the **ActionEvent** events generated by these components is to make the basic application implement the interface. The class declaration could be:

```
public class MyApp extends Frame implements ActionListener
```

Skipping over the creation and placement of the components, the following code fragment shows how to add the application as an **ActionListener** to the components, most likely in the **MyApp** constructor:

```
button1.addActionListener( this );
button2.addActionListener( this );
textField1.addActionListener( this );
```

Your **MyApp** class has to have an **actionPerformed** method to satisfy the **ActionListener** interface. In that method you can find out which component generated the event with code such as the following:

```
public void actionPerformed( ActionEvent evt ){
  Object source = evt.getSource() ;
  if( source == button1 ) doButton1();
  if( source == button2 ) doButton2();
  if( source == textField1 ){
     processEntry( textField1.getText() );
  }
}
```

It is essential that you know how to get information from an event and process it in the various listener interface methods.

An alternative to making your application the **ActionListener** is to use an anonymous inner class. Inner classes are ideally suited to implement listener interfaces because they have access to all of the containing class variables. Using the previous example application, the code to create and add an **ActionListener** looks like this:

```
ActionListener al = new ActionListener(){
  public void actionPerformed( ActionEvent evt ){
    Object source = evt.getSource() ;
    if( source == button1 ) doButton1();
     ...// etc as before
    }
  }
} ; // end inner class creation
button1.addActionListener( al );
button2.addActionListener( al );
textField1.addActionListener( al );
```

Item Selection And Item Events

The **java.awt.ItemSelectable** interface specifies methods of interface objects that have one or more items that can be selected. Typical AWT controls implementing **ItemSelectable** include **List**, **Choice**, and **Checkbox**. When the selection status of an item changes, these controls generate an **ItemEvent** that is communicated to **ItemListener** objects.

An **ItemListener** has the following single method:

```
public void itemStateChanged( ItemEvent evt )
```

When processing an **ItemEvent,** you can find out which control had a changed item with **getSource** and then compare the result of the **getID** method with the constants **ItemEvent.SELECTED** and **ItemEvent.DESELECTED**. The actual list item whose state changed can be obtained with the **ItemEvent** method:

```
public Object getItem( )
```

If you have a **List** that presently has a selected item and you click on another item, any **ItemListener** first gets an **ItemEvent** with an **id** of DESELECTED, followed by an event for the newly selected item with an **id** of SELECTED.

Controls And AdjustmentEvent Events

The **java.awt.Scrollbar** and **javax.swing.JScrollBar** class objects generate **AdjustmentEvent** events. Classes creating **AdjustmentEvent** events are expected to implement the **java.awt.Adjustable** interface. The **AdjustmentListener** interface defines one method:

```
public void adjustmentValueChanged( AdjustmentEvent e )
```

Methods of interest in the **AdjustmentEvent** class are:

➤ **getAdjustable** This returns the object that generated the event.

➤ **getAdjustmentType** This returns an **int** value that can be compared with constants in the **AdjustmentEvent** class to determine the user action that caused the value to change.

➤ **getValue** This method returns an **int** primitive value for the control setting.

You might expect that the **javax.swing.JSlider** control generates **AdjustmentEvent** events, but the designers chose to have it generate **ChangeEvent** events. This class is derived directly from **EventObject** and is not part of the **AWTEvent** hierarchy, so you don't have to worry about it for the exam.

Component Events

In addition to being generated when certain changes affect **Component** objects, the **ComponentEvent** class is the parent of several event classes. The **ComponentEvent** class defines the method as follows:

```
public Component getComponent()
```

The **ComponentListener** interface defines the methods **componentHidden**, **componentMoved**, **componentResized**, and **componentShown**. For convenience, there is also a **ComponentAdapter** class. Here is an example of code using an inner class derived from **ComponentAdapter** to detect when a window has been resized:

```
addComponentListener( new ComponentAdapter() {
  public void componentResized(ComponentEvent e ){
      System.out.println("Resized");
  }
  } ) ;
```

The FocusEvent Class

FocusEvent events are generated whenever an interface component gains or loses the user input focus. The component with the focus is the one that will receive a key event if the user types something. This component is indicated with different conventions, depending on the operating system for AWT components or on the installed look and feel for Swing components. To determine whether focus has been gained or lost, compare the result of the **getID** method with the constants **FocusEvent.FOCUS_GAINED** and **FocusEvent.FOCUS_LOST**.

The **FocusEvent** class also defines the following method:

```
public boolean isTemporary()
```

This method returns **true** if the loss of focus is temporary. A temporary loss of focus can occur when a second window comes to the top. The component regains focus when the first window comes to the top again. The **FocusListener** interface defines **focusGained** and **focusLost** methods. There is also a **FocusAdapter** that has empty versions of these two methods.

When the user is filling in text fields, the loss of focus event is frequently used as a signal to start parsing or otherwise processing the input. Obviously, the programmer should check to see if the loss of focus is only temporary before starting this process.

The WindowEvent Class

Changes in certain aspects of the status of a window generate **WindowEvent** events. The **WindowListener** interface defines the following methods to handle these events:

➤ **windowActivated** Called when the window has been brought to the front of the user's desktop and has the focus.

➤ **windowOpened** Called the first time a window is displayed.

➤ **windowClosed** Called when the window has been closed and cannot be reopened.

➤ **windowClosing** Called when the user has tried to close the window. This is the programmer's last chance to save data. If the method does not specifically exit the program, nothing will happen.

➤ **windowIconified** Called when the window has been put in the minimized state. Exactly how a minimized window behaves depends on the operating system.

➤ **windowDeiconified** Called when the window is restored after being iconified.

➤ **windowDeactivated** Called when the window loses the focus through being closed, being minimized, or through another window gaining the focus.

Note that there is no **WindowEvent** generated when a window is resized. You can attach a **ComponentListener** to catch the **ComponentEvent** events caused by resizing.

Here is typical code used to create an inner class derived from **WindowAdapter** to provide for closing an application derived from **java.awt.Frame**:

```
addWindowListener( new WindowAdapter() {
   public void windowClosing( WindowEvent evt ){
      setVisible( false ) ;
      System.exit( 0 );
   }
} ) ;
```

Note that if an application is closed in the **windowClosing** method by using **System.exit,** no more events of any kind will be processed.

The MouseEvent And KeyEvent Classes

The abstract **InputEvent** class has two subclasses you will use a lot: **MouseEvent** and **KeyEvent.** The following reviews the hierarchy that leads to these classes:

```
java.util.EventObject
  |
  +-- java.awt.AWTEvent
        |
        +-- java.awt.event.ComponentEvent
              |
              +-- java.awt.event.InputEvent
                    |
                    +-- java.awt.event.KeyEvent
                    |
                    +-- java.awt.event.MouseEvent
```

The **InputEvent** class adds the following methods to those it inherits:

➤ **consume()** This sets a **boolean** variable named **consumed** in the event, which subsequent listeners can examine.

➤ **getModifiers()** This returns an **int** that encodes various keyboard and mouse button modifier flags. Constants for these flags are defined in the **InputEvent** class.

➤ **getWhen()** Returns a **long** primitive value of the system timestamp for the creation of the event. This is the same time as returned by **System.currentTimeMillis** method.

➤ **isAltDown()** Returns the state of the Alt key that existed when the event was created. Note that not all operating systems support all of these special flags.

➤ **isAltGraphDown()** Returns the state of the Alt+Graph key that existed when the event was created.

➤ **isConsumed()** Returns true if this event's **consume** method has been called.

➤ **isControlDown()** Returns the state of the Ctrl key that existed when the event was created.

➤ **isMetaDown()** Returns the state of the Meta key that existed when the event was created.

➤ **isShiftDown()** Returns the state of the Shift key that existed when the event was created.

The constants defined in the **InputEvent** class that you can use to interpret the value returned by **getModifiers** are keyboard- or mouse-related. The keyboard-related constants are **SHIFT_MASK, ALT_MASK, CTRL_MASK, META_MASK,** and **ALT_GRAPH_MASK.** The mouse-related constants are **BUTTON1_MASK, BUTTON2_MASK,** and **BUTTON3_MASK.** Obviously, the underlying operating system and hardware determine which of these constants is useful.

Each bit in the 32-bit **int** returned by **getModifiers** is set independently, so you perform a bitwise AND with a constant to determine whether the condition exists. For example, the following operation results in a boolean value of **true** if the Shift key was depressed when the event **evt** was generated:

```
( evt.getModifiers() & InputEvent.SHIFT_MASK ) != 0
```

The MouseEvent Class

In addition to the timestamp and modifiers added in the **InputEvent** class, **MouseEvent** objects carry x and y coordinates as **int** primitive values. Here are the methods provided in the **MouseEvent** class for accessing these coordinates and other properties:

➤ **getX()** Returns the horizontal position of the event as an **int** measured in pixels from the left edge of the source component. If the event is a mouse drag outside the component, position values may be negative.

➤ **getY()** Returns the vertical position of the event as an **int** measured in pixels from the top edge of the source component.

➤ **getPoint()** Returns the x and y coordinates as a **Point** object.

➤ **getClickCount()** Returns an **int** number of clicks associated with the event. This number is determined by operating system conventions, not Java.

➤ **isPopupTrigger()** Returns true if the event is a trigger for a popup menu under operating system conventions.

➤ **translatePoint(int x, int y)** Modifies the stored location by adding these values. This method is used to translate the event to the coordinate system of another component.

➤ **paramString()** This routine returns a **String** describing the event.

Mouse events are the only events that have two types of listener interface, the **MouseMotionListener** and the **MouseListener** interfaces, and two types of adapter class, **MouseMotionAdapter** and **MouseAdapter**. The methods in **MouseMotionListener** are:

➤ **mouseDragged(MouseEvent evt)** This handles events produced when the mouse is moved with a button pressed. You can determine which button is pressed by looking at the value returned by the **getModifiers** method. Note that mouse-dragged events are sent to a component *only* if the drag was started in the component. Furthermore, events continue to be sent to the component long after the drag has exited the component.

 While the drag is in operation, *no* other component gets **MouseEvent** events. When the mouse button is finally released, the component where the mouse drag started gets a mouse-released event.

➤ **mouseMoved(MouseEvent evt)** This handles events produced when the mouse is moved without any button pressed.

The **MouseListener** interface handles mouse events that are more likely to be of interest to a programmer. The **MouseListener** interface defines the following methods:

➤ **mouseClicked(MouseEvent evt)** This handles the event created when a mouse button is depressed. The value returned by **getModifiers** can be used to determine which button was pressed by comparison with constants in the **InputEvent** class.

➤ **mouseEntered(MouseEvent evt)** This event goes to a component when the mouse first enters the component, whether or not a mouse drag is in progress.

➤ **mouseExited(MouseEvent evt)** This event goes to a component when the mouse leaves the component, whether or not a mouse drag is in progress.

➤ **mousePressed(MouseEvent evt)** Any press of a mouse button causes an event going to this method.

➤ **mouseReleased(MouseEvent evt)** When a mouse button is released, an event goes to this method. Note that the event modifiers reflect the state of the mouse buttons after the release, so you can tell which button was released only if you have stored information from previous events.

The KeyEvent Class

The three kinds of key events are processed by three methods in the **KeyListener** interface:

➤ **keyPressed(KeyEvent evt)** Every press of a key causes an event to be sent to this method.

➤ **keyReleased(KeyEvent evt)** Every release of a key causes an event to be sent to this method.

➤ **keyTyped(KeyEvent evt)** The event processed by this method is created only when one or more key events has generated a character.

Each **KeyEvent** carries a key code that can be obtained with the following method:

```
public int getKeyCode();
```

The **KeyEvent** class defines a huge number of key codes for both normal characters and special keys, such as the function key, cursor control keys, and modifiers. Although some of these codes coincide with ASCII codes for characters, you should use the method

```
public char getKeyChar()
```

to determine the Unicode character from a **KeyEvent** in the **keyTyped** method. Some other methods of interest in the **KeyEvent** class are as follows:

```
public void setKeyChar( char ch )
public void setModifiers( int mod )
```

These methods allow you to completely change a **KeyEvent** before it goes to a **TextComponent** such as a **TextField**. For instance, if you want to ensure that all alphabetic characters added to **textField1** are in uppercase, you could create an anonymous inner class extending **KeyAdapter** as follows:

```
textField1.addKeyListener( new KeyAdapter(){
    public void keyTyped( KeyEvent e ){
      e.setKeyChar( Character.toUpperCase( e.getKeyChar() ));
    }
 } ) ;
```

KeyListener objects are typically used to monitor user input in a **TextField** or similar component. All **KeyListener** objects registered with a **TextField** will see a new **KeyEvent** before a character is added to the text. If a **KeyListener**

calls the **KeyEvent consume** method, the character will not be added to the text field. For example, the following statement creates an anonymous inner class extending **KeyAdapter**, which ensures that only numeric characters can be entered in **textField1**:

```
textField1.addKeyListener( new KeyAdapter(){
    public void keyTyped( KeyEvent e ){
      if( !Character.isDigit( e.getKeyChar()) )e.consume();
    }
} ) ;
```

The TextEvent Class

Rather than monitor individual **KeyEvent** events, you can simply use a **TextEventListener**. This interface has a single method:

```
public void textValueChanged( TextEvent evt )
```

This event is generated only when the text contained in the control is actually changed. One use of a **TextEventListener** is to look up a key word while a user has the word only partially entered.

Event Processing Review

Event handling in Java can get pretty complicated. The following reviews the steps involved in event processing:

1. The operating system decides that certain events belong to a Java application and communicates them to the JVM. Exactly how much processing is done by the operating system depends on the type of component. Components created by operating system peers have much of their low-level event processing done by the operating system, but Swing components have low-level events processed by Java.

2. The JVM creates event objects and directs them to a specific component according to various rules. For instance, the component having the current focus gets key events, but the screen location is used to direct mouse events.

3. If the particular kind of event is enabled, **processEvent** in **java.awt.Component** (or in a class overriding **processEvent**) is called. The default behavior of **processEvent** is to call a more specific event processing method according to the type of the event object.

4. If any listeners for this type of event are registered with the component, the appropriate method in each listener is called with the reference to

the event object. Each registered listener gets called, but the order in which they are called is not guaranteed.

As a programmer, you have an opportunity to process an event at several points in this chain. You can override **processEvent** or one of the other process methods in **Component,** you can write a class implementing one of the listener interfaces, or you can create a custom version of one of the adapter classes.

Practice Questions

Question 1

> Which of the following statements about adapter classes are true?
> [Check all correct answers]
>
> ☐　a. Adapter classes may provide a default processing of
> an event.
>
> ☐　b. Every listener interface has a corresponding adapter
> class.
>
> ☐　c. All methods in adapter classes are empty.
>
> ☐　d. Adapter classes are named according to the event they
> process.

Answers c and d are correct. Adapters provide empty method implementations for all methods in a particular interface. Therefore, answer a is incorrect. Adapters are not provided for interfaces with only one method. Therefore, answer b is incorrect.

Question 2

> If you want to prevent the character represented by a **KeyEvent**
> from being added to a **TextField**, what should you do in the
> **keyTyped** method of a listener getting the event?
>
> ○　a. Execute the **KeyEvent** object's **consume** method.
>
> ○　b. Return **true** from the **keyTyped** method.
>
> ○　c. Call the **KeyEvent** object's **setKeyChar** method with a
> zero value.
>
> ○　d. Get the current text from the **TextField**, remove the last
> character from the **String**, and reset the text.

Answer a is correct. The purpose of the **consume** method is to prevent further processing of the input event. All listener interface methods have a void return type. Therefore, answer b is incorrect. Answer c would change the character but would not prevent it from being added. Therefore, answer c is incorrect. When a **KeyListener** gets the event, it has not yet been processed by the **TextField**. Therefore, answer d is incorrect.

Question 3

When you add a **KeyListener** to a **Button** component, which of the following statements are true? [Check all correct answers]

- ❏ a. You must also call the Button's **enableEvents** method with the correct constants to enable key and mouse click events.

- ❏ b. You must also call the Button's **enableEvents** method with the constant **AWTEvent.KEY_EVENT_MASK**.

- ❏ c. The **KeyListener** must provide **keyPressed**, **keyReleased**, and **keyTyped** methods.

- ❏ d. The act of adding the listener ensures that key events are enabled for the **Button**.

Answers c and d are correct. The **addKeyListener** method in the **Button** object turns action events on. Note that the addKeyListener method is in the Component class so all AWT components can have KeyListeners. Therefore, answers a and b are incorrect.

Question 4

Which of the following statements about **ActionEvent** events is *wrong*?

- ○ a. There is only one method in **ActionListener** that takes an **ActionEvent**.

- ○ b. When you are entering text into a **TextField**, typing the Enter key causes an **ActionEvent**.

- ○ c. When you are in an application, clicking the window close control causes an **ActionEvent**.

- ○ d. **Scrollbar** objects do not generate **ActionEvent** events.

Answer c is the only incorrect statement and is thus the correct answer. Window controls are a special case and generate **WindowEvent** events.

Question 5

There are seven kinds of **MouseEvent** events and two kinds of listener that handle mouse events. From the following list of method signatures, select the methods found in the **MouseListener** interface. [Check all correct answers]

❑ a. public void mouseEntered(MouseEvent e)

❑ b. public void mouseDragged(MouseEvent e)

❑ c. public void mouseReleased(MouseEvent e)

❑ d. public void mousePressed(MouseEvent e)

Answers a, c, and d are correct. **mouseDragged** is in the **MouseMotionListener** interface. Therefore, answer b is incorrect.

Question 6

What value is returned by the **MouseEvent** method **getX()**?

○ a. An **int** primitive value representing the horizontal position of the mouse event relative to the left edge of the **Component** generating the event.

○ b. A **long** primitive value representing the horizontal position of the mouse event relative to the left edge of the **Component** generating the event.

○ c. An **int** primitive value representing the horizontal position of the mouse event relative to the left edge of the application window.

○ d. An **int** primitive value representing the horizontal position of the mouse event relative to the left edge of the container holding the **Component** generating the event.

Answer a is correct. The position information in a **MouseEvent** is relative to the upper-left corner of the object generating the event. Like all screen position calculations, the x position is an **int** value. Therefore, answer b is incorrect. The **MouseEvent** position information is generated at the component level; no attempt is made to convert to other coordinate systems. Therefore, answers c and d are incorrect.

Question 7

When an **AdjustmentListener** gets an **AdjustmentEvent** event from a **Scrollbar**, which **AdjustmentEvent** class method is used to retrieve the current setting of the **Scrollbar**?

- ○ a. public int getPosition()
- ○ b. public int getValue()
- ○ c. public float getPosition()
- ○ d. public float getValue()

Answer b is correct. The method **public int getPosition()** does not exist. Therefore, answer a is incorrect. A **Scrollbar** value is an **int**. Therefore, answers c and d are incorrect.

Question 8

Your user interface has a **java.awt.Choice** component that displays a list of colors the user can select to set the application foreground color. Which kind of listener should you attach to this component in order to be notified of a new color selection?

- ○ a. ItemListener
- ○ b. ActionListener
- ○ c. SelectionListener
- ○ d. MouseEventListener

Answer a is correct. Selecting or deselecting an item in a **Choice, List,** or menu creates an **ItemEvent** that is sent to an **ItemListener**. **ActionEvent** events are not generated in a **Choice**. Therefore, answer b is incorrect. There is no such thing as a **SelectionEvent**. Therefore, answer c is incorrect. It would be very difficult to interpret mouse events in terms of item selection in the **Choice**. Therefore, answer d is incorrect.

Question 9

> The following code illustrates testing the modifiers of a
> **MouseEvent** to detect the left mouse button being depressed:
>
> ```
> public void mouseClicked( MouseEvent evt ){
>   if( (evt.getModifiers() &
>        XXXXXX.BUTTON1_MASK) != 0 ) {
>     System.out.println("Left button" );
>   }
> }
> ```
>
> However, XXXXXX has been substituted for the class name for the
> **BUTTON1_MASK** constant. Which of the following classes could
> be used to replace XXXXXX and result in working code? [Check
> all correct answers]
>
> ❑ a. AWTEvent
>
> ❑ b. ComponentEvent
>
> ❑ c. InputEvent
>
> ❑ d. MouseEvent

Answers c and d are correct. The modifier constants are defined in **InputEvent** and inherited by **MouseEvent**. Answers a and b are ancestors of **InputEvent** and thus do not have access to these constants.

Question 10

> A **TextEvent** is generated when a user changes the position of the
> editing cursor in a **TextField**.
>
> ○ a. True
>
> ○ b. False

Answer b is correct. This is a false statement. A **TextEvent** is generated only when the text content is changed, no matter what the sequence of low-level events.

Need To Know More?

 ftp://ftp.javasoft.com/docs/tutorial.zip

At this site, you can find and download an excellent tutorial in HTML form. The section on writing event listeners is excellent and includes many examples.

 http://java.sun.com/products/jdk/1.2/index.html

From this Web site, you can download the Java API documentation in Javadoc-generated form. Although this site changes a lot, it is a good starting point.

Java IO

Terms you'll need to understand:

- √ The **File** class
- √ **InputStream**
- √ **OutputStream**
- √ **Filter**
- √ **Reader**
- √ **Writer**
- √ Object serialization
- √ **Socket**
- √ UTF encoding

Techniques you'll need to master:

- √ Using Java **File** objects to get information on files and directories
- √ Chaining stream objects
- √ Reading local and Web server files
- √ Reading and writing Java objects
- √ Communicating between programs with sockets

For access to local files, Java provides classes for both random and sequential access of text and data files. Special methods are provided to support internationalization of programs by reading a variety of character formats into Java's standard Unicode format. In addition to reading and writing primitive values, the serialization mechanism lets you store the complete state of an object in a file and rebuild the object on demand.

From the beginning, Java has been aware of networks. The extensive library of network-related classes makes it easy for even the beginning programmer to write programs that communicate over networks.

How Java Handles Files

The **java.io.File** class is the central organizing principle for manipulation of file systems in an operating-system-independent fashion. The primary use of a **File** object is to manipulate directory and file names. The **File** class knows about the conventions of the particular operating system on which the JVM is running, and in fact, has constants for the file separator character that are set by the JVM. Here are the constructors for **File** objects:

```
1. File( File parent, String path )
2. File( String path )
3. File( String parent, String path )
```

Note that in the preceding code, **path** may contain a directory name, a file name, or a combination. A **File** contains an *abstract pathname* that can represent either a directory or a path plus a file name. Paths can be either relative to the current user directory or absolute.

File Methods For Directories

If you have a **File** object representing a directory, you can use it to get a list of files and subdirectories as either an array of **File** objects or an array of **String** objects. Note that all methods that get file system information check with the security manager and may throw a **SecurityException** if the program does not have clearance to access the file system. That is how applets are prevented from accessing a user's file system. Getting directory information is illustrated in this code fragment, where **filter** is an object implementing the **FileNameFilter** interface:

```
1. File start = new File( "C:\\java" ); // the java directory
2. File[] grp = start.listFiles() ;
3. File[] selgrp = start.listFiles( filter ) ;
4. String[] names = start.list() ;
5. String[] selnames = start.list( filter );
```

To implement the **FileNameFilter** interface, a class simply has to have an **accept** method that is handed a **File** object and a **String** file name, and returns **true** if the file belongs in the list. There is also a **FileFilter** interface in which the **accept** method is handed a **File** object.

Here are some of the methods you can use with a **File** object such as those returned by lines 2 and 3 in the preceding code:

➤ **boolean exists()** Returns **true** if the directory or file exists.

➤ **boolean isDirectory()** Returns **true** if the **File** represents a directory.

➤ **boolean isFile()** Returns **true** if the **File** represents a normal file.

You can also get an array of **File** objects representing the file system roots with the **listRoots** method. On a Windows system, the roots are the individual drives, such as "A:\", "C:\", and so on.

Although **File** objects can deal with absolute paths or paths relative to the "current" directory, there is no method in **File** to change the current directory. It is best to determine the current directory from the system properties as follows:

```
String currentDir = System.getProperty("user.dir") ;
```

Using that information, you can then create absolute paths.

File Methods For Files

Here are some of the most useful instance methods related to files in the **java.io.File** class. Each one of these may throw a **SecurityException** if the current program does not have clearance to access file system data:

➤ **boolean canRead()** Returns **true** if the current program is allowed to read the file.

➤ **boolean canWrite()** Returns **true** if the current program is allowed to write to the file.

➤ **long length()** Returns the length of the file as a **long** primitive.

➤ **long lastModified()** Returns a **long** primitive representing the date the file was last modified. The value is milliseconds since the beginning of January 1, 1970, compatible with the **currentTimeMillis** method in the **java.lang.System** class.

➤ **boolean delete()** This method attempts to delete a file or directory and returns **true** if it succeeds.

➤ **boolean createNewFile()** Creates a new empty file with this name unless a file with this name already exists. Returns **true** if a new file was created.

 Remember, creating a **File** object with the path and file name of a file does not do anything to the file itself. In order to open the file, you will have to pass the **File** object to a constructor for one of the other classes in the **java.io** package.

InputStream And OutputStream

InputStream and **OutputStream** are the **abstract** classes at the base of the hierarchy of Java classes that represent streams of 8-bit bytes. The basic requirement of a class extending **InputStream** is that it can read the next **byte** of data from a source. Likewise, an extension of **OutputStream** must be able to write a single **byte** of data. From this simple base, Java constructs a wide variety of classes. Here are some of the commonly used extensions:

➤ **FileInputStream** The constructor takes a file name or **File** object and opens the file for reading.

➤ **FileOutputStream** The constructor opens an existing file or creates a new one. One of the constructors lets you append data to the end of an existing file, but generally any existing data is written over.

➤ **ByteArrayInputStream** This class lets you read a **byte** array as if it were a file.

➤ **ByteArrayOutputStream** With one of these, you can write an arbitrary sequence of data to a memory buffer that automatically expands as needed.

Creating input and output streams with network connections will be discussed later in this chapter. The following section looks at what you can do with a stream.

Stream Filters

Unless your program requires only reading and writing bytes, you will be using a stream filter. A filter connects to an **InputStream** or **OutputStream** and performs some transformation on the data or provides some additional functionality. For example, in the following code fragment, a **DataInputStream** object interprets a stream of bytes from the **FileInputStream** as **double** primitive values:

```
double d[] = new double[100] ;
try {
FileInputStream fis = new FileInputStream( "mydata.bin" );
DataInputStream dis = new DataInputStream( fis ) ;
for int i = 0 ; i < 100 ; i++ ){
  d[i] = dis.readDouble();
}
}catch(IOException e ) {}
```

The following code fragment constructs a chain of output stream objects in which the **DataOutputStream** provides the methods to output primitive values, and the **BufferedOutputStream** stores the bytes in a buffer and writes buffer loads to the file via the **FileOutputStream** object:

```
try {
FileOutputStream fos = new FileOutputStream( "moredata.bin" );
BufferedOutputStream bos = new BufferedOutputStream( fos, 4096 );
DataOutputStream dos = new DataOutputStream( bos );
  // assume lots of data writing goes on here
dos.flush() ; // also flushes the buffered stream
dos.close() ;
```

 For programming advanced input/output methods in Java, it is essential to understand this approach of chaining together stream-handling classes.

By extending the **InputStream** or **OutputStream** classes, you can turn just about anything into a stream of bytes that will fit right into the powerful classes in the **java.io** package. Alternately, you can extend **FilterInputStream** or **FilterOutputStream** to create classes that modify a stream of bytes and are compatible with the basic Java IO classes.

Buffered Streams

A basic **InputStream** can read the next byte in a file, but can't back up. Furthermore, reading a file one byte at a time can be very inefficient if each read has to call routines in the underlying operating system. The **BufferedInputStream** class tackles the efficiency problem by reading blocks of bytes into a buffer and then supplying the sequence of bytes without having to go to the operating system.

Input streams that store some of the stream data, such as **BufferedInputStream**, support the **mark** and **reset** methods. These methods allow a limited ability to back up in an **InputStream**. Here are the **InputStream** methods involved in this capability:

➤ **boolean markSupported()** Returns **true** if this stream supports **mark** and **reset**.

➤ **void mark(int byteCt)** Marks the current position in this stream and tells the stream to be prepared to be able to back up **byteCt** bytes.

➤ **void reset()** Attempts to reset the reading point of the stream back to the marked location. If this is impossible, an **IOException** is thrown.

As you can see, the **mark** and **reset** capability is very limited and does not provide much flexibility. The programmer must carefully plan to ensure that resetting beyond the capability of the stream is not required. The **mark** and **reset** methods exist in all classes derived from **InputStream**, but unless **markSupported** returns **true**, they are do-nothing methods.

Here are the classes in the **java.io** package that support some degree of buffering:

➤ **PushbackInputStream** This class supports the capability of *unreading* a single byte, but does not support **mark** and **reset**.

➤ **BufferedInputStream** This class attempts to fill a buffer every time it reads from a source. It supports **mark** and **reset**.

➤ **BufferedOutputStream** Bytes written to this stream are stored in a buffer until the buffer is full or the **flush** method is called. Closing the stream calls **flush** automatically. The default buffer size is 512 bytes, but you can specify another size in the constructor. There is no equivalent of **mark** and **reset** in output streams, so if you want a class that *unwrites* bytes, you will have to code it yourself.

The PrintStream Class

You have probably already used this class extensively because the default **System.out** stream is a **PrintStream**. This class knows how to output text representations of various primitive values correctly. All output is in the form of 8-bit bytes in the default encoding of the operating system. A **PrintStream** traps all **IOExceptions** and sets an internal flag when one occurs.

This class does not correctly handle Unicode characters that use the high byte of a 16-bit character. To discourage the continued use of **PrintStream**, the constructors for the class were deprecated in Java 1.1, but Sun removed the deprecation tag for Java 2. The other methods are not deprecated because you need to be able to use them with the **System.out** stream. Programmers are encouraged to use the **PrintWriter** class instead of **PrintStream**.

Streams And Characters

As you will recall, Java uses 16-bit Unicode characters in **String** objects and the **char** primitive to support internationalization. However, all of the Java source code files in the standard library and those written by typical development environments are in 8-bit bytes, and they typically use the 7-bit ASCII code. When an object such as a **DataInputStream** interprets ASCII text into 16-bit characters, it simply adds an all-zero high byte, and when a **PrintStream** writes 16-bit characters, it simply drops the high byte.

The UTF-8 encoding system neatly bridges between the world of 7-bit ASCII and 16-bit Unicode. A UTF-8 encoded text file consists of bytes that are interpreted according to some simple rules. If the high bit of a byte is zero, it is considered an ASCII character, but if the high byte is one, it must be interpreted as part of a multi-byte sequence that creates a 16-bit character. The Unicode characters between '\u0020' and '\u007F' are equivalent to ASCII and the ISO8859-1 (Latin-1) encoding.

A single character may end up encoded in one, two, or three bytes. Because there is no direct equivalence between the number of characters encoded with UTF-8 in a file and the number of bytes, the reading and writing methods use a special format.

➤ **void writeUTF(String s)** This method, specified in the **DataOutput** interface, writes the length of the **String** as a 2-byte unsigned integer, then writes the bytes encoding the characters.

➤ **String readUTF()** This method, specified in the **DataInput** interface, first reads 2 bytes to get the count of the number of characters to follow, then reads and interprets the stream until that many characters have been decoded and placed in the **String**.

There are also a variety of other character encoding systems that got started long before the Unicode standard was created. Java provides for reading and writing streams of these characters via classes that extend the **abstract java.io.Reader** and **java.io.Writer** classes.

The Reader And Writer Classes

Classes derived from **Reader** and **Writer** can take into account the locale information provided by the operating system, or they can use a specified locale when converting between Unicode and other character system. The following code fragment indicates how a Java program could write a file using ISO8859-8 (Hebrew) encoding:

```
try {
  FileOutputStream fos = new FileOutputStream( "sometext.txt" );
  OutputStreamWriter osw = new OutputStreamWriter( fos,
    "ISO8859-8" );
  // various write operations go here
  osw.close();
}catch( UnsupportedEncodingException ee ){
  System.out.println("Encoding ISO8859-8 not supported");
}catch( IOException ie ){
  System.out.println( ie );
}
```

Here are some of the **Reader**- and **Writer**-related classes you are likely to encounter:

➤ **BufferedReader** This object reads ahead in a character input stream to improve efficiency.

➤ **BufferedWriter** This object stores characters in a buffer and writes the entire buffer when it is full or when the **flush** method is called.

➤ **CharArrayReader** With this class, an array of **char** can be turned into a character stream.

➤ **CharArrayWriter** This class writes to an array of **char** that is automatically expanded as needed.

➤ **FileReader** This class is provided for convenience in reading character files. It is effectively an **InputStreamReader** combined with a **FileInputStream**. The default character encoding is assumed.

➤ **FileWriter** This class is effectively an **OutputStreamWriter** combined with a **FileOutputStream**. It assumes the default character encoding.

➤ **InputStreamReader** The bridge between byte streams and character streams. It can use the default encoding or one specified by name.

➤ **OutputStreamWriter** Writes characters to an **OutputStream** of bytes, using a specified encoding or the default.

➤ **PrintWriter** This is the **Writer**-derived analog to the **PrintStream** class.

➤ **LineNumberReader** This object provides a buffer and counts lines as it reads a stream, and can provide the line number of the present position in the stream.

DataInput And DataOutput Interfaces

Classes implementing the **DataInput** or **DataOutput** interfaces must provide methods for reading or writing all of the Java primitive types. Note that the standard Java format for writing integer primitives is "big-endian"—that is, the most significant byte is written first. This is the opposite of the usual approach in the Intel/DOS/Windows environment, so, if your Java method must read native files, you may have to provide special methods for interpreting the byte stream in a different order.

In addition to writing individual primitive values, these interfaces provide for reading and writing arrays of bytes, **String** objects, and the special UTF-8 encoded character stream format.

Streams And URLs

From the beginning, Java has had many classes designed for communicating on the World Wide Web using the HTTP protocol recognized by Web servers and browsers. A **URL** object represents the address of a resource on the World Wide Web, and includes information on the host computer, the protocol to be used, and the resource name. A **URL** may address a simple Web page, or it may include data being submitted to a process on the Web server.

In the environment of a Java applet, you can use the following methods to get specific **URL** objects:

➤ **getDocumentBase()** Returns the **URL** for the Web page in which the applet is embedded.

➤ **getCodeBase()** Returns the **URL** for the directory on the server that the applet class file came from. This may be different from the document base if the <APPLET> tag used a CODEBASE parameter to point to the applet source.

The following code fragment illustrates getting an **InputStream** for data provided by a request to a Web server by an applet. Calling the **openStream** method attempts to open a connection to the Web server with a **URL** for a specific file. If all goes well, the Web server sends that file using the HTTP protocol and the programmer can read data from the resulting **InputStream**.

```
URL theUrl = new URL( getDocumentBase(), "mydata.bin" );
InputStream ins = theUrl.openStream();
```

Note that this code would have to be enclosed in a **try-catch** structure because **openStream** may throw an **IOException**. Because it may take some time for the server to respond, code like this should always be in a **Thread** that is separate from the JVM event-processing **Thread**.

The RandomAccessFile Class

One of the major divisions in the **java.io** package is between this class and all other classes. A **RandomAccessFile** object can both read and write data to any part of a file. All other file-reading and file-writing classes view files as streams of bytes that must be read from the beginning of the file. **RandomAccessFile** objects are created with a *mode* **String**, which can either be "r" for read-only or "rw" for read and write. The following constructors will attempt to create a file if the mode is "rw" and the file does not already exist:

```
RandomAccessFile( File f, String mode )
RandomAccessFile( String filename, String mode )
```

These constructors can throw a **FileNotFoundException** or a **SecurityException**.

A **RandomAccessFile** has a file pointer that determines where in the file the next read or write operation will occur. When the file is initially opened, this pointer is at 0 (the beginning of the file). After that, it is positioned where the last read or write ended. You can position this pointer with the **seek** method.

In addition to methods for reading an arbitrary number of bytes into a buffer, the **RandomAccessFile** class implements all of the methods called for by the **DataInput** and **DataOutput** interfaces. This means that there are methods for reading and writing all Java primitives plus **String** objects.

Object Serialization

Using object serialization, you can permanently store a Java object in a file or transmit it over a network to another Java program. Classes indicate that they make objects that can be serialized by implementing the **java.io.Serializable** interface. Serialization is at the core of all sorts of interesting Java applications. Writing an object is as simple as this example:

```
try {
 FileOutputStream fos = new FileOutputStream( "currentObject" );
 ObjectOutputStream oos = new ObjectOutputStream( fos );
 oos.writeObject( theObj );
 oos.close();
} catch(Exception e){}
```

Any system that has a copy of the class file for the class that **theObj** belongs to could now read the "currentObject" file with the **readObject** method of an **ObjectInputStream** and reconstitute the object. The object that is serialized may be quite complex, with many references to other objects. The serialization process takes care of writing all of the linked objects and also keeps track of all objects that have been written so that no duplication occurs.

You do not have to accept Java's method of serialization. If you have a more efficient method, just make your custom class implement the **java.io.Externalizable** interface. The **writeObject** method will then call your **writeExternal** method, and the **readObject** method will call your **readExternal** method to serialize the object.

Zip Files And JAR Files

Java Archive (JAR) files provide a compact way to store a number of classes or other data resources. The format used in a JAR file is that of the familiar zip utility. Classes in the **java.util.zip** and **java.util.jar** packages provide methods for reading and writing data with stream methods that decompress or compress files. In addition to file names, a JAR or zip file may contain path information, essentially creating a directory system within a single file.

The JAR file format adds a *manifest* file to the zip format. This file gives extra information about each of the data items in the file. Extra information may include digital signatures to positively identify applications as coming from a known source.

Client/Server Programming

It is surprisingly easy to program communication between computers using Java's network classes. A **java.net.Socket** object represents one end of a TCP/IP-based communication link between two programs. The programmer does not have to worry about the details of the TCP/IP protocol. Once a **Socket** has established a connection, it can be used to create input streams and output streams that receive and transmit streams of bytes.

The draft objectives for the exam actually included a section on socket programming, but this got dropped in the final release. I am leaving this material in the book because it illustrates significant points about using streams and handling exceptions.

Here is some code from a simple client class in which the constructor creates a socket connection to a given port on a given host and opens streams for communication. Note that because the streams are connected to **Reader** and **Writer** objects, this connection could only be used for character streams and not binary data:

```
1.     // instance variables
2.   Socket sok ;
3.   OutputStreamWriter oswri ;
4.   InputStream ins ;
5.   BufferedReader bread ;
6.
7.   SimpleConnect( String host, int port ) throws IOException {
8.     sok = new Socket( host, port );
9.     oswri = new OutputStreamWriter( sok.getOutputStream() );
10.    InputStreamReader isr = new InputStreamReader(
11.           ins = sok.getInputStream() );
12.    bread = new BufferedReader( isr );
13.    System.out.println("Streams created" );
14. }
```

The constructor will block at line 8 until a connection is established or an exception occurs. For this reason, applications involving network connections usually create separate **Threads** to establish a connection and do the actual data transmission and reception. If you used the system **Thread** that handles user events and screen painting to execute the **SimpleConnect** constructor, your application could be unresponsive for a long time.

On The Server Side

For the preceding code to establish a connection, there must be a server application on the host computer listening for a connection on that port. In Java this can be done with a **java.net.ServerSocket** object. The following code fragment shows the constructor for a simple server class that listens at a given port:

```
// instance variables
ServerSocket listenSok ;
Socket clientSok ;
boolean working ;

SimpleServer( ) throws IOException {
   listenSok = new ServerSocket( portn );
   working = true ;
}
```

After the **ServerSocket** is constructed, the server application executes the following method, which blocks at line 5 until a client application tries to establish a connection:

```
1.  void listen() {
2.    System.out.println("Listening");
3.    while( working ){
4.      try {
5.        clientSok = listenSok.accept();
6.        System.out.println("Client connect port:" +
7.              clientSok.getPort() );
8.        handleClient();
9.      }catch(IOException ex ){
10.        System.out.println("listen: " + ex );
11.     }
12.   } // end while
13. }
```

When a **ServerSocket** accepts a connection, it creates a **Socket** to be used for the actual communication. In the preceding code, the **handleClient** method is executed by the same **Thread** that created the **clientSok Socket**. This means that only one client could be handled at a time. In servers that need to handle multiple clients, a new **Thread** would be created for each client.

Datagram Sockets

The TCP/IP protocol used by **java.net.Socket** is actually two protocols that work at different levels. The Internet Protocol (IP) is responsible for trying to get packets to their destination, whereas the Transmission Control Protocol (TCP) performs error checking, requests retransmission of damaged or missing packets, and acknowledges packet receipt. This extra processing consumes network bandwidth and processing power.

For applications that don't mind losing an occasional packet, such as audio transmissions, the User Datagram Protocol (UDP) is much more efficient. This protocol is sometimes referred to as the *Unreliable* Datagram Protocol because it simply sends and receives packets of bytes without worrying about lost data or missing packets. It's up to the programmer to provide interpretation of the packets.

A **DatagramPacket** object encapsulates all details of a single packet transmission, including the network addresses of the source and destination, the port on the destination machine, and the actual data bytes. A new object should be created for every packet sent.

Packets are both sent and received on a **DatagramSocket** object, which listens on an assigned port number. When sending, you must supply the socket with a **DatagramPacket** that has been addressed and filled with data bytes. When receiving, you must supply a new **DatagramPacket** object, which the **DatagramSocket** will fill. It is up to the programmer to ensure that the byte array supplied for receiving a packet is large enough, or data will be lost.

Listing 15.1 shows an example of processing a **DatagramPacket** in an application. This method performs the trivial task of receiving a packet (line 13), interpreting the byte array as a **String** (line 16), converting it to uppercase and retransmitting it (line 19). Note how the source information in the received packet (lines 14 and 15) is used to set the address in the transmitted packet (line 20).

Listing 15.1   An example of sending and receiving UDP datagrams.

```
1. // bufsz is a int giving the buffer size
2. // listenSoc is a DatagramSocket listening at a specified port
3. void listen() {
4.    byte[] buf = new byte[ bufsz ] ;
5.    DatagramPacket recDG ;
6.    DatagramPacket sendDG ;
7.    InetAddress fromaddr ;
8.    int fromport ;
9.    String tmp ;
10.   while( working ){
11.     try {
12.        recDG = new DatagramPacket( buf, bufsz );
13.        listenSok.receive( recDG );
14.        fromport = recDG.getPort();
15.        fromaddr = recDG.getAddress();
16.        tmp = new String( buf, 0, recDG.getLength() );
17.        tmp = tmp.toUpperCase();
18.        byte[] sendbuf = tmp.getBytes();
19.        sendDG = new DatagramPacket( sendbuf, sendbuf.length,
20.               fromaddr, fromport );
21.        listenSok.send( sendDG );
22.     }catch(IOException ex ){
23.         System.out.println("listen: " + ex );
24.     }
25.   }
26. }
```

Exceptions Thrown By IO Classes

Security-related exceptions may be thrown if a program does not have clearance to perform certain operations. In addition, a large number of possible exceptions descended from the **IOException** class can be thrown by input/output methods. Here are some of the ones you are most likely to encounter:

➤ **EOFException** Thrown when an input method hits an unexpected end of file. Some classes return a special value rather than throwing the exception.

➤ **FileNotFoundException** Thrown when a file specified by a **String** or **File** could not be opened.

➤ **InterruptedIOException** Thrown when a **Thread** performing an IO operation is interrupted. The exception object has a field indicating how many bytes had been transferred before the interruption.

➤ **MalformedURLException** Thrown when an attempt to create a stream from a **URL** is unable to interpret the data as a valid address.

➤ **ObjectStreamException** The abstract class that is the base for all exceptions specific to serializing objects.

Review

I have only been able to skim the high points of working with Java IO classes. Here are some of the most important points to remember:

➤ **File** Remember that creating **File** objects doesn't change the file system.

➤ **InputStream and OutputStream** The majority of Java IO classes are related to processing streams of bytes. Sources for objects derived from the **abstract InputStream** and **Outputstream** classes include local files, HTTP connections, and **Sockets**.

➤ **Filters and chaining** Classes that transform and interpret streams are called filters. Stream processing objects can be chained to provide a variety of functions.

➤ **Reader and Writer** These classes read and write Unicode characters and support locale-dependent interpretation of text files. They are not used for reading and writing binary data.

➤ **RandomAccessFile** This class is completely separate from the world of streams, but it does provide the methods of both the **DataInput** and **DataOutput** interfaces.

➤ **Socket and ServerSocket** With these classes, you can implement TCP/IP communication between client and server applications. A **Socket** object provides an **InputStream** and an **OutputStream**.

➤ **DatagramSocket** This class can send and receive blocks of bytes in the UDP (User Datagram Protocol) format over networks.

Practice Questions

Question 1

What happens to the file system when the following code is run and the **myFile** object is created? Assume that **name** represents a valid path and file name for a file that does not presently exist. [Check all correct answers]

```
File createFile( String name ){
  File myFile = new File( name ) ;
  return myFile ;
}
```

❑   a. A new empty file with that name is created but not opened.

❑   b. The current directory changes to that specified in **name**.

❑   c. A new empty file with that name is created and opened.

❑   d. None of the above.

Answer d is the only correct answer. Creating a **File** object does not do anything to the file system.

Question 2

A Java programmer proposes to accomplish random access to a file that exists on a Web server with the following code in an applet. What is the result of trying to compile and run this code?

```
1. URL newU = new URL( getDocumentBase(),
   "thedata.txt" ) ;
2. RandomAccessFile raf = new
   RandomAccessFile( newU );
```

○   a. The compiler objects to the constructor in line 2.

○   b. The compiler objects to the constructor in line 1.

○   c. The code compiles but gets a security exception when it runs.

○   d. The code compiles and the **RandomAccessFile** is created when it runs.

Answer a is correct. Line 1 shows correct creation of a URL, but there is no way to create a **RandomAccessFile** from a **URL**. The basic reason is that there is no protocol for random access to files via HTTP.

Question 3

> Which of the following statements about the default **System.out** stream are correct? [Check all correct answers]
>
> ❑ a. System.out is a PrintStream.
>
> ❑ b. System.out is an OutputStream.
>
> ❑ c. System.out is a FilterOutputStream.
>
> ❑ d. System.out throws IOException exceptions if it encounters an error.

Answers a, b, and c are correct because **System.out** is a **PrintStream** and **PrintStream** inherits from **FilterOutputStream**, which inherits from **OutputStream**. **PrintStream** objects never throw **IOExceptions**. Therefore, answer d is incorrect.

Question 4

> Which approach would you use to create an **InputStream** for data being transmitted through a **DatagramSocket**?
>
> ○ a. Call the **DatagramSocket getInputStream** method.
>
> ○ b. Custom programming would be required to do error checking and create the stream of bytes required by an **InputStream**.
>
> ○ c. It is impossible to create an **InputStream** to work with a **DatagramSocket**.

Answer b is correct because the Java library does not supply methods to do additional processing of any kind on UDP packets. Answer c is incorrect because the **InputStream** methods could be accomplished by custom programming. Answer a is incorrect because **DatagramSocket** does not have a **getInputStream** method. **DatagramSocket** just sends and receives packets.

Question 5

Which of the following objects can't be used in the constructor of
a **DataInputStream** object?

○ a. **FileInputStream**

○ b. **RandomAccessFile**

○ c. **BufferedInputStream**

○ d. **ByteArrayInputStream**

Answer b is correct. The **RandomAccessFile** class already implements the
DataInput interface methods and cannot be used as an **InputStream**.

Question 6

Which of the following statements about encoding a character
stream using UTF-8 is correct?

○ a. A single Java character may end up as 1, 2, or 3 bytes
      when encoded.

○ b. A single Java character will always occupy 2 bytes when
      encoded.

○ c. A single Java character will always occupy either 2 or 3
      bytes when encoded.

○ d. A single Java character may end up as 1, 2, 3, or 4 bytes
      when encoded.

Answer a is correct. Normal ASCII characters are encoded as a single byte,
whereas others occupy 2 or 3 bytes but never more.

Question 7

When an **Applet** uses an **InputStream** created by a **URL**, which
network protocol is involved?

○ a. UDP

○ b. ISO8859-1

○ c. HTTP

○ d. Multicast

Answer c is correct. The **URL openStream** method establishes a connection with a Web server using the HTTP protocol. Answer b, "ISO8859-1", is the local string for ASCII encoding of characters. Answer a, UDP, stands for User Datagram Protocol, used only with Datagram transmission. Answer d, Multicast, is a method of sending Datagrams to multiple addresses.

Question 8

When serializing a complex object with an **ObjectOutputStream**, what precautions must a programmer take?

○ a. The object cannot have any circular references. In other words, if object A has a reference to object B, B must not have a reference to A because the process will enter an endless loop.

○ b. The total size of the object must be less than 65,535 bytes.

○ c. The object or a parent must implement the **Serializable** or **Externalizable** interface.

○ d. The object must inherit from the **Serializable** class.

Answer c is correct. Answer a is incorrect because the **ObjectOutputStream** resolves circular references correctly. Answer b is incorrect because there is no limit on the size of the object to be serialized. Answer d is incorrect because **Serializable** is an interface, not a class.

Question 9

You have created a **File** object that corresponds to a file on your hard disk. What is returned when you call the **lastModified** method of this **File** object?

○ a. A **long** primitive value representing the date the file was last modified as the number of seconds since the start of January 1, 1970.

○ b. A **long** primitive value representing the date the file was last modified as the number of milliseconds since the start of January 1, 1970.

○ c. A **java.util.Date** object representing the date the file was last modified.

○ d. A **String** formatted with the last modified date in the default style for your operating system.

Answer b is correct. The value returned is in milliseconds, even if the underlying operating system does not measure time to that precision. You could create a **Date** object with the value returned, but the actual value is a **long** primitive.

Question 10

Which of the following Java entities are not **abstract** classes or interfaces? [Check all correct answers]

❑ a. InputStream

❑ b. PrintStream

❑ c. Socket

❑ d. Reader

❑ e. DataInput

Answers b and c are the only entities that are concrete classes. **InputStream** and **Reader** are abstract classes and **DataInput** is an interface.

Need To Know More?

 Farley, Jim. *Java Distributed Computing*. O'Reilly & Associates, Inc. Sebastopol, CA, 1998. ISBN: 1-56592-206-9. Chapter 2 offers a good review of writing network-aware programs in Java.

 Flanagan, David. *Java in a Nutshell, 2nd Edition*. O'Reilly & Associates, Inc. Sebastopol, CA, 1997. ISBN: 1-56592-262-X. This is the most compact desktop reference book documenting the Java language. Chapter 9 covers object serialization.

 ftp://ftp.javasoft.com/docs/tutorial.zip

An excellent tutorial in HTML form can be downloaded from this site.

 http://www.iso.ch/

This is the primary Web site of the International Organization for Standardization (ISO), the body responsible for, among other things, standards for encoding various character sets.

Sample Test

In this chapter I will review some pointers to help you develop a successful test-taking strategy for the Sun Certified Programmer for the Java 2 Platform exam. Following the pointers is a sample test of 59 questions covering the published objectives for the exam. Based on feedback we have gotten on these questions, this test is similar to or slightly harder than the real one. The answers are discussed in Chapter 16.

Questions, Questions, Questions

There should be no doubt in your mind that you are facing a test full of specific and pointed questions. There are very few questions that would be considered simple. At the risk of repeating myself, the most important thing is to thoroughly read and understand the question.

This does not mean that you should always start with a minute examination of the question text. If a question appears to be long and complex, and especially if it involves some sample code, read the possible answers first. This will give you a clue as to what to look for when reading the question.

Picking Proper Answers

Obviously, the only way to pass any exam is to select enough of the right answers to obtain a passing score. In this case that is 42 out of the 59 questions. Actually, due to those questions having multiple correct answers, you must pick a lot more than 42 correct answers. The test questions appear in random order, and many elements or issues that receive mention in one question may also crop up in other questions. It's not uncommon to find that an incorrect answer to one question is the correct answer to another question, or vice-versa. Take the time to read every answer to each question, even if you recognize the correct answer to a question immediately. That extra reading may spark a memory or remind you about some aspect of Java that will help you on another question elsewhere in the exam.

You can revisit any question as many times as you like. If you're uncertain of the answer to a question, check the box that's provided to mark it for easy return later on. You should also mark questions you think may offer information that you can use to answer other questions. The testing software is designed to let you mark every question if you choose; use this framework to your advantage. Everything you will want to see again should be marked; the testing software can then help you return to marked questions quickly and easily.

Deciding What To Memorize

It is very important that you know the Java keywords inside and out. The correct interpretation of access modifiers is an essential part of a surprising number of questions. The Cram Sheet provided in the front of the book is great for reviewing the most commonly encountered keywords. You will have to identify your own weaknesses by carefully analyzing the questions you get wrong on the sample questions in the chapters and the sample test. Feel free to add your own notes to The Cram Sheet.

Preparing For The Test

The best way to prepare for the test—after you've studied—is to take at least one practice exam. We've included one here in this chapter for that reason; the test questions are located in the pages that follow (and unlike the preceding chapters in this book, the answers don't follow the questions immediately; you'll have to flip to Chapter 16 to review the answers separately).

Give yourself 90 minutes to take the exam, keep yourself on the honor system, and don't look at earlier text in the book or jump ahead to the answer key. When your time is up, or you've finished the questions, you can check your work in Chapter 16. Pay special attention to the explanations for the incorrect answers; these can also help to reinforce your knowledge of the material. Knowing how to recognize correct answers is good, but understanding why incorrect answers are wrong can be equally valuable.

Naturally, the book can not simulate the computer administered test. If you have not taken one of these tests before and are nervous about it, try our online mock exam at http://www.lanw.com/java/javacert/.

This Java applet emulates the computer administered test with a randomly selected set of questions.

Taking The Test

Relax. Once you're sitting in front of the testing computer, there's nothing more you can do to increase your knowledge or preparation. Take a deep breath, stretch, and start reading that first question.

There's no need to rush; you have plenty of time to complete each question and to return to those questions that you skip or mark for return. If you read a question twice and remain clueless, you can mark it and move on. Both easy and difficult questions are intermixed throughout the test in random order. Don't cheat yourself by spending too much time on a hard question early in the test, thereby depriving yourself of the time you need to answer the questions at the end of the test.

After your first pass through the test, and before returning to marked questions for a second visit, figure out how much time you've got per question. As you answer each question, remove its mark. Continue to review the remaining marked questions until you run out of time, or you complete the test.

The Sample Test

This sample test covers the same general categories as the Sun Certified Programmer for the Java 2 Platform exam in approximately the same proportion. In the real test, you will have 90 minutes to answer about 59 questions. Pay close attention to the difference between questions taking a single answer, which are indicated with options having circles, and those that may have multiple correct answers, showing options with squares. Remember that questions showing squares may have anywhere from one to all answers correct. Take notes about the question topics you feel unsure of so you can optimize your cramming before the real test.

> *Note: Keywords and other code terms, such as class and method names, are not shown in bold in the test questions because they are not shown in bold in the actual test.*

Question 1

Given the following definition of the Demo class and the DerivedDemo class

```
1. public class Demo extends Object {
2.    String Title;
3.    public Demo( String t ){
4.       Title = t;
5.    }
6.    public void showTitle() {
7.      System.out.println( "Title is " + Title );
8.    }
9. }
10. class DerivedDemo extends Demo {
11.    public void setTitle( String  tt )
          { Title = tt ; }
12. }
```

what happens if we try to compile this code, create a DerivedDemo object, and immediately call the showTitle method of that object?

○ a. The message "Title is null" is written to standard output.

○ b. The compiler complains about the DerivedDemo class.

○ c. A NullPointerException is thrown in line 7.

Question 2

Which of the following class declarations are not correct Java declarations? [Check all correct answers]

❑ a. public synchronized class FastClass extends Thread

❑ b. private protected class FastClass

❑ c. public abstract class FastClass

❑ d. class FastClass extends Thread

Question 3

You are writing a toolkit of classes in the "wesayso" package to be used by other programmers in your company. Because of security considerations, you don't want other programmers to subclass your VitalDataAccess class, but you will have to provide for access by classes in other packages. How should this class be declared?

○ a. protected static class VitalDataAccess extends Object

○ b. public final class VitalDataAccess extends Object

○ c. public abstract class VitalDataAccess extends Object

○ d. public static class VitalDataAccess extends Object

Question 4

Given the following partial listing of the Widget class

```
1. class Widget extends Thingee{
2.    static private int widgetCount = 0;
3.    static synchronized int addWidget(){
        widgetCount++;
4.        return widgetCount;
5.    }
6.    String wName;
7.    public Widget( int mx, String T  ){
8.      wName = "I am Widget #" + addWidget();
9.    }
10.  // more methods follow
```

what is the significance of the word "private" in line 2? [Check all correct answers]

❏ a. Because widgetCount is private, only methods in the Widget class can access it.

❏ b. Because widgetCount is private, only the addWidget method can access it.

❏ c. If another class tries to access widgetCount, a runtime exception will be thrown.

❏ d. Because widgetCount is private, only methods in the Widget class and any derived classes can access it.

Question 5

The following lists the complete contents of the file named Derived.java:

```
1.  public class Base extends Object {
2.      String objType ;
3.      public Base(){  objType = "I am a Base
           type" ;
4.      }
5. }
6.
7. public class Derived extends Base {
8.     public Derived() { objType = "I am a
          Derived type";
9.     }
10.    public static void main(String args[] ){
11.        Derived D = new Derived();
12.    }
13. }
```

What will happen when this file is compiled?

○ a. Two class files, Base.class and Derived.class, will be created.

○ b. The compiler will object to line 1.

○ c. The compiler will object to line 7.

Question 6

Given the following listing of the Widget class

```
1. class Widget extends Thingee{
2.    static private int widgetCount = 0;
3.    public String wName;
4.    int wNumber;
5.
6.    private static synchronized int
          addWidget(){
7.       return ++widgetCount;
8.    }
9.    public Widget(){
10.      wNumber = addWidget();
11.   }
12. }
```

what happens when we try to compile the class and use multiple Widget objects in a program that uses multiple Threads to create Widget objects?

- ○ a. The class compiles, and each Widget will get a unique wNumber reflecting the order in which the Widgets were created.

- ○ b. The compiler objects to the addWidget call of a static method in line 10.

- ○ c. A runtime error occurs in the addWidget method.

- ○ d. The class compiles and each Widget will get a wNumber, but we cannot guarantee that the number will be unique.

Question 7

In the following class definitions, which are in separate files, note that the Widget and BigWidget classes are in different packages:

```
1. package conglomo;
2. public class Widget extends Object{
3.     private int myWidth;
4.     XXXXXX void setWidth( int n ) {
5.         myWidth = n;
6.     }
7. }
    // the following is in a separate file
8. import conglomo.Widget ;
9. public class BigWidget extends Widget {
10.    BigWidget() {
11.        setWidth( 204 );
12.    }
13. }
```

Which of the following modifiers, used in line 4 instead of XXXXXX, would allow the BigWidget class to access the Widget.setWidth method (as in line 11)? [Check all correct answers]

❑ a. private

❑ b. protected

❑ c. blank—that is, the method declaration would read void setWidth(int n)

❑ d. public

Question 8

Given the following code fragment with a continue to a labeled statement, predict the printed output:

```
1. int i, j;
2. lab: for( i = 0; i < 6; i++ ){
3.        for( j = 5; j > 2; j-- ){
4.          if( i == j ) {
5.            System.out.print(" " + j );
                continue lab;
6.          }
7.        }
8.     }
```

○ a. Output will be 3 4 5.

○ b. Output will be 3 4.

○ c. Output will be 3.

○ d. The statement on line 5 is never reached, so there is no output.

Question 9

You are writing a set of classes related to cooking and have created your own exception hierarchy derived from java.lang.Exception as follows:

```
Exception
    +-- BadTasteException
            +-- BitterException
            +-- SourException
```

BadTasteException is defined as an abstract class.

You have a method eatMe that may throw a BitterException or a SourException. Which of the following method declarations will be acceptable to the compiler? [Check all correct answers]

❑ a. public void eatMe(Ingredient[] list) throws BadTasteException

❑ b. public void eatMe(Ingredient[] list) throws BitterException, SourException

❑ c. public void eatMe(Ingredient[] list) may throw BadTasteException

❑ d. public void eatMe(Ingredient[] list)

Question 10

Given the following code fragment

```
switch( x ) {
  case 100 :
    System.out.println( "One hundred" );break;
  case 200 :
    System.out.println( "Two hundred" );break;
  case 300 :
    System.out.println( "Three hundred" );break;
}
```

(continued)

Question 10 *(continued)*

choose all of the declarations of x that will not cause a compiler error. [Check all correct answers]

❑ a.
```
byte x = 100 ;
```

❑ b.
```
short x = 200 ;
```

❑ c.
```
int x = 300 ;
```

❑ d.
```
long x = 400 ;
```

Question 11

Which of these statements about the value that appears in a switch statement is correct? [Check all correct answers]

❑ a. The value can be of type char.

❑ b. The value can be of type byte.

❑ c. The value can be of type long.

❑ d. The value can be of type boolean.

Question 12

Which of the following loop expressions will not compile? Assume there are no other variable declarations inside the method containing the expression. [Check all correct answers]

❑ a.
```
int t = 10 ;
while( t ){
    System.out.print(" - " + t-- );
}
```

❑ b.
```
while( x > 0 ){
  int x = 1 ; x--;
}
```

❑ c.
```
int i = 0;
do { System.out.print(" - " + i++ );
}while( i < 10 );
```

Question 13

Here is part of the hierarchy of exceptions that may be thrown during file IO operations:

```
Exception
    +-- IOException
            +-- FileNotFoundException
```

Suppose you had a method X that is supposed to open a file by name and read data from it. Given that X does not have any try-catch statements, which of the following options are true? [Check all correct answers]

❑ a. The method X must be declared as throwing IOException or Exception.

❑ b. The method X must be declared as throwing FileNotFoundException.

❑ c. Any method calling X must use try-catch, specifically catching FileNotFoundException.

❑ d. No special precautions need be taken.

Question 14

Which of the following statements about finalize methods are incorrect? [Check all correct answers]

❑ a. The purpose of a finalize method is to recover memory and other system resources.

❑ b. The purpose of a finalize method is to recover system resources other than memory.

❑ c. You should always write a finalize method for every class.

❑ d. The order in which objects are created controls the order in which their finalize methods are called.

Question 15

Here is a method that creates a number of String objects in the course of printing a countdown sequence:

```
1. public void countDown()
2.    for( int i = 10 ; i >= 0 ; i-- ){
3.       String tmp = Integer.toString( i );
4.       System.out.println( tmp );
5.    }
6.    System.gc()
7.    System.out.println( "BOOM!" );
8. }
```

When the program reaches line 7, how many of the String objects created in line 3 will have been garbage collected? Assume that the System.out object is not keeping a reference.

○ a. None.

○ b. There is no way to tell.

○ c. 10.

○ d. 11.

Question 16

Which of the following statements about Java garbage collection is a true statement? [Check all correct answers]

❑ a. The following code will start the garbage collection mechanism:
```
System.gc();
Thread.yield();
```

❑ b. Calling Runtime.getRuntime().gc() will probably start the garbage collection mechanism, but there is no guarantee.

❑ c. The garbage collection Thread has a low priority.

❑ d. The method by which Java determines that a chunk of memory is garbage is up to the implementer of the Java Virtual Machine.

Question 17

You are writing code for a class that will be in the default package and will use the graphic components in the AWT package. Select the correct code fragment to start the source code file.

```
Fragment A
    import java.awt.*;
Fragment B
    package default ;
    import java.awt.*;
Fragment C
    import java.awt.*;
    package default;
```

○ a. Code Fragment A

○ b. Code Fragment B

○ c. Code Fragment C

Question 18

What is the range of values that can be stored in a short primitive variable?

○ a. 0 to 65535

○ b. -32768 to 32767

○ c. -32767 to 32768

Question 19

Given the following method definition in a class that otherwise compiles correctly

```
1. public boolean testAns( String ans , int n ){
2.    boolean rslt;
3.    if( ans.equalsIgnoreCase("YES") &&
          n > 5  ) rslt = true;
4.    return rslt;
5. }
```

what will be the result of trying to compile the class and execute the testAns method with inputs of "no" and 5?

○ a. A runtime exception will be thrown in the testAns method.

○ b. A result of false will be returned.

○ c. A compiler error will prevent compilation.

○ d. A result of true will be returned.

Question 20

Given that a class, Test, declares a member variable named "Scores" as an array of int as follows

```
int Scores[];
```

which of the following code fragments would correctly initialize the member variable Scores as an array of 4 int with the value of zero if used in the Test constructor? [Check all correct answers]

❏ a. int Scores[] = {0,0,0,0} ;

❏ b. Scores = new int[4] ;

❏ c. Scores = new int[4] ;

   for(int i = 0 ; i < 4 ; i++){ Scores[i] = 0 ; }

❏ d. Scores = { 0,0,0,0 };

Question 21

Given the following code for the Demo class

```
public class Demo {
  private String[] userNames;
  public Demo(){ userNames = new String[10];
  }
  public void setName( String s, int n ){
        userNames[n] = s;
  }
  public void showName( int n ){
    System.out.println( "Name is " +
      userNames[n]);
  }
 public String getName( int n ){return
    userNames[n];}
}
```

what would be the result of calling the showName method with a
parameter of 2 immediately after creating an instance of Demo?

O a. Standard output would show "Name is null".

O b. A NullPointerException would be thrown, halting the
       program.

O c. An ArrayIndexOutOfBoundsException would be thrown,
       halting the program.

O d. Standard output would show "Name is ".

Question 22

Given the following code fragment from a class definition, which
of the following statements is true? [Check all correct answers]

```
1.  int Aval  = 0x65;
2.  byte Bval = 065;
```

❏ a. The variable Aval has been initialized with a hexadecimal
       format literal, and Bval has been initialized with an octal
       format literal.

❏ b. Both Aval and Bval contain 65.

❏ c. The logical test Aval > Bval   would evaluate True.

❏ d. The compiler would report a NumberFormatException on
       line 1.

Question 23

The following program is compiled and then run with this command line:

```
>java Demo alpha beta gamma

 public class Demo {
   public static void main(String args[] ){
     int n = 1;
     System.out.println( "The word is " +
       args[ n ] );
   }
 }
```

What happens?

○ a. "The word is alpha" is written to standard output.

○ b. "The word is beta" is written to standard output.

○ c. "The word is gamma" is written to standard output.

○ d. The runtime system reports an error in the main method.

Question 24

What happens when we attempt to compile and run the following code?

```
1. public class Logic {
2.    static long sixteen = 0x0010;
3.    static public void main( String args[] ){
4.       long N = sixteen >> 4;
5.       System.out.println( "N = " + N );
6.    }
7. }
```

○ a. The compiler will object to line 4 combining a long with an int.

○ b. The program will compile and run, producing the output "N = 0".

○ c. The program will compile and run, producing the output "N = 1".

○ d. A runtime exception will be thrown.

Question 25

Given the following object hierarchy and code for the upgrade method

```
java.lang.Object
    |
    +----mypkg.BaseWidget
                |
                +----TypeAWidget

// the following is a method in the BaseWidget
class
1. public TypeAWidget upgrade( ){
2.    TypeAWidget  A = (TypeAWidget)  this;
3.    return A;
4. }
```

choose the result of trying to compile and run a program containing the following statements:

```
5.   BaseWidget B = new BaseWidget();
6.   TypeAWidget A =  B.upgrade();
```

○ a. The compiler would object to line 2.

○ b. A runtime ClassCastException would be generated in line 2.

○ c. After line 6 executes, the object referred to as A will in fact be a TypeAWidget.

Question 26

Given the following code fragment, what will happen when we try to compile and run the showSmall method?

```
1. public void printArray( long[] x ){
2.    for(int i = 0 ; i < x.length ; i++ ){
3.       System.out.println("# " + i + " = " +
          x[i] );
4.    }
5. }
6. int[] small = { 1,2,3,4,5,6,7,8,9,0 };
7. public showSmall() {
8.     printArray( small );
9. }
```

○ a. The code compiles and the JVM automatically promotes the int array to a long array.

○ b. The compiler complains that there is no method matching the use in line 8.

○ c. The code compiles but a runtime ClassCastException is thrown in line 8.

Question 27

In the following code fragment from an applet, we know that the getParameter call may return a null if there is no parameter named size. Which logical operator should replace X in line 5 to ensure that a NullPointerException is not generated if tmp is null?

```
1. int sz ;
2. public void init(){
3.    sz = 10;
4.    String tmp = getParameter( "size" );
5.    if( tmp != null X tmp.equals( "BIG" ))
         sz = 20;
6. }
```

○ a. Replace 'X' with '&'.

○ b. Replace 'X' with '&&'.

○ c. Replace 'X' with '|'.

○ d. Replace 'X' with '||'.

Question 28

What happens on trying to compile and run the following code?

```
1. public class EqualsTest{
2.   public static void main( String args[] ){
3.     float A = 1.0F / 3.0F ;
4.     if( ( A * 3.0) == 1.0F )
         System.out.println( "Equal" );
5.     else System.out.println( "Not Equal" );
6.   }
7. }
```

❍ a. The program compiles and prints "Not Equal".

❍ b. The program compiles and prints "Equal".

❍ c. The compiler objects to line 3.

❍ d. The compiler objects to using == with primitives in line 4.

Question 29

Given that we have a method scale defined as follows, where scalex and scaley are int constants

```
public Point scale( int x, int y ){
   return new Point(
     ( int )( x / scalex ),( int )( y / scaley ) );
}
```

what will happen when we call this method with double primitives instead of int as in the following fragment?

```
1. double px = 10.02;
2. double py = 20.34;
3. Point thePoint = scale( px, py );
```

❍ a. A compiler error is caused in line 3.

❍ b. The program compiles but a runtime cast exception is thrown.

❍ c. The program compiles and runs.

❍ d. The compiler objects to line 1.

Question 30

What happens on trying to compile and run the following code?

```
1. public class EqualsTest{
2.   public static void main( String args[] ){
3.     Long L = new Long( 7 );
4.     Integer J = new Integer( 7 );
5.     if( L.equals( J ) )
        System.out.println( "Equal" );
6.     else System.out.println( "Not Equal" );
7.   }
8. }
```

○ a. The program compiles and prints "Equal".

○ b. The program compiles and prints "Not Equal".

○ c. The compiler objects to line 5.

○ d. A runtime cast error occurs at line 5.

Question 31

The GenericFruit class declares the following method to return a float calculated from a serving size:

```
public float calories( float serving )
```

A junior programmer writing the Apple class, which extends GenericFruit, proposes to declare the following overriding method:

```
public double calories( double amount )
```

What result do you predict?

○ a. It won't compile because of the different return type.

○ b. It won't compile because of the different input type in the parameter list.

○ c. It will compile but will not override the GenericFruit method because of the different parameter list.

Question 32

You are designing an application to recommend dog breeds to potential pet owners. To maximize the advantage of working in an object-oriented language, you have created a Dog class, which will be extended by classes representing different kinds of dogs. The following code fragment shows the class declaration and all of the instance variables in the Dog class:

```
1. public class Dog extends Object {
2.    float avgWeight;
3.    float avgLifespan;
4.    String breedName;
```

Which of the following would be reasonable variable declarations for the SportingDog class, which extends Dog? [Check all correct answers]

❏ a. private float avgWeight ;

❏ b. private Dog theDog ;

❏ c. String[] hunts ;

❏ d. String breedName ;

Question 33

In the following code for a class in which methodA has an inner class

```
1. public class Base {
2.    private static final int ID = 3;
3.    public String name;
4.    public void methodA( int nn ){
5.      final int serialN = 11;
6.      class inner {
7.        void showResult(){
8.          System.out.println( "Rslt= " + XX );
9.        }
10.     } // end class inner
11.     new inner().showResult();
12.   } // end methodA
13. )
```

which variables would the statement in line 8 be able to use in place of XX? [Check all correct answers]

❑ a. The int ID in line 2

❑ b. The String name in line 3

❑ c. The int nn in line 4

❑ d. The int serialN in line 5

Question 34

The GenericFruit class declares the following method to return a float calculated from a serving size:

```
public float calories( float serving )
```

A junior programmer writing the Apple class, which extends GenericFruit, proposes to declare the following overriding method:

```
public double calories( float amount )
```

What result do you predict?

○ a. It won't compile because of the different return type.

○ b. It won't compile because of the different name in the parameter list.

○ c. It will compile but will be incompatible with other uses of the method because you can't cast the double return type to float.

○ d. It will compile and be compatible with other uses of the calories method.

Question 35

Given a base class and a derived class defined as follows

```
public abstract class BaseTest extends Object
implements Runnable
public class AdvancedTest extends BaseTest
```

what will happen when we try to compile the following method?

```
1. public boolean checkTest( Object obj ){
2.   if( obj instanceof BaseTest ) return true;
3.   System.out.println( "Not a BaseTest" );
4.   if( obj instanceof Runnable ) return true;
5.   System.out.println( "Not Runnable" );
6.   return false;
7. }
```

○ a. The compiler objects to the use of an abstract class in line 2.

○ b. The compiler objects to the use of an interface in line 4.

○ c. The code compiles just fine.

Question 36

You have written a class extending Thread, which does time-con-suming computations.

In the first use of this class in an application, the system "locked up" for extended periods of time. Obviously you need to provide a chance for other Threads to run. Here is the run method that needs to be modified. Select all of the statements that could be inserted at line 5 to allow other Threads a chance to run. [Check all correct answers]

```
1. public void run(){
2.    boolean runFlg = true;
3.    while( runFlg ){
4.       runFlg = doStuff();
5.
6.    }
7. }
```

❑ a.
```
5.    yield();
```

❑ b.
```
5.    try{ sleep( 100 );
}catch( InterruptedException e ){}
```

❑ c.
```
5.    suspend( 100 );
```

❑ d.
```
5.    wait( 100 );
```

Question 37

You need to create a class that implements the Runnable interface to do background image processing. Out of the following list of method declarations, select all of the methods that must appear in the class to satisfy the Runnable interface requirements. [Check all correct answers]

❑ a. public void start()

❑ b. public void run()

❑ c. public void stop()

❑ d. public void suspend()

Question 38

You have an application that executes the following line:

```
Thread myT = new Thread();
```

Select all of the following statements that are correct. [Check all correct anwers]

❑   a. The Thread myT is now in a runnable state.

❑   b. The Thread myT has the priority of the Thread that executed the construction statement.

❑   c. If myT.start() is called, the run method in the class where the construction statement appears will be executed.

❑   d. If myT.stop() is called, the Thread can later be started with myT.start() and will execute the run method in the Thread class.

Question 39

Here is a partial listing of a class to represent a game board in a networked game. It is desired to prevent collisions due to more than one Thread using the addPic method to modify the array of Image references.

```
1.  class Board extends Object{
2.    Image[] pics = new Image[64];
3.    int active = 0;
4.    public boolean addPic( Image mg, int pos ){
5.      synchronized(XXX)
6.      { if( pics[pos] == null ){
7.        active++ ; pics[pos] = mg; return true;
8.        }
9.        else return false;
10.     } // end synchronized block
11.   } // end addPic method
12.   // remainder of class
```

Select all of the alternatives for line 5 that would accomplish this. [Check all correct answers]

❑   a. 5.   synchronized(this)

❑   b. 5.   synchronized(pics)

❑   c. 5.   synchronized(mg)

❑   d. 5.   synchronized(active)

Question 40

You are working on an applet that does animation. There is a single object animC, derived from java.awt.Canvas, which holds all the animation data and a memory image. There is a single Thread, animT, which uses this data to create a new image for the next animation frame and then calls the following method:

```
1. synchronized void waitForPaint(){
2.    painted = false; repaint();
3.    while( !painted ){
4.      try{ wait();
5.      }catch(InterruptedException x){}
6.    }
7. }
```

The paint method in animC executes the following code after the new animation frame has been shown:

```
synchronized(this){painted = true; notify();}
```

After animT has entered waitForPaint and before the paint method has been executed, which of the following statements is true? [Check all correct answers]

❏ a. Other Threads cannot modify data in the animC object.

❏ b. Other Threads can only modify data in the animC object using synchronized methods.

❏ c. Other Threads can modify data in the animC object using synchronized or unsynchronized methods.

❏ d. If the animT Thread is interrupted, it will exit the waitForPaint method.

Question 41

Select all of the following methods that are not instance methods of the Thread class, or are instance methods deprecated in Java 2. [Check all correct answers]

❑ a. start()

❑ b. stop()

❑ c. run()

❑ d. suspend()

❑ e. sleep(long msec)

❑ f. toString()

❑ g. join()

Question 42

You are using a Panel to contain a set of five buttons. To ensure that at least a portion of each button is displayed even when the Panel has been resized to an area too small to show the full area of all buttons, which layout manager should you use?

○ a. new GridLayout(1,5)

○ b. new FlowLayout(FlowLayout.LEFT)

○ c. new GridBagLayout(5)

○ d. new CardLayout()

Question 43

You are writing a simple utility application based on Frame. This application will have a menu bar, a label, and a text field. You have decided to do without a layout manager.

Which of the following statements will be required in the constructor to place the label at the top left corner of the Frame, with 5 pixels of clearance below the menu bar and 5 pixels in from the left border? Assume that label1 has already been constructed and added to the Frame. [Check all correct statements.]

❑ a. setLayout(null);

❑ b. setLayoutManager(null);

❑ c. label1.setLocation(5, 5);

❑ d. label1.setLocation(getInsets().left + 5, getInsets().top + 5);

Question 44

When you are building a menu system, the highest level of organization is the MenuBar. Which class handles the next level of organization?

○ a. java.awt.MenuComponent

○ b. java.awt.MenuItem

○ c. java.awt.Menu

○ d. java.awt.PopupMenu

Question 45

Which of the following layout managers does not alter the height of a component? [Check all correct answers]

❑ a. BorderLayout

❑ b. GridBagLayout

❑ c. CardLayout

❑ d. FlowLayout

Question 46

Select all of the following constant names that are valid positioning options in the GridBagConstraints class. [Check all correct answers]

❑ a BOTH

❑ b. EAST

❑ c. NORTHEAST

❑ d. NONE

Question 47

Once created, some Java objects are "immutable," meaning that they cannot have their contents changed. Which of the following classes produce immutable objects? [Check all correct answers]

❑ a. java.lang.Double

❑ b. java.lang.StringBuffer

❑ c. java.lang.Boolean

❑ d. java.lang.Math

Question 48

Given an object created by the following class

```
1. class Example extends Object{
2.   public void  Increment( Integer N ){
3.     N = new Integer(  N.intValue() + 1 );
4.   }
5.   public void Result( int  x ) {
6.     Integer X = new Integer( x );
7.     Increment( X );
8.     System.out.println( "New value is " + X
);
9.   }
10. }
```

what happens when a program calls the Result method with a value of 30?

○ a. The message "New value is 31" goes to the standard output.

○ b. The message "New value is 30" goes to the standard output.

○ c. Neither a nor b occurs.

Question 49

What happens when we compile and run code containing the following lines:

```
1. Integer A, B, C;
2. A = new Integer( 3 );
3. B = new Integer( 4 );
4. C = A + B;
5. System.out.println( "Final value " + C );
```

○ a. The code compiles and prints "Final value is 7" when run.

○ b. The code compiles but generates a runtime exception in line 5.

○ c. The compiler balks at line 4.

○ d. The code compiles and prints "Final value is null".

Question 50

Given the following method in an application

```
1. public String setFileType( String fname ){
2.   int p = fname.indexOf( '.' );
3.   if( p > 0 ) fname = fname.substring( 0,p );
4.   fname += ".TXT";
5.   return fname;
6. }
```

and given that another part of the class has the following code

```
7.   String TheFile = "Program.java";
8.   File F = new File( setFileType( TheFile ) );
9.   System.out.println( "Created " + TheFile );
```

what will be printed by the statement in line 9?

○ a.
   Created Program.java

○ b.
   Created Program.txt

○ c.
   Created Program.java.txt

Question 51

What happens when this method is called with an input of "Java rules"?

```
1. public String addOK(String S){
2.   S += " OK!";
3.   return S;
4. }
```

○ a. The method will return " OK!" ;

○ b. A runtime exception will be thrown.

○ c. The method will return "Java rules OK!".

○ d. The method will return "Java rules".

Question 52

Which of the following code fragments are legal Java code? [Check all correct answers]

❑ a.
```java
String A = "abcdefg";
A -= "cde";
```

❑ b.
```java
String A = "abcdefg";
A += "cde";
```

❑ c.
```java
Integer J = new Integer( 27 );
J -= 7;
```

❑ d.
```java
Integer J = new Integer( 27 );
J--;
```

Question 53

What happens when we try to compile and run code containing the following lines:

```java
1. Float A = new Float( 1.0F );
2. String S = "value is " + A;
3. System.out.println( S );
```

○ a. The compiler objects to line 2.

○ b. The program compiles and prints "value is 1.0".

○ c. A runtime exception occurs in line 2.

Question 54

Which of the following AWT components can generate an ActionEvent?

○ a. java.awt.List

○ b. java.awt.Scrollbar

○ c. java.awt.Canvas

○ d. java.awt.Panel

Question 55

Which of the following Collections classes can return object references in the order of addition? [Check all correct answers]

☐ a. java.util.ArrayList

☐ b. java.util.Hashtable

☐ c. java.util.Map

☐ d. java.util.Collection

Question 56

Which of the following interfaces in the java.util package does java.util.Hashtable implement?

○ a. java.util.HashMap

○ b. java.util.Map

○ c. java.util.SortedSet

○ d. java.util.Iterator

Question 57

The Math.random() method returns what kind of primitive value?

○ a. An int with values randomly distributed between Integer.MIN_VALUE and Integer.MAX_VALUE.

○ b. A float with values randomly distributed between 0.0 and 1.0.

○ c. A double with values randomly distributed between 0.0 and 1.0.

○ d. A long with values randomly distributed between Long.MIN_VALUE and Long.MAX_VALUE.

Question 58

What kind of stream is the System.out object?

○ a. java.io.BufferedWriter

○ b. java.io.PrintStream

○ c. java.io.FileWriter

○ d. java.io.OutputStreamWriter

Question 59

Which of the following events has a matching adapter class that implements the appropriate listener interface? [Check all correct answers]

❑ a. java.awt.event.MouseEvent

❑ b. java.awt.event.KeyEvent

❑ c. java.awt.event.ActionEvent

❑ d. java.awt.event.FocusEvent

❑ e. java.awt.event.ItemEvent

Answer Key

1. b	16. b, c, d	31. c	46. b, c
2. a, b	17. a	32. c	47. a, c
3. b	18. b	33. a, b, d	48. b
4. a	19. c	34. a	49. c
5. b	20. b, c	35. c	50. a
6. a	21. a	36. a, b	51. c
7. b, d	22. a, c	37. b	52. b
8. a	23. b	38. b	53. b
9. a, b	24. c	39. a, b	54. a
10. b, c	25. b	40. c	55. a
11. a, b	26. b	41. b, d, e	56. b
12. a, b	27. b	42. a	57. c
13. a	28. a	43. a, d	58. b
14. a, c, d	29. a	44. c	59. a, b, d
15. b	30. b	45. d	

Question 1

Answer b is correct because the **DerivedDemo** class does not define a constructor; the compiler expects to find a default constructor in the **Demo** class. The expected form of a default constructor is one with no arguments (which we don't have in the **Demo** class), causing a compiler error. Answer a could occur if other problems were fixed because the member variable "Title" is initialized to **null**. Answer c would never occur because the **String** concatenation process will add "null" if the object reference is **null**.

This question demonstrates how important it is when taking a test not to jump to conclusions about the question. On reading the code, you might think the question is going to be about access to variables, but it turns out to be about the absence of a constructor.

Question 2

Answers a and b are correct. Answer a is correct because **synchronized** cannot be used as a class modifier. Answer b is correct because neither of these keywords can be used as a class modifier. Answer c is incorrect because this is a valid declaration; **abstract** is used for a class having one or more **abstract** methods. Answer d is also incorrect because this is a legal class declaration. In general, you can expect test questions that ask you to identify incorrect code, so read the question carefully.

Question 3

Answer b is correct because the **final** modifier is used with class declarations to ensure that the class cannot be extended. Answers a and d are incorrect because the **static** modifier cannot be used with class declarations, only with methods and variables. Answer c is incorrect because the modifier **abstract** implies that the class *must* be extended.

Question 4

Answer a is correct; the **private** keyword restricts access to within the class. Answer b is incorrect because there may be other methods in the class. Answer c is incorrect because it is the compiler that recognizes the **private** keyword and controls access. All access considerations are taken care of by the compiler, not the runtime system. Answer d is incorrect because derived classes cannot see **private** variables in the parent. You are just about guaranteed to run into access modifier questions and questions that say to check all correct answers but only have one correct answer on the test.

Question 5

Answer b is correct; the compiler error message is:

Public class Base must be defined in a file called "Base.java".

Although it is common for a single Java source file to generate more than one class file on compilation, two **public** classes cannot occupy the same Java source file. Answer a does not occur; the compiler will object because the **public** class name does not match the file name. Answer c is incorrect, but if the source file had been named Base.java, answer c would be correct.

Question 6

Answer a is correct. The use of **synchronized** in line 6 ensures that number assignment will not be interrupted, no matter how many **Threads** are trying to create **Widget** objects. Answer b is incorrect because line 10 is in the correct form, although **Widget.addWidget** could also be used. Answer c is incorrect because the **addWidget** method has no code that can generate a runtime error. Answer d is incorrect because the use of **synchronized** in line 6 ensures that number assignment will not be interrupted, no matter how many **Threads** are trying to create **Widget** objects.

Question 7

Answers b and d are correct. Answer b is correct because the **protected** modifier allows access by derived classes as well as classes in the same package. Answer d is correct because the **public** modifier allows access by all. Answer a is incorrect because **private** prevents any access from another class. Answer c is incorrect because the default access allows only access within the same package.

Question 8

Answer a is the correct answer. Every time the statements on line 5 execute, the **continue** resumes the loop started on line 2. A complicated loop logic question such as this is likely on the test. Don't panic—use the scratch paper to work through the loop logic if necessary.

Question 9

Answers a and b are correct. Answer a is acceptable because **BadTasteException** is more general than **BitterException** or **SourException**. The alternative of answer b that lists each exception separated by commas is also acceptable. Answer c is incorrect; "may throw" is not a legal expression. Answer d is incorrect because these exceptions don't descend from **RuntimeException**; they must be declared in the method declaration.

Question 10

Answers b and c are correct. The type used in the **switch** statement must accommodate all of the values in the **case** statements. For this reason, both b and c are acceptable. There are two considerations that the compiler checks; the variable in the **switch** statement must be capable of assuming all of the values in the **case** statements, and it must be convertible to an **int**. Answer a is incorrect; x cannot be a **byte** type because the **case** constants 200 and 300 are not compatible. Answer d is incorrect because **switch** statements cannot use **long** values. You would have to have a specific cast: **switch((int)x)** before the compiler would accept it.

Question 11

Answers a and b are correct; a **char** or **byte** can be used, but only if all the **case** statement constants are in the correct range. Answer c is incorrect because a **long** cannot be used in a **switch** statement. This restriction is related to the fact that the compiler constructs a table with 32-bit entries that point to the code for each case to handle a **switch** statement. This also explains why case values must be evaluated as constants at compile time. Answer d is obviously incorrect; only integer types can appear in a **switch** statement.

Question 12

Answers a and b are correct. The code in answer a fails to compile because **t** is not a **boolean**. Only an expression resulting in a **boolean** value can be used in a **while** test. Answer b fails to compile because **x** is defined only inside the code block and is not available to the **while** test. If x had been defined elsewhere, the compiler would object to the second definition inside the loop. Answer c is incorrect because the code in answer c does compile.

Question 13

Answer a is correct. Answer b is incorrect because of inheritance; declaring **IOException** is sufficient. Answer c is incorrect due to a bit of a trick in the statement; there are alternatives to using **try-catch**. For example, the calling method *could* be declared as throwing **IOException**, thus passing responsibility for catching the exception back up the calling chain. Answer d is incorrect because **IOException** exceptions are "checked"—they must be declared and caught.

Question 14

Answers a, c, and d are correct. Answer a is correct because the statement is incorrect. Memory is recovered by garbage collection, and finalizers are for other resources. Answer c is correct because the statement is incorrect; objects that do not use system resources other than memory do not need finalizers. Answer d is correct because the statement is incorrect; there is no guarantee about the order of object finalization. Answer b is incorrect because the statement is correct.

Question 15

Answer b is the correct answer because there is no way to tell when the garbage collector **Thread** will run. The programmer cannot count on garbage collection starting at once. The language specs say that the JVM will make a "best effort," but this does not guarantee anything.

Question 16

Answers b, c, and d are correct. As discussed in the previous answer, the code may start the garbage collector, but there is no guarantee. The Java Virtual Machine assigns a low priority to the garbage collection thread. Answer d is correct because picking the best garbage collection method is left up to the individual JVM implementer. Answer a is incorrect.

Question 17

Answer a is correct. The default package is what you get when there is no package statement. Answer b is incorrect because it tries to put the class in a package named "default," which will cause a compiler error because **default** is a Java keyword (used in switch statements). Answer c not only uses the wrong **package** statement but also puts it in the wrong position. Any **package** statement must be the first non-comment statement in a Java source code file.

Question 18

Answer b is correct and answer c incorrect. To remember whether the negative or positive range is larger, think of the byte range -128 to 127 and recall that the high bit is used as a sign bit. Answer a is incorrect because **short** variables are signed; 0 - 65535 would be unsigned.

Question 19

Answer c is correct; the compiler recognizes that the local variable **rslt** will not always be initialized. Answers a, b, and d are prevented because the class will not compile as written.

Question 20

Answers b and c are correct. Answer b works because primitive number arrays that are member variables are automatically initialized to zero when constructed. Note that this is not true of variables declared inside methods. Answer c works but the loop would be necessary only if an initial value other than zero was required. Answer a is incorrect because it creates an initialized array but it is a local variable, not the member variable. Note that the question says "in the Test constructor." Problems related to duplicate variable declarations are difficult to catch. Answer d is incorrect because initialization by means of a bracketed list can be used only in the statement that declares the variable.

Question 21

Answer a is correct. The constructor creates a new array of type **String[]** in which every item has a null value. Answer b is incorrect because a **NullPointerException** would be thrown only if the constructor had not created the array. Note that c is incorrect; the array index 2 is legal because the array has been constructed with a size of 10. Answer d does not occur because the **String** conversion process substitutes the word "null" when it finds a **null** reference, not a blank.

Question 22

Answers a and c are correct. The hexadecimal literal evaluates to 101 decimal, and the octal literal evaluates to 53 decimal. Answer b is incorrect because line 1 uses a hexadecimal literal and line 2 an octal literal. Answer d is spurious because it is the Java runtime that reports exceptions, not the compiler.

Question 23

Answer b is correct because the index of "alpha" is zero. This also explains why answers a and c are incorrect. The **args String** array, like all Java arrays, is addressed starting with zero. Answer d is incorrect because the runtime system finds the **main** method without problem. At least one question involving the correct signature of the main method and the interpretation of the command line is likely to occur on the test.

Question 24

Answer c is correct. The shift operation is legal. Answer a does not occur because the 4 represents the number of bits to be shifted. Because shifts greater than the number of bits in a **long** do not make sense, shifts are always **int** values. Answers b and d are incorrect because the shift operation is legal. The bit pattern for the hex constant, when right-shifted four positions, leaves a single bit on in the one position. If you are not used to working in binary, be sure to get in some practice before the test.

Question 25

Answer b is correct; the Java runtime checks all class casts for compatibility. A base class cannot be cast to a derived class type. Answer a does not occur because of the explicit cast in line 2. If this cast were removed, the compiler would object. Answer c is incorrect and is there to see if you are paying attention—objects never change their type, no matter what the type of the reference.

Question 26

Answer b is correct. The compiler knows that the signature of the **printArray** method requires an array of **long** primitives. Answer a is incorrect; array types do not have a hierarchy and cannot be cast to another array type. You may be thinking of the automatic promotion of an **int** primitive to **long**. Answer c is incorrect because the compiler can detect the error. When dealing with arrays, be sure to remember that an array is an object whose type includes the type of the primitive or reference variable it can contain.

Question 27

Answer b is correct; this is the "short-circuited" AND operator that does not evaluate the second term if the first one results in **false**. Answer a is incorrect; this operator would attempt to run the **equals** method on the **tmp** variable even if it were **null**, causing a **NullPointerException**. Answers c and d are incorrect because these two OR operators would attempt to run the **equals** method on the **tmp** variable even if it were **null**, causing a **NullPointerException**.

Question 28

Answer a is correct because a floating-point number cannot exactly represent the fraction 1/3—multiplying by 3 does not recover the original number. This also explains why answer b is incorrect. You should be extremely careful when testing for equality between two floating-point numbers. Answer c does not occur because the compiler has no problem with this initialization of variable A. Answer d does not occur because == can be used with primitives and reference variables.

Question 29

Answer a is correct; the compiler will not convert a **double** to an **int** without a specific **cast**. Answer b is incorrect because the program does not compile and because cast exceptions are thrown only by reference variable casts. Answer c is incorrect because the code does not compile. Answer d does not occur because line 1 is the correct way to initialize a double primitive value. A numeric constant with a decimal point is automatically assumed to be a double.

Question 30

Answer b is correct; the test results in a **false** value because J is not a **Long Object**. This also explains why answer a is incorrect. All of the reference variable **equals** tests compare content only after they have determined that the input **Object** is of the correct class. Answers c and d do not occur because the signature of the **equals** method will take any **Object** reference.

Question 31

Answer c is correct; this declaration will not override the one in **GenericFruit** because of the different parameter list. Answers a and b are incorrect. The compiler will consider this an overloaded method name, so it will compile.

Question 32

Answer c is correct; this array of **String** objects could be used to store the names of game animals the **SportingDog** is used to hunt. Answers a and d are incorrect; shadowing the base class **avgWeight** and **breedName** variables would only cause trouble without gaining anything. Answer b is incorrect because there is no need for **SportingDog** to "have a" **Dog** because it "is a" **Dog** by inheritance. Sun literature frequently mentions the distinction between "is a" and "has a," so you may see these terms on the test.

Question 33

Answers a, b, and d are correct. Answers a and b are correct because inner classes can access any static or member variable in the enclosing class. Answer d is correct because, although it is a local variable, it is declared **final**. Answer c is incorrect because the local variable **nn** is not declared **final**. This special usage of the keyword **final** causes the compiler to provide storage for this variable in a permanent location. This is necessary because an inner class object created in a method may outlive the method.

Question 34

Answer a is correct; the compiler sees an attempt to override the **calories** method in the parent class because the method name and input parameter type are the same. However, overriding methods cannot have a different return type, so a compiler error results. Answer b is incorrect because the name used in the parameter list is not part of the method signature; it is the variable type that is significant. Answers c and d are incorrect because the code will not compile. Note how the slight differences in wording between this question and Question 31 make a large difference in outcome. Be sure you can spot the difference between overloading and overriding a method.

Question 35

Answer c is correct. The compiler has no trouble with this method code. Answer a is incorrect because an **abstract** class can be used in **instanceof** tests. Answer b is incorrect because an interface can be used in **instanceof** tests. Knowing how the **instanceof** operator is used is essential to programming in Java, so if you missed this one, go back and review.

Question 36

Answers a and b are correct. Answer a is correct because **yield** will let the thread scheduling mechanism run another **Thread**. Answer b is correct because **sleep** will allow time for other threads to run. Answer c is incorrect; there is no **suspend** method with a time input. The **suspend()** method (with no input parameter) would permanently suspend your **Thread**, and of course, **suspend** is a deprecated method anyway. Answer d is incorrect: It would not compile as written because calls to **wait** must provide for catching **InterruptedException**. Furthermore, the call to **wait** would have to be in a **synchronized** code block, and provision would have to be made for **notify** to be called, or the **Thread** would **wait** forever.

> *Note: It is an essential part of this question that the **run** method is in a class extending **Thread** because both **yield** and **sleep** are static methods in the **Thread** class. If this **run** method were in a **Runnable** class, the syntax Thread.yield() and Thread.sleep() would be required.*

Question 37

Answer b is the only correct answer. The only method required by **Runnable** is **run**.

Question 38

Answer b is the only correct answer. The priority of the new **Thread** will be that inherited from the **Thread** that called the constructor. Answer a is incorrect; the **Thread** is in the "new" state, so **start()** must be called to put it in the runnable state. Answer c is incorrect because **myT** is a **Thread** object created without a reference to a **Runnable** object, the **run** method in the **Thread** class will be executed. The **run** method in **Thread** is, of course, an empty method, so nothing would happen. Answer d is incorrect because once a **Thread** has been stopped, it cannot be restarted.

Question 39

Answers a and b are correct. Answer a would work because it would obtain a lock on the entire **Board** object, and answer b would work because it would obtain a lock on the **pics** array. Answer c would not work because having a lock on the **mg Image** would not protect the array. Answer d would not even compile because **synchronized** statements must have an object reference and **active** is a primitive variable.

Question 40

Answer c is correct. When **animT** calls **wait**, the lock on the **animC** object is released. Answers a and b are incorrect. Other **Threads** can modify data in **animC** using any method because **animT** does not hold a lock on the object while in the **wait** state. Answer d is incorrect because when a **Thread** is interrupted, an **InterruptedException** is thrown. Because this exception is caught inside the **while** loop, **animT** will re-enter the **wait** method.

Question 41

Answers b, d, and e are correct. Answer b is correct because **stop** is a deprecated method. Answer d is correct because **suspend** is a deprecated method. Answer e is correct because **sleep** is a **static** (class) method, not an **instance** method. Answer a is incorrect because **start** is an instance method of **Thread**, which makes a new **Thread** runnable. Answer c is incorrect because the **run** method is an instance method of **Thread**. Answer f is incorrect because all Java objects have a **toString** instance method so **Thread** does too. Answer g is incorrect because **join** is a **Thread** instance method. The convoluted way this question is stated should convince you of how important it is to read the question carefully.

Question 42

Answer a is correct; a **GridLayout** will attempt to display an equal portion of each button when resized. Answer b is incorrect because a **FlowLayout** will leave out buttons that don't fit. Answer c is incorrect because this is not a valid **GridBagLayout** constructor. Answer d is incorrect because a **CardLayout** shows only one component at a time.

Question 43

Answers a and d are correct. For answer a, because **Frame** has a default **BorderLayout**, you will have to set the layout manager to **null** or the **Label** will end up filling the Center position. Answer d shows the correct way to position the label with compensation for the **Frame** insets. Answer b is incorrect because it uses a bogus **setLayoutManager** method that does not exist. Questions that state bogus method names are possible on the test. Answer c is incorrect because it does not take the **Insets** into account. If you don't compensate for the **Insets**, the menu bar will partially or completely cover the label.

Question 44

Answer c is correct. **MenuItem** objects are attached to **Menu** objects that are attached to a **MenuBar**. Answer a is incorrect. **MenuComponent** is the **abstract** class that the other menu-related classes inherit from. Answer b is incorrect because a **MenuItem** is the object that you actually select. Answer d is incorrect because a **PopupMenu** is a **MenuItem** container that can be attached to any **Component**. Although you could attach a **PopupMenu** to a **MenuBar**, that is not the usual convention.

Question 45

Answer d is correct. A **FlowLayout** attempts to fit in components without changing their height. Answer a is incorrect because the East, West, and Center components of a **BorderLayout** have their height changed. Answer b is incorrect because a **GridBagLayout** typically alters both height and width of components. Answer c is incorrect because components in a **CardLayout** are resized to fit the container.

Question 46

Answers b and c are correct because both are positioning options. EAST causes a component to be positioned on the right edge of the available area, centered vertically. NORTHEAST causes a component to be positioned at the upper-right corner of the available area. Answer a is incorrect. BOTH is a resizing option, not a positioning option; it allows a component to be stretched in both directions. Answer d is not a positioning option. NONE is a resizing option; it prevents a component from being resized.

Question 47

Answers a and c are correct. **Double** and **Boolean** are "wrapper" classes that produce an immutable object. Answer b is incorrect because the **StringBuffer** class is provided with many methods for manipulating its contents. It is the **String** class that creates immutable objects. Answer d is incorrect. The **Math** class cannot be used to create an object; it consists entirely of **static** methods. This is an important item to remember when you see a question involving a **Math** class method.

Question 48

Answer b is correct. Inside the **Increment** method, the reference to N is local. The **Integer** created with 31 has nothing to do with the reference to X in the **Result** method. This also explains why answer c is incorrect. Answer a is incorrect. Although a new **Integer** object with an **int** value of 31 is created, it does not affect the object X in the **Result** method.

Question 49

Answer c is correct. The "+" operator is not defined for **Integer** objects, only for **String** objects. Answers a, b, and d are incorrect because line 4 causes a compiler error.

Question 50

Answer a is correct. **TheFile** still refers to the same immutable **String** object created in line 7. Answers b and c are incorrect because the manipulations inside the **setFileType** method cannot alter the original object.

Question 51

Answer c is correct; the += assignment creates a new **String** concatenating the original **String** text with the literal. Therefore, answer a is incorrect. Answer b is incorrect because the += assignment is perfectly legal. Furthermore, if it were illegal, the compiler would have caught the problem. Answer d is incorrect because although it is true that the original input **String** is unchanged, the statement in line 2 creates a new **String** object. You are practically guaranteed to get at least one question that involves knowing legal **String** operations.

Question 52

Only answer b is correct. **String** is the only class for which an assignment operator "+=" is defined. This operation constructs a new **String** assigned to variable A. Answer a is incorrect because the "-=" operator is not defined for **String** objects. Answers c and d are incorrect because there are no arithmetic operators defined for **Integer** objects. Remember that **Integer** objects cannot be changed, so answer d is not legal no matter how plausible it looks.

Question 53

Answer b is correct. The compiler recognizes that the "+" requires **String** concatenation. This also explain why answer a does not occur. Answer c does not occur because the compiled code uses the **Float.toString()** method to convert the value stored in **A** to a **String**.

Question 54

Answer a is correct. An **ActionEvent** is generated when an item in a **List** is double-clicked. Answer b is incorrect; a **Scrollbar** generates an **AdjustmentEvent** when moved. Answers c and d are incorrect because **Canvas** and **Panel** can't generate an **ActionEvent**. **ActionEvents** are considered "semantic" events because the raw mouse or keyboard events are interpreted in terms of the logic implemented by the **Component** that gets the event.

Question 55

Answer a is correct. **ArrayList** maintains an internal list in the order of addition. **ArrayList** is the new class closest to the original Java **Vector** class. Answer b is incorrect; the order of elements in a **Hashtable** depends on the treatment of key hashcodes. Answer c is incorrect because **Map** is an interface that does not require the order of addition to be retained. Answer d is incorrect. **Collection** is the root of the collection interface hierarchy. It does not require the order of addition to be retained.

Question 56

Answer b is correct; **Hashtable** implements the **Map** interface. Answer a is incorrect: **HashMap** is a concrete class, not an interface. Answer c is incorrect because **SortedSet** is an interface that requires the contents to be sorted, whereas **Hashtable** does not sort. Answer d is incorrect because the **Iterator** interface is used by classes that iterate over a collection.

Question 57

Answer c is correct and a, b, and d are incorrect because **Math.random** returns a **double** value. This value may equal 0.0 but will always be less than 1.0.

Question 58

Answer b is the correct answer. **System.out** is a **PrintStream**. In general, the use of **PrintStream** is discouraged in Java 2 because it does not properly handle Unicode characters, but **System.out** remains a **PrintStream** for compatibility with older programs. The classes in answers a, c, and d are all designed to correctly handle Unicode characters.

Question 59

Answers a, b, and d are correct. Answer a is correct because there are in fact two adapters that take **MouseEvent** events, **MouseAdapter** and **MouseMotionAdapter**. Answer b is correct because there is a **KeyAdapter** class. Answer d is correct because there is a **FocusAdapter** class with two methods. Answer c is incorrect because the **ActionListener** interface specifies only one method, **actionPerformed**, so there is no need for an adapter. Answer e is incorrect because the **ItemListener** interface specifies only one method, **itemStateChanged**, so there is no need for an adapter. Note that in general, adapters are provided only where the listener interface specifies two or more methods.

Glossary

. . . .

100% Pure Java—Classes and applications meeting Sun's criteria for total independence from underlying operating system support may display this label.

absolute positioning—If a **Container** has a **null** layout manager, the programmer may position and size **Component** objects in pixel coordinates. This is called absolute positioning.

abstract (Java keyword)—Classes or methods defined as **abstract** define a runtime behavior, but do not provide a complete implementation. You cannot create an object from an **abstract** class, but an object created from a class extending the **abstract** class can be referred to with the **abstract** class name. When applied to member methods, it declares that the implementation of the function must be provided by subclasses, unless they are also declared as **abstract** classes. Any class that contains **abstract** methods must be declared **abstract**. An **abstract** class can't be declared **final**.

abstract pathname—The operating system-independent internal representation of a path inside a **File** object. It consists of an optional prefix string, typically representing a disk drive, plus a list of zero or more names. The last name in the list may represent a directory or file.

accessibility—The **javax.accessibility** package specifies interfaces to connect user interface components with assistive technologies that make it easier for people with disabilities to interact with Java applications.

adapter—The **java.awt.event** package has a number of classes provided for convenient creation of event listeners. These "adapter" classes provide empty methods that fulfill the requirements of various event listeners. For example, the **KeyAdapter** class implements the **KeyListener** interface, so if you need a class that implements **KeyListener**, you can extend **KeyAdapter**.

Adjustable (interface)—The **java.awt.Adjustable** interface defines methods for dealing with scrollbar-like controls.

anonymous class—A local class that is declared and instantiated in one statement. The term anonymous is appropriate because the class is not given a name.

applet—A Java program that runs almost independently of the operating system within a JVM provided by a Web browser. An applet is normally distributed or downloaded as part of a Web page from a central Web server, and then the applet executes on the client machine. Browser security limits an applet's access to the client-machine file system and other resources.

application—A Java program that runs on a user's system with full access to system resources—as opposed to an applet, which is strictly limited by the security restrictions in a Web browser. By convention, the start-up class for an application must have a **main** method.

Application Services—Sun's category for a range of interface improvements considered to be part of the JFC (Java Foundation Classes).

ArithmeticException—A runtime exception thrown by the JVM (Java Virtual Machine) when integer division by zero occurs. Note that floating-point division by zero does not cause an exception.

array—A collection of data items, all of the same type, in which each item is uniquely addressed by a 32-bit integer index. Java arrays behave like objects, but have some special syntax. Java arrays begin with the index value 0.

Arrays class—This class in the **java.util** package contains many **static** methods for operations on arrays of primitives and object references.

ASCII (American Standard Code for Information Interchange)—A widely used encoding standard for text and control characters. Java uses Unicode internally, but appears externally to be using ASCII, because the printing characters of ASCII are a subset of Unicode.

assignable—An object reference is assignable to a reference variable if it is the same type as the variable or has the variable as an ancestor in the class hierarchy. A primitive type is assignable to a variable if it can be converted to that type without a specific **cast**.

assignment—Operators that place a value in a variable, such as the = and += operators, are assignment operators.

atomic—A sequence of computer operations is said to be atomic if it cannot be interrupted by another **Thread**.

automatic variable—A variable that is declared inside a method. It is called automatic because the memory required is automatically provided when the method is called. Local variable is the preferred term.

bitwise—A bitwise operator performs an operation on Java integer primitive types on an individual-bit basis.

break—A Java keyword that is used in two contexts. The plain **break** statement simply causes execution to continue after the present code block. When used with a statement label, **break** causes execution to continue after the code block that is tagged by the label. Contrast this behavior with that of the **continue** keyword.

byte—The 8-bit integer-type primitive used in Java. Java treats a **byte** as a signed integer.

Byte class—The wrapper for 8-bit byte primitive values.

bytecode—Essentially, an instruction for the JVM in a platform-independent format. The Java compiler reads Java source code and outputs class files containing bytecodes.

cast—A Java expression explicitly changes the type of the expression to a different type by using the **cast** syntax, which consists of the new type in parentheses. **Cast** is also a reserved word in Java, but is not currently used.

catch—The Java keyword **catch** is used to create a block of code, or "clause," to be executed when a specific exception is thrown in a block of code set up by a **try** statement. Each **catch** must specify the type of exception caught.

CGI (Common Gateway Interface)—The conventions that govern data communication between a Web server and auxiliary programs. For example, Web search requests to search engines such as Yahoo use the CGI convention.

char—The integer primitive variable that Java uses to represent Unicode characters. A **char** variable is treated as a 16-bit unsigned integer, whereas all other integer primitives are treated as signed.

Character class—The wrapper for 16-bit **char** primitive values.

checked exception—Those exceptions for which the compiler requires you to provide explicit handling code.

class—An object-oriented programming term that defines the implementation of objects that can inherit or share certain characteristics. In Java, all program behavior is defined by classes, and all classes descend from the **Object** class. Think of a class as a blueprint for creating objects; just as you can create more than one building from a blueprint, you can create more than one object from a class.

Class (class)—This class in the **java.lang** package allows you to find out the runtime type of any object. An instance of this class is created for every class and interface in a running Java program as the JVM loads the program.

class file—The compilation of a Java class results in a class file. The name of the file matches the name of the class and the file type is ".class".

class method—A method that is declared **static** and thus is attached to the class as a whole. Some Java classes, such as **Math,** are used entirely through class methods.

class modifiers—Java keywords **public, abstract,** and **final** that define characteristics of a class.

class variable—A variable that is attached to a Java class rather than to an instance of the class. Variables that are declared **static** are class variables.

ClassCastException—This exception is generated when the JVM detects that an attempt has been made to cast an object reference to an incompatible type.

clone method—A method in the **Object** class that can create a copy of an object.

Collection interface—This interface defines the basic behavior for objects in the Collections API (application programming interface).

Collections API (application programming interface)—The set of classes and interfaces, new for Java 2, that provide a wide array of methods for manipulating of collections of objects.

Color (class)—The **java.awt.Color** class encapsulates the red, green, and blue intensities of a screen color. In addition, **Color** has an alpha component that represents opacity.

Comparator interface—By implementing this interface, your custom class can make use of the large number of sorting and searching methods in the **Arrays** class.

completeness—Whether a behavior is fully developed or needs to be further developed by subclasses. In an incomplete, or **abstract,** class, the implementation of some or all behavior is left to subclasses. A **final** class is considered the end of a hierarchy and can't be subclassed.

Component (class)—The **java.awt.Component** class is the parent of all non-menu screen components in the AWT. This is an **abstract** class so **Component** objects are never created directly.

constraints—In layout managers that implement the **LayoutManager2** interface, a constraint is an object passed to the layout manager that directs the way a particular component is treated. For example, the **String** "North" in a **BorderLayout** is a constraint.

constructor—A special type of member function that is called when an instance of a class is created. The constructor performs many steps to initialize data storage.

constructor chaining—One constructor calling another constructor. Java enforces a set of rules on chaining constructors, to ensure that superclasses get a chance to perform default processing.

Container (class)—The basic functionality of all AWT containers stems from this class. In addition to the functions it inherits from **Component**, a **Container** object has a list of all components it contains and may have a layout manager that controls arranging these components.

contentPane—In the Swing primary container classes such as **JFrame**, interface components are added to the **contentPane** container rather than directly to the **JFrame**.

continue—This Java keyword is used in two contexts. When used inside a looping construct, the plain **continue** statement causes execution to continue with the next innermost loop execution. When used with a statement label, **continue** transfers control to the labeled loop. Contrast this behavior with that of the **break** keyword.

controller—In the Model-View-Controller design pattern, controller functions communicate user input to the model and view(s).

conversion—In a Java expression, changing the type of the expression by one of several methods. Conversion can occur when assigning the results of an expression to a variable, when invoking a method with a specific **cast**, or in a numeric expression. Java also provides for converting any type to a **String** in **String** expressions.

daemon Thread—Threads may be tagged as daemon threads by the **setDaemon** method to distinguish them from user threads. Daemon threads are generally JVM utilities such as the garbage collection **Thread**. The name comes from typical Unix usage.

deadlock—A situation in which two or more **Thread** objects are unable to proceed because each holds a resource the other needs.

decorator—A design pattern in which a core class has additional functions added by an attached object rather than by subclassing.

decrement—The decrement operator (--) subtracts one from the primitive numeric variable to which it is attached. This operator can be used with all primitive numeric types.

deep copy—This term is used when describing the cloning of objects. A deep copy must be made by creating new copies of all objects referred to by the original object.

delegate—In the Swing convention, the object that handles look and feel for a component is called a delegate. From the point of view of the Model-View-Controller design pattern, a delegate combines view and controller functions.

delegation—The Java 1.1 event model is sometimes referred to as a delegation model because event-generating components delegate event handling to specific event listeners, as opposed to the original event model in which the component generating the event had no connection to the eventual handler.

deprecated—Disapproved of—a number of methods in Java 2 that are left over from earlier versions are tagged in the JDK 1.2 documentation as deprecated. Some are deprecated because an improved naming convention has been adopted and some because their use has been found to be harmful. Note that these methods are still in the library in JDK version 1.2 but are not guaranteed to be there in subsequent versions.

deserialize—To reconstitute a Java object that was stored by serialization; typically performed by an **ObjectInputStream**.

Dimension (class)—The width and height of a component are typically read and set with **java.awt.Dimension** objects. For instance, in the **setMinimumSize** method, a **Dimension** object is passed.

doclet—A Java program written with classes in the **sun.tools.javadoc** package that can customize javadoc output. (See javadoc.)

double—The 64-bit floating-point primitive type used in Java.

Double class—In addition to being the wrapper for 64-bit **double** primitive values, this class has special constants such as **NaN**, used to detect various problems with floating-point arithmetic as discussed in Chapter 3.

drag-and-drop—The part of the JFC supporting transfer of data between Java applications and between Java and native applications using the dragging and dropping metaphor.

dynamic method lookup—The JVM locates the correct method to call at runtime, based on an object's actual type, not the type of the reference that is used.

editable—You can control whether the user can edit the text displayed in a **TextArea** or **TextField** with the **setEditable** method.

enabling events—The **enableEvents** method in **java.awt.Component** is called to specifically enable events as determined by an event mask. Events are also enabled when specific listeners are added to a **Component**.

encapsulation—Encasing information and behavior within an object so that its structure and implementation are hidden to other objects that interact with it.

Enumeration interface—The interface in Java 1.0 that specifies how a collection will generate a series of the elements it contains using the **nextElement** and **hasMoreElements** methods. The **Iterator** interface in Java 2 is intended to replace **Enumeration**.

equals—The **equals** method compares one object reference with another and returns **true** if the objects are equal in content. The default **equals** method in the **Object** class returns **true** if both references refer to the same object. Classes such as **String** provide an **equals** method that checks for equality of content.

Error (java.lang.Error)—This class, which is a subclass of **Throwable**, is the parent of all Java error classes. Errors generally signal a condition from which the program cannot recover, as opposed to exceptions that may be recoverable.

event listener—Any object that has an interest in user interactions with a particular control can register with that control as an event listener for specific events. When the event occurs, each listener for that type of event is notified.

event mask—The event mask in a **Component** object determines the types of events it will generate. Constants corresponding to the various events are defined in the **java.awt.AWTEvent** class.

Exception (java.lang.Exception)—This class, which is a subclass of **Throwable**, is the parent of all Java exceptions. The compiler will insist that all **Exceptions**, except those that descend through the **RuntimeException** branch of the hierarchy, must be provided for in the code.

extends—The Java keyword used in the definition of a new class to indicate the class from which the new class inherits.

field—A variable that defines a particular characteristic of a class.

File (class)—The **java.io.File** class manages directory and file pathnames, not actual data files. **File** objects can be used as input to methods that do open files, but the main purpose of the class is to manipulate names in an operating-system-independent fashion.

file separator—The character used to separate the components of a path and file name. Because Windows and Unix use different symbols, the only portable way to build a path and file name is with the system-specific constants provided in the **File** class.

final—Java keyword that declares that a class can't be subclassed. When applied to a member method, it declares that the method can't be overridden by subclasses. When applied to a member variable, it declares that the variable is a constant; after its value has been set, it can't be changed. A **final** class can't be declared **abstract**.

finalize—The **finalize** method of an object is executed by the Java garbage collection mechanism when the memory occupied by the object is about to be reclaimed. The **Object** class has a do-nothing **finalize** method, so all Java objects inherit a **finalize** method.

finally—The **finally** keyword is used to attach a code block that must always be executed to a **try** block.

float—The 32-bit floating-point primitive type used in Java.

Float class—In addition to being the wrapper for 32-bit float primitive values, it also defines several important constants.

Font (class)—A **Font** object represents a particular font face characterized by the family plus style information and point size.

font family—From a typographic point of view, fonts are characterized by a design style or font family such as Times Roman or Courier.

garbage collection—The process by which the JVM locates and recovers memory occupied by objects that can no longer be used by the program.

Graphics (class)—The **java.awt.Graphics** class provides a context for drawing components and images on the screen. All drawing is done through a **Graphics** or **Graphics2D** object.

Graphics2D (class)—The **java.awt.Graphics2D** class extends **Graphics** and is used throughout Java 2.

hashcode—In general computing terms, a hashcode is a characteristic number generally derived from the contents of a data item. Operations on this number allow a program to locate a data item much faster than any search method.

hashCode method—Every object in Java has a **hashCode** method that generates an **int** primitive value. The **Object** class provides a simple method that, in most implementations, just returns the reference value that points to the object. By overriding this base method, the designer can create an optimized hashcode.

Hashtable class—A **Hashtable** object stores **Object** references indexed by "key" objects using the hashcode of the key. Typically used to store references with a **String** key, but any class implementing the **hashCode** method will work as a key.

heavyweight components—Interface components that make use of a corresponding operating system peer are called heavyweight components.

IDE (Integrated Development Environment)—A programming system that integrates several programming tools in the same package. An IDE typically includes a source code editor, a compiler, a debugger, project tracking functions, and graphic screen-design functions.

IEEE (Institute of Electrical and Electronics Engineers)—A professional society that maintains various standards for computer hardware and software, among others.

implements—The keyword used in a class declaration to precede a list of one or more interfaces. When more than one interface is implemented, the names in the list are separated by commas.

import—An **import** statement in a Java source code file tells the Java compiler in which package to look for classes that are used in the code. The **java.lang** package is automatically imported; all others must be specified in **import** statements.

increment—The increment operator (++) adds one to the primitive variable to which it is attached. This operator can be used with all primitive numeric types.

IndexOutOfBoundsException—This exception is generated when an attempt is made to address an array element that does not exist. The **ArrayIndexOutOfBoundsException** and **StringIndexOutOfBoundsException** are subclasses of this class.

init (applet method)—By convention, the initial class of a Java applet is expected to have an **init** method. The JVM in the Web browser calls the **init** method after the applet object has been created but before it is displayed.

initialize, initialization—Setting a starting value for a variable.

inner classes—A class or interface that is nested within another class. Inner classes have access to all member fields and methods of their enclosing class, including those declared as **private**.

InputStream (class)—The **abstract** base class in the **java.io** package for many classes that read data as a stream of bytes.

Insets (class)—The border widths on all four sides of a container are typically represented by a **java.awt.Insets** object.

instance—An object of a particular class is called an instance of that class.

instance fields—Member fields that are distinct for each instance of a class.

instance methods—Member methods that can be executed only through a reference to an instance of a class.

instance variable—A variable that is part of an instance of a class, as opposed to a class (or static) variable that is part of the class itself.

instanceof—This logical operator is used in expressions to determine whether a reference belongs to a particular type. The operator expects a reference on the left and a reference type on the right. If the reference can legally be cast to the reference type, the operator returns **true**.

int—The 32-bit integer primitive type used in Java. Note that **int** primitives are always treated as signed integers.

Integer class—The wrapper for 32-bit **int** primitive values.

interface—In Java, an interface is similar to a class definition, except that no detailed implementation of methods is provided. A class that implements an interface must provide the code to implement the methods. You can think of an interface as defining a contract between the calling method and the class that implements the interface.

interrupt—An instance method of the **Thread** class. The results of calling this method depend on the state of the **Thread**. If it is in a **sleep** or **wait** state, it is awakened and an **InterruptedException** is thrown; if not, the interrupted flag is set.

interrupted (Thread private variable)—This flag is set to **true** if a **Thread** is interrupted. It can be accessed only by the **interrupted** and **isInterrupted** methods.

interrupted (Thread static method)—A **static** method used by the currently running **Thread** to determine whether it has been interrupted.

InterruptedException—This exception can be generated when a **Thread** that is sleeping or waiting is interrupted. The **Thread** cannot continue with what it was doing but must handle the exception.

IOException—The parent class for all exceptions associated with input-output processes such as opening and reading a file.

isInterrupted—An instance method of the **Thread** class by which a **Thread** can be interrogated to see if it has been interrupted.

Iterator interface—This interface is intended to take the place of the **Enumeration** interface as the preferred way to examine elements in a collection. It provides methods similar to those in **Enumeration** but with shorter names, and adds a **remove** method.

JAR (Java ARchive)—This format enables a single file to contain a number of resources such as class files or images. The basic format is that of the well-known zip utility, but it has some Java-specific additions.

Java 2D—This is Sun's term for a group of classes providing many advanced graphic methods.

javac—The program that starts the Java compiler.

javadoc—The Java utility for automatic documentation. Source code with comments in the correct format can be processed by the javadoc utility, which creates HTML-formatted reference pages. If this processing is done correctly, your application documentation is merged with the documentation for the rest of the language.

JComponent (class)—The **javax.swing.JComponent** class is the base class for the Swing visual components. The immediate ancestor of **JComponent** is **java.awt.Container**; thus, a **JComponent** object can contain other components.

JDK (Java Development Kit)—The package of utilities, a class library, and documentation that you can download from the **www.javasoft.com** Web site. You may see the JDK for the Java 2 platform referred to as the 1.2 version.

JFC (Java Foundation Classes)—A group of five toolkits for various aspects of advanced user interface building. Most of these classes were developed as add-ons for Java 1.1 but are now integrated into Java 2. These classes are in five groups called Swing, Java 2D, Accessibility, Drag & Drop, and Application Services.

join—This instance method in the **Thread** class is provided to coordinate **Threads**. The **Thread** executing the method waits for the **Thread** whose method is called to die.

JVM (Java Virtual Machine)—The part of the Java runtime environment that interprets Java bytecodes and connects your program to system resources. The specifications for the JVM are public and have been used to create Java interpreters on a variety of systems.

label—A Java statement can be labeled with an identifier followed by a colon. Labels are used only by **break** and **continue** statements.

layout manager—The generic term for an object that can control the position and size of screen components within a **java.awt.Container** object. The **LayoutManager** and **LayoutManager2** interfaces in the **java.awt** package define the methods one of these objects must provide. Chapter 10 focuses on layout managers.

lightweight components—Interface components that do not have an operating system peer are called lightweight components. All screen drawing and event processing for lightweight components is carried out by the JVM.

List interface—This interface provides for an ordered collection of object references not to be confused with the **java.awt.List** class, which creates a listbox.

listener—In the Java 1.1 event model, a listener is an object that receives a certain class of events because it has registered with the generating component. Listeners are defined as interfaces so that any class can implement the listener interface and receive events.

local class—An inner class that is defined within a member method. Not only does the local class have access to all class members, it also has access to local variables that are declared **final**.

local variable—A variable declared inside a code block. (See also **automatic variable**.)

lock—A variable associated with each object that can be manipulated only by the JVM. For a **Thread** to execute a **synchronized** code block, it must have ownership of the lock belonging to the **synchronized** object.

long—The 64-bit integer primitive type used in Java. Note that **long** primitives are always treated as signed integers.

Long class—The wrapper for 64-bit **long** primitive values.

low-level event—This term is used for events close to the raw events provided by the operating system, such as mouse movements.

main (application method)—By convention, the initial class of a Java application must have a **static** method named **main**. The JVM executes this method after loading the class, to start the application.

manifest—Every JAR file has a contained manifest file that carries additional information about the other files in the JAR. This can include digital signatures, encryption information, and a variety of other data. The **java.util.jar.Manifest** class is used to give the programmer access to the data in a manifest.

Map interface—A class implementing this interface must associate key objects with value objects. Each key must be unique. The **Hashtable** class implements the **Map** interface.

maximumSize—Components descended from **JComponent** can have this parameter set with the **setMaximumSize** method.

MAX_PRIORITY—A constant in the **Thread** class.

member—A field, function, or inner class that is declared as part of a class. The class encapsulates the member and can control access to the member.

member class—An inner class that isn't declared as **static** and isn't declared within a member method.

MenuComponent (class)—All **java.awt** classes used to display screen menus descend from **java.awt.MenuComponent**.

method—Java code is organized into methods that are named and declared to have specific input parameters and return types. All methods are members of a class. (See **member**.)

method signature—The combination of a method's name and parameters, which distinguishes it from other methods. The return type isn't included as part of the signature.

minimumSize—Components descended from **JComponent** can have this parameter set with the **setMinimumSize** method. Layout managers will not attempt to give the component less than this amount of space.

MIN_PRIORITY—A constant in the **Thread** class.

model—In the Model-View-Controller design pattern, the model object contains the data.

modulo, modulus—The modulus (also called modulo) operator (%) returns the result of the division of the left operand by the right operand. This operator can be used with integer and floating-point types.

monitor—The mechanism by which the JVM uses object locks to control access by **Threads** to objects.

multiple-inheritance—Subclassing more than one class, which isn't allowed in Java.

multitasking—When an operating system, such as Windows NT, appears to be running several programs simultaneously, it is multitasking. Each program runs separately with its own memory and resources.

multithreading—When there are several independent paths of execution within a program, it is multithreading. Each thread may have access to the main memory and resources of the entire program.

name space—The total set of names for classes, methods, and other program items that the Java compiler has to keep track of to uniquely identify an item.

NaN (Not a Number)—A special floating-point constant used to represent the results of arithmetic operations that don't have a correct numerical representation, such as division by zero. **NaN** constants are defined in the **Float** and **Double** classes. The only way to determine whether a numerical result is **NaN** is with the **isNaN** method. Trying to test for the **NaN** value with the == operator or **equals** method does not work.

narrowing conversion (primitives)—Conversions of primitive types that may lose information are called narrowing conversions. For instance, converting an **int** to a **byte** simply discards the extra bits.

narrowing conversion (reference type)—A conversion of a reference type to a subclass, for instance, from **Object** to **String**, is a narrowing conversion. The Java compiler insists on explicit **casts** and installs a runtime check on all narrowing conversions. At runtime, a **ClassCastException** is thrown if the conversion is not legal.

NEGATIVE_INFINITY—A constant defined in the **Float** and **Double** classes; it is the result of floating-point division of a negative floating-point primitive by zero.

nested top-level inner class or interface—An inner class that is declared **static** and treated the same as any other Java outer class. These inner classes don't have access to the **static** members of the enclosing class.

new—The Java keyword that is used to indicate construction of a new object or array.

NORM_PRIORITY—A constant in the **Thread** class.

notify—A method in the **Object** class that makes one of the **Threads** on the object's wait list become runnable. Note that the **Thread** will not actually run until the JVM scheduling mechanism gives it a chance.

notifyAll—Similar to **notify**, but it makes all **Threads** on the object's wait list become runnable.

null—The special literal value used for the value of a reference variable that hasn't been initialized. Note that **null** has no interpretation as a primitive variable.

object—A specific instance of a class.

Observable—A class in the **java.util** package that provides basic methods for adding and notifying objects implementing the **Observer** interface. In the **Observer-Observable** design pattern, the object containing data.

Observer—An interface in the **java.util** package specifying the **update** method. This is the method that **Observable** objects use to notify **Observers**.

OutputStream (class)—The abstract base class in the **java.io** package for the classes that write data as a stream of bytes.

overloading—A class can have more than one method with a given name provided the parameter lists are different. This is called overloading the method name.

overriding—If a method in a subclass has the same return type and signature as a method in the superclass, the subclass method is said to override the superclass method.

package—A group of affiliated Java classes and interfaces. Packages organize classes into distinct name spaces. Classes are placed in packages by using the **package** keyword in the class definition. A package limits the visibility of classes and minimizes name collision.

parent—A class that is the immediate ancestor of another class by inheritance. Also known as the superclass.

path separator—The character used to separate paths in a list such as the Windows environment variable PATH. Because this varies between operating systems, the **File** class has a constant that you should use rather than hard-coding a particular character.

peer—The operating system object corresponding to a Java AWT interface object is called a peer.

pointer—A mechanism used in C for indirect access to objects and variables. Java does not allow pointer manipulations, so give up your clever C programming tricks!

polymorphic—In object-oriented programming, this refers to the ability of an object to have many identities, based on its inheritance, interfaces, and overloaded methods.

POSITIVE_INFINITY—A constant defined in the **Float** and **Double** classes; it is the result of floating-point division of a positive floating-point primitive by zero.

preferredSize—Components descended from **JComponent** have this parameter, which may be set with the **setPreferredSize** method. Those layout managers that respect **preferredSize** will attempt to allow the **Component** to occupy this space.

primary container—One of the Swing objects that has an operating system peer and can serve as the basis for an independent window.

primitive—The following Java types: **boolean, char, byte, short, int, long, float,** and **double**. These are not objects, and variables of these types are not object references. Primitive values are accessed and stored directly in binary form rather than through the object reference system.

priority—All **Threads** have a priority, a numeric value from 1 to 10, which is used by the JVM to decide which **Thread** runs next. Not all operating systems provide the full range of priorities that the language prescribes.

private—Variables and methods that are tagged with the **private** keyword can be accessed only by methods that are declared within the same class.

promotion—The compiler's use of widening conversion of a number to the type required by a particular operation. For example, a **byte** primitive being used as an index to an array will be promoted to **int** for the purposes of the operation.

protected—Variables and methods that are tagged with the keyword **protected** can be accessed only by methods of classes in the same package or by methods within classes derived from that class (in other words, classes for which that class is the superclass).

protocol—A set of rules governing a transaction.

public—Java keyword that modifies the visibility of classes and members, so that they may be accessed by all objects, regardless of the package to which they belong.

random access—Having random access to a file means that the programmer can move a file pointer to any spot in the file and begin reading or writing. This is in contrast with streams, which can be read only from beginning to end.

Reader (class)—The **abstract** base class in the **java.io** package for classes that read data as a stream of 16-bit Unicode characters.

reference—In Java, the programmer never works directly with the physical memory address of an object, but instead works with an object reference. The JVM is responsible for fetching and storing object data indirectly through the reference.

reference variable—Except for primitives, all variables in Java are referred to indirectly and thus are called reference variables. Objects, classes, interfaces, and arrays are reference variables.

Reflection API (application programming interface)—Classes that make up this API allow a program to discover the constructors, methods, and variables available in any class and the interface the class implements.

resume—The **Thread** instance method used to allow a suspended **Thread** to continue. This method is deprecated.

RMI (Remote Method Invocation)—The technology that enables one Java program to execute a method on an object resident on another system.

Runnable—An interface in the **java.lang** package that defines the **run** method used by **Threads**.

RuntimeException (java.lang.RuntimeException)—This class is the parent of all of the exceptions that do not have to be declared in a method **throws** clause.

scope—The attribute of an identifier that determines its accessibility to other parts of the program.

semantic event—This term is used in contrast with "low-level" events. A semantic event incorporates some additional logic.

serialize—To turn a Java object into a stream of bytes, typically using an **ObjectOutputStream**.

Set interface—An extension of the **Collection** interface holding object references with the restriction that the set prevents duplication of references so every reference is unique.

shallow copy—A copy produced by the **clone** method in the **Object** class is shallow because it simply copies reference variables' values.

short—The 16-bit integer primitive variable type. Remember that **short** variables are always treated as signed integers.

Short class—The wrapper for 16-bit **short** primitive values.

sign bit—The most significant bit in the Java **byte**, **short**, **int**, and **long** primitives. If this bit is turned on, the number is interpreted as a negative number.

signature—A method's name and the type and order of parameters in its argument list constitute its signature.

singleton—A design pattern in which only one instance of a class can be created and access to this instance is controlled by a **static** class method.

sleep—The **Thread** calling this **static** method of the **Thread** class sleeps for the number of milliseconds specified.

socket—Connections over a network between computers are represented on each end as sockets. A socket has a computer address and a port number so a given computer can support many sockets.

Socket (class)—An object of the **java.net.Socket** class represents a single socket connection and can provide an **InputStream** and **OutputStream** for communication through the socket.

SortedSet interface—An extension of **Set** that keeps references in a sorting order as determined by the **compareTo** method, which each object in the set must implement.

stack trace—The formatted text output that can show the history of how a particular **Thread** came to be executing a method that created an exception or error.

start (applet method)—By convention, the JVM in a Web browser calls an applet's **start** method after the initial display of the applet and whenever the Web page containing the applet is re-exposed.

static—Tags a method or variable as belonging to the class rather than to an instance of the class.

static fields—Member fields of a class for which one, and only one, copy exists, regardless of the number of instances of that class.

static methods—Member methods of a class that can be executed without the need to reference a particular instance of that class.

stop—This **Thread** instance method causes a **ThreadDeath** error to be thrown, thus bringing a **Thread** to an abrupt end. The method is deprecated due to unpredictable results in certain circumstances.

stream—One of the ways Java looks at inputs and outputs such as files is as a sequence or stream of bytes. In contrast with random access, streams can be read only from beginning to end with limited or nonexistent ability to back up.

StringIndexOutOfBoundsException—Methods in the **String** class throw this exception if an out-of-range character position is specified.

subclass—A class that extends another class directly or indirectly. In Java, all classes (with the exception of **Object** itself) are subclasses of the class **Object**.

super—The Java keyword used to refer to parent class constructors, methods, or variables.

superclass—In the Java class hierarchy, an ancestor of a class; the immediate ancestor is the direct superclass. (See also **extends** and **parent**.)

suspend—A **Thread** instance method that halts a **Thread** until the **resume** method is called. This method is deprecated because the suspended **Thread** can keep a lock on an object, thus creating a deadlock condition.

Swing—The set of advanced interface components developed as improvements over the original AWT components. Swing components were an optional add-on for Java 1.1 but are part of the standard extensions for Java 2.

synchronized—The Java keyword that activates the monitor mechanism for a method or a block of code.

System class—The **System** class is composed of **static** methods and variables initialized by the JVM when a program starts in order to provide a variety of utility functions.

Thread—The **java.lang.Thread** class encapsulates and defines the behavior of a single thread of control within the JVM.

ThreadDeath—A special error used to bring a **Thread** to a halt.

ThreadGroup—The JVM uses these objects to define a set of **Thread** objects and conduct operations on the set as a whole.

throw—The Java statement that throws an exception; it must have an associated **Throwable** object.

Throwable (java.lang.Throwable)—The class that is the parent of all Java error and exception classes.

throws—This Java keyword is used in method declarations to introduce a list of exceptions that the method may throw.

time stamp—Mouse and keyboard events, which are descendents of **InputEvent**, carry a **long** primitive variable that gives the system time when the event was created. This is generally called a time stamp.

toString—All reference types have a **toString** method, which the Java compiler uses when evaluating statements in which **String** objects and the + operator appear.

try—A **try** statement creates a block of code in which an exception may occur. There must be one or more associated **catch** clause(s) following the **try**.

type—The interface to an object. In object-oriented programming, an object's interface is sometimes separated from its implementation, leading to a distinction between class and type.

UDP (User Datagram Protocol)—A packet communication protocol providing simple communication between programs. UDP is unreliable in the sense that a packet may be totally lost, but if the packet is successfully received, the data inside is reliable.

unary—Operators that affect a single operand. An example is the ++ increment operator.

unchecked exception—Those exceptions that descend from **RuntimeException** are called unchecked because the compiler does not require you to provide explicit handling code for them.

Unicode—The international standard for representing alphabets. Java uses Unicode so that writing programs that are compatible with any locale is easier. Java uses the 2.0 version of this standard (**http://www.unicode.org**), in which the ASCII standard codes are represented with the usual values.

URL (class)—The **java.net.URL** class represents a Uniform Resource Locator. With a valid **URL**, you can open an **InputStream** and read a resource from a Web server.

user Thread—Any **Thread** not tagged as a daemon **Thread**.

variable shadowing—Variables in the same scope can block direct access to other variables with the same identifier.

Vector class—A **Vector** object holds an extensible array of **Object** references.

view—In the Model-View-Controller design pattern, a view creates a particular presentation of the model data. A single model may have many views.

viewport—The logical window through which part of the view object in a **JViewPort** is seen.

visibility—The level of access granted to other classes.

wait—A method in the **Object** class. A **Thread** calling this method releases its lock on the object, becomes inactive, and is placed on the object's wait list. Calls to an object's **wait** method must be in a block of code synchronized on the object.

wait list—A list of **Threads** attached to a particular object waiting for notification.

wait set—Another term for a wait list.

widening conversion—Conversions of primitive types are called widening conversions when the conversion does not lose magnitude information. For example, converting a **short** to a **long** loses no information. A conversion of reference types from a subclass to a class higher up the class hierarchy is a widening conversion. For example, any reference can be converted to an **Object** reference, because **Object** is the root of the entire Java hierarchy.

widget—Programmer slang for a user interface component such as a button.

wrapper classes—A generic term for classes that correspond to each of the primitive types and provide various utility functions related to those types. For example, the **Float** class that corresponds to **float** primitives.

Writer (class)—The **abstract** base class for classes that write data as a stream of 16-bit characters.

Index

R

S